FIREARMS
AND
FORTIFICATIONS

THE REPUBLIC OF SIENA AND HER TERRITORY
DURING THE SIXTEENTH CENTURY.

The squares mark towns that were
chosen to be defended in February 1554 (see chapter 4).

FIREARMS
&
FORTIFICATIONS

Military Architecture and Siege Warfare in Sixteenth-Century Siena

SIMON PEPPER
and
NICHOLAS ADAMS

University of Chicago Press

Chicago and London

Simon Pepper teaches at the University of
Liverpool's School of Architecture. He is the
author of *Housing Improvement: Goals and
Strategy* (1971). Nicholas Adams is associate
professor in the Department of Art and
Architecture, Lehigh University.

The University of Chicago Press, Chicago 60637
The University of Chicago Press, Ltd., London
© 1986 by The University of Chicago
All rights reserved. Published 1986
Printed in the United States of America

95 94 93 92 91 90 89 88 87 86   5 4 3 2 1

Library of Congress Cataloging-in-Publication Data

Pepper, Simon.
    Firearms and fortifications.

    Bibliography: p.
    Includes index.
    1. Fortification—Italy—Siena—History—16th century.
2. Artillery—Italy—Siena—History—16th century.
3. Attack and defense (Military science)—History—16th
century.   4. Siena (Italy)—History, Military.
I. Adams, Nicholas.   II. Title.
UG430.S54P47   1986   355.7'0945'58   85–24673
ISBN 0–226–00535–6

In Memory

JUDITH HOOK

Scholar and Friend

CONTENTS

ILLUSTRATIONS

Acknowledgment is made in parentheses to the author of the photo or line drawing, or the owner of the copyright. Where the location of the work and the photo credit is the same, only one listing is given.

ACKNOWLEDGMENTS

Acknowledgments are a way to recall moments of intellectual friendship, a way to call attention to one's place in the scheme of things, and a chance to tell the reader the history of the book now open in front of his or her eyes.

The two authors were brought together by Paul Barolsky, a colleague of Simon Pepper at the University of Virginia and teacher of Nicholas Adams at Cornell University. It was on the basis of an encounter in the Archivio di Stato in Siena, now almost ten years ago, that the process was begun to stitch together two dissertations on the architectural defense of Siena in the early and mid-sixteenth century.

The authors have also been helped immeasurably by friends of another sort. Jill Moore spent considerable time with the authors in the archives. Her transcriptions, neat, clean, and precise, form the basis for many of the sections that had to be written afresh when it was decided to make a book. Jill Moore's critical interest in this project, so far from her own expertise in the notarial archives of Genoa, was of incalculable value. And Anna and Robin Adams provided the support and distraction of family life: the pleasures of work increased by knowing that any success could be shared.

Others showed great fortitude in reading sections of the book and providing the authors with the chance to make many improvements. Some read chapters of dissertations, others read chapters from what was proposed as a book; all comments were most welcome: Samuel Berner (University of Virginia), Kathleen Weil-Garris Brandt (New York University), Horst de la Croix (San Jose State), Sir John Hale (University College London), Quentin Hughes (University of Liverpool), Daniela Lamberini (University of Florence), the late Wolfgang Lotz (Biblioteca Herziana, Rome), Joseph Rykwert (Cambridge University).

Individuals on both sides of the Atlantic also aided the authors with conversation and discussion: Samuel K. Cohn (Brandeis University), Alberto Cornice (Soprintendenza delle Belle Arti, Siena), Robert Farrell (Cornell University), Kurt Forster (Getty Museum), the late L. H. Heydenreich, Anna and Mario Luccarelli (Siena), Henry A. Millon (CASVA, Washington), Marvin Trachtenberg (New York University), Richard Tuttle (Newcomb College).

Archivists and librarians were generous with their time and enthusiasm for the project. In particular we must thank Sonia Fineschi, director of the Archivio di Stato, Siena, and her assistants, notably Nello Barbieri and Erminio Jaconna in the study room. Thanks are also due the staffs of the British Library, London; the Stephen Chan Library at the Institute of Fine Arts, New York; the Archivio di Stato, Florence; the Biblioteca Comunale, Siena; the Biblioteca Herziana, Rome; and the Kunsthistorisches Institut, Florence.

Financial support came from a number of sources. Nicholas Adams's travels were aided by grants from the National Gallery Chester Dale Fellowship, the Samuel H. Kress Fellowship Fund, and Institute of Fine Arts Fellowship Awards. Support was also provided by the College of Arts and Science at Lehigh University and its dean John Hunt. Simon Pepper was supported by the Bernard Webb Studentship at the British School in Rome and by Liverpool University Research Funds, which enabled continued visits to Italy. Both authors are grateful for these research funds.

Finally the reader's attention is directed to the dedication page. Judith Hook was a comrade in the archives, the model of the committed scholar, and a person whose energy and enthusiasm for life was boundless. We shall all miss her.

INTRODUCTION

Early Modern Europe witnessed revolutionary changes in the conduct of war. Technical developments influenced both campaign strategy and operational tactics, while economic and political factors combined to make warfare, waged comprehensively in all seasons, a routine reality. It is our intention in this book to explore one part of this revolution by looking closely at the fortifications and tactics of siege warfare that evolved in response to more effective gunpowder artillery. The early part of the study is necessarily general in scope, for here we deal synoptically with fifteenth- and sixteenth-century developments in the design and supply of artillery and the consequent evolution of a bastioned military architecture, an architecture that eventually became commonplace over the entire continent of Europe and among the colonies of Africa and the New World. The core of the book consists of an examination of the design and construction of fortifications in one central Italian state, the republic of Siena. This is coupled with accounts of three important sieges, which put the defenses of the republic to the test of battle in a series of campaigns that by the year 1559 had finally ended Siena's independence and brought her extensive territories under the control of Cosimo de' Medici and ultimately into the Granducato della Toscana. In the case of Siena we may examine what a medium-sized state of modest means could do to cope with the changes in warfare.

During the second quarter of the sixteenth century the defensive face of Siena was changed. Between 1527 and 1532 she was equipped with new bastions designed by Baldassarre Peruzzi; a citadel begun by the Spaniards in 1550 and subsequently incorporated into the city enceinte; and extensive outworks constructed by the Sienese and their French allies immediately before and during the great siege of 1554–55. These works formed the largest architectural complex in the republic and were defended against Spanish and Florentine forces for fifteen months in one of the longest and most savage sieges of the Italian Wars, before Siena succumbed finally to starvation. The main towns in her dominio were also defended. Montalcino, located some twenty miles to the south of Siena, was equipped with substantial earthwork bastions in 1552–53, which successfully resisted an eighty-day siege from a greatly superior Spanish force. Port' Ercole, the main port of entry for French supplies and reinforcements, was defended between 1552 and 1555 by an extensive and unusual system of no less than seven detached forts. All of these fortifications, together with a much larger number of less important works and actions, constitute the raw material for our study. Their value hinges upon the wide variety of different military architectural solutions represented in the sample and upon the fact that all of them may be considered both as major construction projects and as functional buildings that were actually contested in well-documented military operations.

Indeed, these last years of the republic of Siena offer special opportunities for a study of this kind. By no means the most prosperous of Early Modern states, Siena nevertheless controlled a vast tract of land between the often hostile territories of the Papal States to the south and those of Florence, her traditional rival, to the east and north. All of these frontiers (as well as the capital itself) had to be defended along with the southern Tuscan coastline, which was constantly threatened by seaborne Turkish raiders. Siena's fortifications represented an enormous investment in building materials, labor, and professional skill, an investment which, when expressed monetarily, she was barely able to afford. Yet though not a power of the first order, Siena could call on the services of some of Italy's best architects as fortification designers, among whom Francesco di Giorgio Martini, Baldassarre Peruzzi, Pietro Cataneo, and Giovambattista Peloro were all natives of the city. The reports of these architects, together with the vastly more numerous and regular correspondence of the republic's commissioners and ambassadors, provide an excellent and remarkably thorough picture of Siena's fortification building program.

Siena's need for self-defense stemmed not only from geography but from chronic defects in her government. Threats were generated internally by the endemic factionalism that divided the republic's ruling class into what were known as *monti* or *ordini*. Each of the five monti struggling for power in Renaissance Siena took its name from a medieval ruling group: the *Gentilhuomini* or Nobles, the *Noveschi* (comprising families represented in the regime of the Nine), the *Dodici* (or Twelve, who overthrew the Nine in 1355), the *Riformatori* (Reformers, who succeeded the Twelve) and the *Popolari* or Popular party. It was a system, in Judith Hook's words, "whose very existence seemed to institutionalize civic strife" as the monti, acting singly or in combination, sought to win control of the republic's institutions, courts and revenue-yielding offices for the benefit of their own members. Our own period was ushered in by some years of relative stability under the so-called "tyranny" of the Petrucci family who, aided by their fellow Noveschi, had siezed power in 1487 and enforced the most successful and sustained exercise in political control. The death of Rafaello Petrucci in 1522, the brief rule of Fabio Petrucci (1522–24) and the subsequent exile of their followers created a crisis which was to be finally resolved only by the end of the republic itself. Exiled Noveschi seeking to fight their way back into power supported the Medici pope, Clement VII, in a serious but ultimately unsuccessful attack on Siena in 1526 which provoked savage reprisals by the ruling junta of Popolari and Riformatori. The major Italian and international powers were inevitably drawn into the continuous crisis created by Sienese political instability, often, as in 1526, at the instigation of monti seeking advantages for themselves within Siena through alliances without. Although the ruling Popolari and Riformatori identified themselves in 1526 stridently with the Imperial cause, Charles V and his Spanish governors were unable to control their excesses. Moreover, Spanish control of Siena became increasingly heavy-handed and eventually sparked off rebellion. Thus it was that within the last quarter century of its existence, the Sienese republic faced attacks from the Florentine Pope, from its own rebel partisans, from the Turks, and finally from its former protector, the emperor.

Baldassarre Peruzzi's fortifications of 1527–32 were built to remedy specific weaknesses exposed by the attack of 1526 and to meet the continuing threat posed by the exiles. The major test for the republic's defenses came in the years following 1552 when, after expelling the Spanish garrison of the emperor Charles V, Siena allied herself to France and was immediately counterattacked by the emperor's loyal subjects and allies from Naples and the duchy of Florence. At times feigning neutrality, Cosimo de' Medici, duke of Florence, was at all stages the chief supplier of money, provisions, artillery, fortified bases, and reinforcements to the Imperial expeditionary forces attacking Siena. In effect, Cosimo controlled the war, corresponding continuously with Imperial officers in the field and with his own officials and engineers in the army. Dispatch riders using relays of horses could carry messages between Florence and Siena in less than a day, allowing a rapid exchange of information and orders and encouraging the duke to demand briefings on all manner of technical concerns as well as the grand strategy of the war. To the field leaders the duke's meddling memoranda were something of a nuisance. Seen through the letters from the Imperial and Florentine officers, the siege of Siena becomes a real affair of pay and supply problems, technical shortcomings, delays, disagreements, and recriminations. Out of this mass of material it is possible to piece together a detailed account of offensive siege operations. Here the key documents are the letters between Cosimo and Giangiacomo de'Medici, Marquis of Marignano, the general commanding the Spanish and Florentine forces outside Siena for the siege of 1554–55. Their frequency and immediacy constitute a primary record of military leadership rarely encountered in so complete a form.

Although official Sienese records leading up to the period of the siege itself are plentiful, the republic's records of the siege itself are in many ways less revealing than those of the attacking Imperialists. Inside the besieged capital, argument and explanation were by word of mouth, while the difficulty of sending letters through the blockade meant that most of the documents were carefully considered statements, sometimes in code, which often conveyed less of the problems of siege operations than did the hastily scribbled postscripts to Imperial dispatches. These shortcomings are partially compensated, however, by chronicles such as those of the Sienese Alessandro Sozzini and Agnolo Bardi. In addition, the action-packed *Commentaires* of Blaise de Monluc, the French military governor in Siena during much of the siege, provide a somewhat more objective account of events and allow us to check the accuracy of the Sienese patriots. Only in the final weeks of the siege, however, was the government of the republic of Siena cut off completely from its territory. For most of the war a stream of letters flowed into Siena from outlying fortresses and towns, giving a vivid and often exciting picture of defensive siege warfare in the dominio.

The only category of source material that is in short supply are original architectural drawings. This is not altogether surprising since models were often used to explain the more complex permanent fortifications, and many of the temporary works were thrown up hastily without proper drawings and leveled soon after the fighting; some drawings may even have been destroyed in the construction process. Hence, for physical records of vanished works we have, from time to time, been compelled to rely on sources of a less precise nature. Some of the works and actions are illustrated in contemporary printed treatises. A number of the more important fortifications from the 1550s were recorded on the painted wooden book covers commissioned by the Sienese finance ministry, the Biccherna, some of them painted by Maestro Giorgio di Giovanni, one of the Sienese artist-architects most closely involved in their design and construction. Others appear in the wartime scenes depicted by Giorgio Vasari's ceiling panels and wall frescoes for the Palazzo Vecchio, Florence. History painting of this period is often regarded as more symbolic than realistic; yet Vasari's views accord closely with the written record and, when used with a careful reconstruction of the historical narrative, can yield much useful information on the layout of the siegeworks.

When taken together, therefore, Sienese and Florentine sources provide all the essential ingredients for an account of fortress design and siege warfare that, somewhat unusually, gives equal weight to the problems of both sides involved in the fighting. The situation we have described for Siena generally holds for the other sieges during the Siena campaign at Montalcino and Port' Ércole. Thus the military architecture will be studied as closely as the remains or surviving records allow. But besides physical description and analysis we will be concerned to examine the administration of these works, the time taken to bring them to completion, and the measures adopted to secure labor, materials, and funds for what by any standard was among the greatest public building projects of the age. The activity of Siena's military architects will also be explored; in particular the part played by "civilian" artists, architects, even mathematicians, who served in the wartime emergency beside the professional mercenary soldiers. In short, by concentrating on the building programs and campaigns of a single state, we are attempting to assemble a comprehensive picture of sixteenth-century military architecture in peace and war.

We have tried to contruct our story mindful of the multidisciplinary character of the history and architecture of war. As formal invention, military architecture can be admired or criticized, but it must rapidly be accounted for as an effective or defective instrument on the battlefield; no work of military architecture can exist which fails to mix the useful in with the beautiful. We might, of course, make the same claim for any work of architecture, and yet nowhere else does the Wottonian insistence on firmness seem more appropriate (or the connection with beauty seem more tenuous) than in the study of military architecture. As distinguished from most civil or religious architecture, however, firmness was not something that could be achieved in military architecture once and for all; military imperatives change over time spans of amazing brevity. A work of military architecture has to continue to give service against new artillery, new strategies, and new enemies, and it may have to accommodate new owners and altered battle plans. The life of a fortress may or may not be a long one, but if it was to continue to serve its masters effectively in an unstable world, it had to accept changes and alterations of many sorts. In order to bring it fully to life, military architecture must be studied over time. By concentrating on one city and its territory we hope to reveal changes in military and fortification practice more clearly.

Art history has for many years struggled with distinctions between high and low art. Studies of military architecture in the 1960s, for example, often took an apologetic stance toward their study, arguing, in a normative manner, that it should be the responsibility of the art historian to consider what most architects did most of the time. Thus, when J. S. Ackerman, in his important book on the architecture of Michelangelo, and Ackerman's student Horst de la Croix, in a crucial series of articles (to which extensive reference will be made later on), propounded a new kind of democratic art history, they tended to assume that military architecture, like other aesthetically disadvantaged topics, could only be included in an art history that was written as a history of things—possibly, in the manner suggested by George Kubler in *The Shape of Time* (New Haven, 1962). Although art history seems better disposed to accept subjects like military architecture today, there remains a critical lapse when it comes to the consideration of use and firmness—military architecture's crucial attributes. While study of the aesthetic and symbolic values of military architecture is now not uncommon,[1] study of how fortifications performed as a defense tool is rare. The reluctance to come to grips with military architecture under fire results, in part, from the terms under which fortifications have been accepted as a part of architecture and architectural history. Admired for its machinelike precision and clean lines, one often notes an aestheticized protomodernist interest in symbolic function rather than actual function. The architectural historian Ludwig H. Heydenreich, for example, wrote in his monograph on Leonardo da Vinci: "To our own generation . . . which has learned to appreciate simple, utilitarian forms and clearly planned buildings, so long as their proportions are good, Leonardo's fortresses seem beautiful the more because of their exquisite simplicity and their proportions."[2] In this respect, a study like ours that centers around function conceived of as a specific activity rather than in formal or symbolical terms strikes an altogether different pose.

One result of the art-historical bias against function in many twentieth-century studies of military architecture in Early Modern Europe can be seen in the acceptance of a kind of technological determinism. This bias is revealed most clearly in debates concerning the importance of bastioned military architecture, the so-called Italian manner of fortification. Expressed crudely, the invention of the angle bastion in Italy around 1500, of which much more will be said later on, is often seen as the inevitable response to the new cannon produced in the late fifteenth century; its form is reckoned to be a perfected, indeed almost ineluctable application of mathematical and military principles. It has seemed clear to most historians that those who failed to fortify their towns with the new angle bastions, the product of Renaissance genius, should have been unable to meet the demands of the modern world. In effect, the acceptance of the angle bastion as a technological imperative has ultimately led to a kind of crude linkage between, on the one hand, the independent city-state of medieval Italy with its imperfect techniques of warfare and, on the other, the new artillery and the angle bastions of the nascent modern state.

"The hand-mill gives you society with the feudal lord; the steam-mill, society with the industrial capitalist." Our examination of military architecture under fire in Early Modern Italy leads us to conclusions somewhat different from the kind sometimes represented as deriving from that phrase of Karl Marx.[3] Technological developments, it is often said, only open doors; they compel no one to pass through.

To understand the function of military architecture we must face the ebb and flow of action. In order to do so we have turned to the methods of so-called pure historians. Studies of warfare in Early Modern Italy such as those of Cecil Roth, Frederick Taylor, Michael Mallet, Piero Pieri, and Charles Oman (see bibliography) have been valuable for the kind of information they supply us about what people actually did under arms. We have also used an extensive contemporary literature of old soldiers' reminiscences, diaries, and chronicles; it is the narrative nature of these texts above anything else that makes them valuable for our purposes. Without a measure of understanding of the panic and confusion of the battlefield derived from our sources, all action seems merely chaotic and the reasons for architectural defense will be only vaguely or very generally understood.

While most art-historical writing about military architecture has failed to come to grips with function, for their part pure historians have tended to avoid analysis of the forms of military architecture. Exceptions are found primarily among a school of military historians in Italy who, enflamed by the passion of national unification in the nineteenth century, looked to recreate a glorious past of Italian martial skill. Carlo Promis, Alberto Gugliemotti, and Enrico Rocchi, for example (see bibliography), tried to see fortifications in the context of the battlefield, though they tended to stress the heroic achievements of individual genius in design and in battle rather than the interaction of the sometimes anonymous events of war with military architecture. For us, however, the most important scholarly model is the English historian Sir John Hale. For Hale, military architecture is not just a static adjunct to military affairs. The form of fortification, not just its presence alone, is explained by reference to military policies based in political, social, economic, and military realities. In his studies of the development of the angle bastion, the fortifications of Vicenza, and Florence's Fortezza da Basso, Hale laid out a model of the history of military architecture responding to actual circumstance. And Judith Hook, in an article on fortifications and the end of the Sienese state, sought to apply Hale's method to Sienese defense policies in the sixteenth centruy. For Hook, like Hale, Early Modern fortifications formed military policies as well as resulting from them. Generally speaking, therefore, Hale's work offers the best example of the multidisciplinary model to which we aspire. We approach matters from the other side of the narrow divide, however it is defined, that separates art history from pure history, but to put the matter briefly we too have, like him, tried to combine the art historian's respect for genius and material form with the pure historian's respect for narrative and the overall context for military construction.

We have also taken some intensely practical matters to a level of detail that would hardly have been open to researchers working is less confined fields. How were Siena's defenses constructed? What materials were used? From which directions were attacks on the republic's strongholds expected? How were the attacks actually mounted? What weapons were available to the combatants—both attackers and defenders—and how did they perform? Such questions might suggest that our aim was to write a kind of Rankean military-architectural history *wie es eigentlich gewesen.* On one level, indeed, that kind of history is what we might want to write were it attainable; not because it has any intrinsic value or leads us to moral high ground, but because it offers an invaluable key to the form of things. Although we are frequently unable to answer all of our own questions, enough can be discovered about the weapons, walls, men, and events to give us a somewhat skeptical view of the contemporary printed culture of the military and architectural treatises. As John Keegan has observed, "action is fundamentally destructive of all institutional studies."[4] We will find out not only what every GI or Tommy knows—that a successful operation can result from the most accidental features of the landscape, or the nerve of a key individual—but that the experience of the veteran will generally serve as well, or better, than the formal training of West Point or Sandhurst graduates. Soldiers and military architects of the sixteenth century, equally, did not always fight or build by the book. Our study will try to account for the significance of actual circumstances.

In a sense, our own predisposition in favor of action and its narrative, our stress on the object and the event as the subverter of the print culture, allies us with the French school of historical thought often represented by its most noted journal, *Les Annales,* and its celebrated scholar of the sixteenth century, Fernand Braudel. For besides giving a breathtaking panorama of the Mediterranean world at the end of our own period, Braudel is master of the critical or illuminating incident. Historians of technology with an affinity for Braudel's methods—such as Frederick Lane (himself a pioneer), Carlo Cipolla, and John Francis Guilmartin—have provided us with numerous valuable insights into the complex relationships between war machines, military buildings, and the economic, political, even geographical factors which bear upon their innovation, diffusion, and use in action. For historians of architecture or technology, of course, the goals are not so universal as those of Braudel. For us, an understanding of only a piece of reality will do. Central Italy, then, provides our field; war provides the action; and at the intersection of these two we will find our subject: military architecture and siege warfare in sixteenth-century Siena.

FIREARMS
AND
FORTIFICATIONS

1

FIREARMS AND FORTIFICATIONS

The most significant of all architectural forms evolved during the Renaissance was the angle bastion. By resisting the new artillery and providing platforms for heavy guns it revolutionised the defensive-offensive pattern of warfare, and its speedy adoption by state after state during the sixteenth century dramatically affected the appearance of cities throughout Europe—and further afield. . . . The International Style par excellence of the Renaissance was that of military architecture, and its module was the angle bastion.[1]

The Angle Bastion

THE bastion for which so much has been rightly claimed by Hale was little more than a solid platform projecting in front of a fortress or town walls. Guns mounted on its flanks could sweep the neighboring curtains, so that with a properly planned defensive scheme any assault on the main walls would have to pass through a cross fire from two adjacent flanking batteries. Guns mounted on the faces fired outward to break up siege batteries and, as the contemporary phrase went, to "annoy the enemy" (fig. 1). Semicircular or rectangular gun platforms, of course, were capable of providing an identical combination of artillery positions. But the angled, triangular, or pointed shapes which were to give the characteristic star patterns of Early Modern fortifications were the only forms capable of eliminating the blind spots in the defensive fire plan which were always to be found outside squared or rounded works.[2]

Among the first architectural casualties to effective artillery had been the elaborate superstructures of medieval fortifications, the bracketed machicoulis galleries and timber hoardings from which the defenders had shot down—or dropped heavy objects—on their enemies at the foot of the walls. Once these upper works had been removed, either by architects or by gunfire, effective defense demanded that every inch of the perimeter should be swept by the flankers. Blind spots represented a particular hazard. Any dead ground offered opportunities for sappers to dig or mine their way into a fortress or city. Hence the interest of Renaissance military architects and the preoccupation of their modern critics with the total rationalization of the flanking system and its angled geometry.

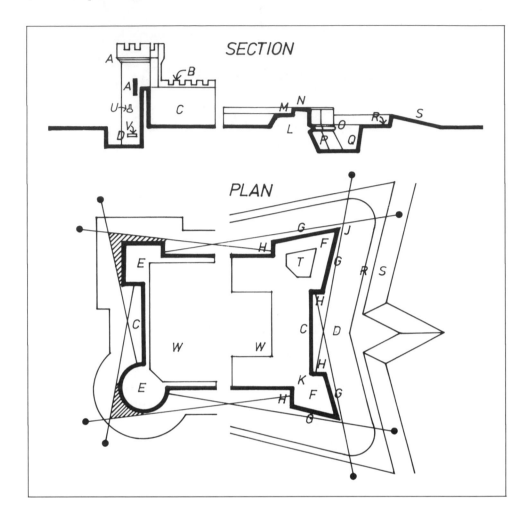

Fig. 1. Medieval and Early Modern Fortification. Diagram contrasts medieval wall and tower defenses (left) with the bastion and rampart system (right). Lines of fire illustrate how the triangular trace avoids blind spots. **A:** Machicolations or machicoulis gallery, bracketed upper-level works allowing defenders to drop heavy objects to the foot of the wall. **B:** *Merli* (Italian) or merlons (English), solid protective components between embrasures. **C:** Curtain, section of wall or rampart between towers or bastions. **D:** Ditch. **E:** Towers, with hatching indicating blind spots. **F:** Bastions, solid gun platforms projecting from the curtains. **G:** Face of the bastion. **H:** Flank of the bastion. **J:** Salient or pointed tip of the bastion. **K:** Gorge or throat of the bastion. **L:** Rampart. **M:** Terreplein or gun platform. **N:** Parapet. **O:** Cordon, moulding dividing vertical and battered sections of a rampart or bastion. **P:** Scarp, battered (sloping) lower section of rampart/bastion. **Q:** Counterscarp, outer wall of ditch. **R:** Covered way, protected infantry position outside the ditch. **S:** Glacis, gently sloping earth bank concealing the covered way and all but the uppermost defensive works. **T:** Cavalier, raised gun platform on rampart or bastion. **U:** Keyhole gunport. **V:** Letterbox gunport. **W:** Enceinte, area enclosed (literally "belted") by a fortification.

Fig. 2. Two Views of the Castel Sant'Angelo, Rome. Note the increase in scale of fortifications during the sixteenth century. *Above:* Works by Antonio da Sangallo the Elder (1492–95), who added octagonal "bastions" or guntowers to the round towers of 1447 at the corners of the early medieval enceinte. *Below:* A simplified air view showing Francesco Laparelli's bastions built 1561–65. The *orecchioni* ("big ears") or curved shoulders and the *traditore* flanks (concealed or traitor flanks) were added in 1630.

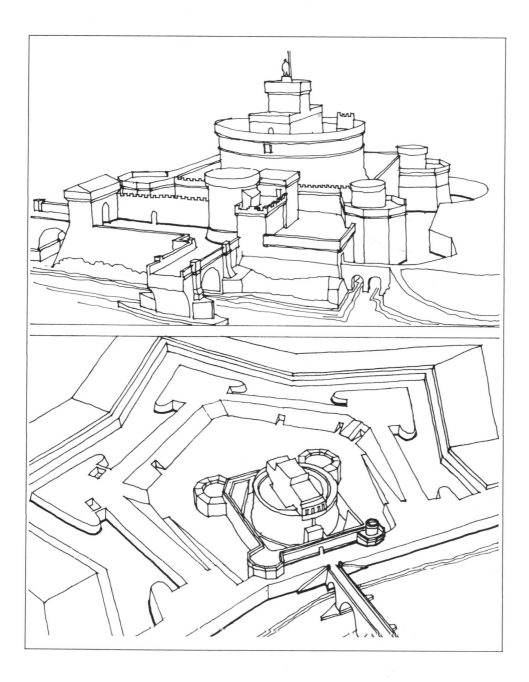

Another concern was the accommodation of artillery. Big guns, in particular, needed solid mountings and plenty of room. Initially these requirements were satisfied by reducing towers to the same level as the walls and reinforcing both elements to give a series of high platforms, connected by broad galleries for the movement of weapons. Although it was a time-honored principle that to overlook one's enemy was preferable to being overlooked, high platforms themselves made vulnerable targets and forced the defenders to angle their fire sharply downward, which was much less effective than a horizontal trajectory. For besides the tendency of balls to fall out of steeply depressed muzzle-loaders, plunging fire—as it has always been called—had to be aimed at foreshortened targets and, unlike horizontal shots, was more likely to strike the ground harmlessly than to hit a secondary target, should it miss its intended mark. All these factors combined in a general tendency toward the lowered profiles of bastioned fortifications, providing less exposed works and lines of fire that eventually would only graze the edge of the ditch in which the fortress was sunk. Room for greater numbers of heavy guns was obtained by enlarging the area of the platform. In its fully developed form the Early Modern bastion assumed gigantic, squat proportions (fig. 2).

There was nothing sudden about the transition from medieval to Early Modern fortifications. The mid-fifteenth-century angled towers identified by Hale in the central Italian hill towns mark the beginnings of the process; but round or polygonal towers were still being constructed well into the early sixteenth century—if by then generally without *merlatura* or machicolations. Early examples of fully integrated angled flanking systems can be found at Poggio Imperiale, Brolio, Nettuno, and Pisa (figs. 3 and 4), around the turn of the century. Another twenty-five years were to pass before the classic angled plan could truly be said to inform all new works. Indeed, only by the second half of the sixteenth century had designers universally abandoned multilevel masonry structures for the fully developed platform bastions, open to the sky, where masonry construction generally served only to shape and retain massive earthworks. By then, the proven success of the new fortifications and the exposition of their virtues in the burgeoning technical literature, a product of the new print culture, had created a climate of opinion that made the bastion the standard against which alternative forms were judged, and generally found wanting.[3] Yet other design ideas were floated during the bastion's long gestation, some of which were clearly important to the development of military architecture. Because all of these schemes were devised with two purposes in mind—to resist artillery and to exploit firearms in their own defense—it is appropriate to begin our study of Siena's fortifications with a discussion of the weapons of Renaissance siege warfare.

Fig. 3. A Corner Bastion at the Fortress of Poggio Imperiale, near Poggibonsi. Built on the Florentine-Sienese border (1495–1513) to guard the main route into Florence by the architects Giuliano da Sangallo and Antonio da Sangallo the Elder, this fortress remains one of the best-preserved Early Modern defense works. Note the straight flanks and obtuse angle of the salient. Its multifaceted face and carefully positioned casemates allow for flanking fire. The fortress, of which this bastion is part, is linked to a curtain wall almost a mile in length, which encircles the crown of the hill.

Fig. 4. The Fortress of Nettuno, (1501–03). One of the Papal fortresses built by Antonio da Sangallo the Elder and Giuliano da Sangallo to defend the western coast of Italy from Turkish marauders. The defenses are arranged to provide fire across each face from flank embrasures well concealed by curved orecchioni. Pronounced scarping of the walls is a more modern feature; but the curved salients and the vestigial machicoulis brackets—used here as decoration—reflect an earlier tradition.

The Weapons of Renaissance Siege Warfare

The first effective artillery pieces appeared in the fourteenth century, and by the early fifteenth century quite large guns were being made from a series of wrought-iron wedges formed into a tube and held together by iron bands, shrunk onto the tube like barrel hoops (Fig. 5).[4] These so-called hooped bombards fired stone balls, often more than twelve inches and sometimes up to three feet in diameter. The difficulty of sealing the rear end of a built-up barrel was avoided by designing most of them as breechloaders, the breech being closed by a variety of plug-and-wedge arrangements which could safely sustain only modest gunpowder charges. By the middle of the fifteenth century, however, much more powerful muzzle-loading bombards were being cast in bronze—using the technology of church bell manufacture.[5] In these guns the breech walls were made thicker than those of the barrel, either by enlarging the casting by the addition of prominent and highly decorated moldings or by reducing the bore to form a smaller powder chamber. Limitations on the size of bronze castings meant that the biggest guns had to be made in two or three sections, transported separately, and assembled on heavy timber flatbeds before firing. Their use was of course limited to static siege warfare. But siege artillery of this kind posed a significant threat to fortified positions. The fall of Constantinople in 1453 to the stone firing bombards of the Turks gave gunnery its most spectacular early achievement.

A few years earlier the French had introduced what was eventually to prove a seminal innovation. Their substitution of cast-iron shot for stone cannonballs allowed the caliber and consequently the size, weight, and cost of guns to be reduced, while at the same time achieving considerable improvement in shot penetration. The brothers Jean and Gaspard Bureau were the artillerists credited with this technical breakthrough and with the subsequent successes of Charles VII's siege train, which, in the single campaigning season of 1449, reduced some sixty English castles to submission.[6] It was a triumph for mobility as well as for increased firepower (fig. 6). Yet even iron-shotted pieces remained cumbersome to transport, as is clear from the early artillery campaigns, such as the epic passage of the Pyrenees by the French siege train in 1462 en route to Barcelona. "It was indeed a remarkable achievement," wrote Guillaume Leseur, "for master Jean Bureau had done this by sheer weight of men . . . [causing] a completely new way . . . to be cut through the rock and the mountains, a way which the Catalans since then have taken to calling 'The French Road.' "[7] Transport operations of this kind made enormous demands on manpower. Isabella of Castille is reported to have employed a work force of six thousand on a causeway bringing guns to the siege of Cambil, one of the minor actions in the *reconquista* of Granada.[8]

Improved mobility was by no means the last of the long-term trends stimulated

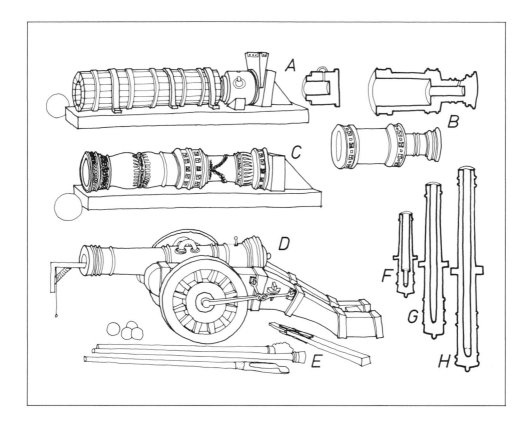

Fig. 5. Siege Artillery of the Fifteenth and Sixteenth Centuries. **A:** Hooped bombard (early fifteenth century), with detachable powder chambers. **B:** Mortar-type bombard (mid-fifteenth century), in cast bronze, sectioned to show reduced bore of the powder chamber. **C:** Bronze bombard (mid-fifteenth century), cast in two sections for easier transport. **D:** Carriage-mounted bronze cannon of the sixteenth century, with "dolphins" for hoisting and gunner's quadrant for determining elevation. **E:** Tools of the gunner's trade (top to bottom): iron-shod spike for traversing the gun, sponge, rammer, and powder ladle. **F:** Perrier, sectioned to show thin barrel walls and reduced-bore powder chamber. **G:** Cannon-type gun with reduced "bell bore" at the breech. **H:** Culverin-type weapon, or "long gun" with thick barrel walls and straight bore.

by the introduction of cast-iron shot. Once shot-casting techniques had been perfected, iron rounds could be mass-produced much more cheaply than stone balls could be sculpted by hand.[9] Standardization of calibers soon became necessary as well as desirable, although it was to be many years before skilled stone cutters ceased to turn out "bespoke" ammunition for the older guns.[10] Finally, the reduction in the deadweight of guns led to their being made with trunnions—lugs cast into the barrel at the point of balance—and mounted permanently on wheeled carriages. Long-distance transport was probably not much easier or faster

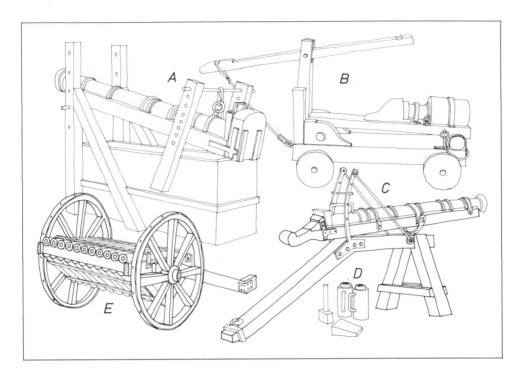

Fig. 6. Defensive Artillery on Fortress Carriages. **A:** Breechloading bombard on fixed carriage set to fire over a high parapet, based on a reconstructed carriage of circa 1500 in the Castel Sant'Angelo, Rome. **B:** Mortar, circa 1500, Castel Sant'Angelo, Rome. This carriage allows the mortar to be elevated (its most common position) as well as depressed to fire steeply downward. **C:** Breechloading bombard, circa 1500, Castel Sant'Angelo, Rome. **D:** Spare chambers for **C**, with mallet and wedge used to secure the chambers in the breech. **E:** An organ or multibarreled piece based on drawings by Leonardo da Vinci. This example has three rotating gun racks, each containing eleven barrels. Although sometimes described as a volley-firing weapon, the simultaneous discharge of eleven barrels could not be achieved with match ignition and would, in any event, ruin the relatively frail carriage. However, a very rapid rate of fire could be achieved from organs of this type.

than before; but wheeled guns could be brought quickly into action, elevated or depressed simply, trained rapidly onto different targets, and used in the field as well as in siege operations.

From this stage, notable tactical successes began to be recorded for the artillery. The 1494 invasion of Italy by Charles VIII provided one of the first large-scale demonstrations of the new weapons' mobility and destructive efficiency as the French siege train managed to keep pace with the army to crack open one fortress after another in the victorious progress to Naples and the equally precipitate retreat to Fornova (1495). At the battles of Ravenna (1512) and Marignano (1515) the artillery inflicted terrible casualties on congested battlefields. But it was the impact of the new artillery in sieges that most impressed contemporaries conscious of witnessing fundamental changes in the pace and grand strategy of war. The analysis of Francesco Guicciardini, the Florentine-born diplomat and historian, who served as papal governor of Parma shortly after the successful defense of that city in 1521, is one of the clearest. In his aphoristic *Ricordi Politici e Civili* he writes: "Before the year 1494, wars were protracted, battles bloodless, the methods followed in besieging towns slow and uncertain, and although artillery was already in use, it was managed with such lack of skill that it caused little hurt. Hence it came about that the rulers of a state could hardly be dispossessed. But the French, in their invasion of Italy, infused so much liveliness into our wars that up to the year 1521, whenever the open country was lost, the state was lost with it."[11] Guicciardini's fuller explanation in his *History of Italy* encompassed not only the technical superiority of the new weapons but the skill of their operators and the logistical efficiency of the royal siege train.

> the French brought a much handier engine made of brass, called Cannon, which they charged with heavy iron balls, smaller without comparison than those of stone made use of heretofore, and drove them on carriages with horses, not with oxen, as was the custom in Italy; and they were attended by such clever men, and on such instruments appointed for the purpose that they almost ever kept pace with the army. They were planted against the walls of a town with such speed, the space between shot was so little, and the balls flew so quick, and were impelled with such force, that as much execution was done in a few hours, as formerly, in Italy, in the like number of days. These, rather diabolical than human instruments, were used not only in sieges, but also in the field, and were mixed with others of a smaller size. Such artillery rendered Charles's army very formidable to all Italy.[12]

Here it becomes necessary to introduce a note of caution. Anyone researching into Early Modern warfare can hardly fail to be impressed by evidence of the highly variable quality of artillery and its short supply. Well into the sixteenth century, lists of the artillery stock holdings in European arsenals included significant numbers of the earlier generations of stone-firing weapons. These guns were still being used in combat as late as the 1550s. Moreover, the bigger guns used for the bombardment of fortifications were by no means the mobile weapons of Guicciardini's account. A full cannon of the mid-sixteenth century weighed, with its carriage, over 8,000 pounds and was moved across country with great difficulty, a factor that in practice was bound to reduce their availability. On a few occasions very large numbers of guns were assembled for major enterprises. Barcelona, it was claimed, mustered more than two hundred guns of all types for the siege of 1462, no doubt disarming many of the ships in port to do so. Figures in excess of a hundred guns are claimed for the artillery trains that accompanied Charles VIII to Naples in 1494 and Emperor Maximilian's expedition against Venice in 1509: heavy weapons formed a small proportion of these totals.[13] In truth, siege batteries of less than a dozen heavy guns were much more common in the first half of the sixteenth century.

By the second half of the sixteenth century the most up-to-date arsenals might contain a few of the cast-iron guns first manufactured on a significant scale by the English in the 1540s.[14] Caliber for caliber these iron weapons were both heavier and less safe to use than bronze artillery. But they cost only about one-third the price of bronze guns,[15] a factor which was to provide the impetus for the almost exponential growth in the number of guns employed in the seventeenth and eighteenth centuries. All of this, however, lay in the future. The sixteenth-century soldier had to make do with very limited numbers of guns, heavy guns being in particularly short supply.

As an example, in the year 1552 the duchy of Florence, one of Italy's more substantial powers, possessed 625 artillery pieces of all types (see table 1).[16] This may sound like a large number, but only 58 were heavy battering pieces; the full cannon-of-battery firing a shot of some 40 pounds and the culverins firing 25-pound shot. Almost half of the battering pieces were concentrated in Florence itself, where 22 cannon and 2 culverins were stored. About three-quarters of these guns formed the siege train in time of war, leaving only about six heavy pieces in the city reserve. Ten heavy guns were to be found in the combined fortress, galleys, and arsenal of Pisa, the principal Florentine military port. Livorno mustered another six, as did the combined fortresses and towers on the exposed island of Elba. However, 13 out of the remaining 18 Florentine fortresses possessed no heavy artillery at all.

Florence's medium artillery far outnumbered her heavy guns. The most numerous medium-weight pieces were the 107 *petreri* or perriers, which, as their name suggests, were designed to fire stone balls of up to some 24 pounds' weight.[17] Stone balls were extremely effective against the frail wooden hulls of Mediterranean galleys, and it is no surprise to find a large concentration of petreri at the naval base of Pisa. They were also employed against batteries in siege warfare and, in theory, were sufficiently light and mobile to use against the smaller medieval fortifications. But the preferred weapon for mobile siege warfare of this kind was the half-cannon, a heavier gun of some 4,500 pounds firing 20- to 30-pound iron shot. Florence possessed only 19 of these useful guns and used some of them intensively in the war against Siena.

The great majority of the Florentine weapons would be classified as light artillery, a category that included the 12-pounder half-culverins and quarter-

Table 1   Florentine Artillery in 1552

Location	Cannon Type								
	Full Cannon	Culverin	Half Cannon	Half Culverin	Quarter Cannon	Perrier	Saker	Falcon	Moschetto
Fortress of Florence	22	2	3	5	—	40	9	13	36
Fortress of Pisa, galleys and arsenal (total)	7	3	5	1	3	40	13	—	54
Fortress of Livorno	2	2	1	2	—	—	6	8	3
Torre Nova at Livorno	—	—	—	—	—	—	2	—	—
Fortress of Gorgona	—	—	—	—	—	—	1	1	2
Tower at Cala Furia	—	—	—	—	—	—	—	1	2
Tower at Castiglioncello	—	—	—	—	—	—	—	1	2
Pietrasanta and Motrone	—	—	—	—	—	—	—	3	6
Fortress and Tower on Elba	2	4	2	4	2	8	7	6	12
Fortress of Volterra	1	—	—	—	2	—	9	6	11
Fortress of Arezzo	3	—	2	3	—	2	6	6	8
Arezzo (surroundings)	—	—	—	—	—	—	—	2	8
Fortress of Cortona	—	—	—	—	1	—	—	1	13
Fortress of Montepulciano	—	—	—	—	1	—	—	2	3
Montepulciano (surroundings)	—	—	—	—	—	—	—	—	8
Fortress at Borgo San Sepolcro	1	3	—	—	1	1	2	3	9
Firenzuola	—	—	—	—	—	—	—	—	2
Montepogiolo	—	—	—	—	—	—	—	—	3
Fortress of Modigliana	—	—	—	—	—	—	3	—	2
Fortress of Castrocaro	—	—	1	1	—	—	1	4	3
Fivizano	—	—	—	—	—	4	—	—	—
Fortress of Pistoia	3	—	3	2	—	8	7	12	12
Empoli	—	—	—	—	—	2	2	—	1
Prato	1	—	2	1	—	2	5	4	6
Colle Val d'Elsa	—	—	—	—	—	—	—	—	8
On Board Ships	—	—	—	—	—	—	—	—	—
Totals	42	16	19	19	10	107	73	75	265

SOURCE: Adapted from D'Addario, "Burocrazia," p. 446.
NOTE: The "cannon" class (full-cannon, half-cannon and quarter-cannon) was distinguished from the "culverin" class (full, half-, and quarter-culverins) by length and weight-of-gun: weight-of-projectile ratio. Generally cannon were shorter and had thinner barrel walls and reinforced breeches (i.e., a powder chamber of reduced bore). The culverins, often known as "long guns" or *artiglieria longa* were relatively longer and had thicker barrel walls. This made them heavier than cannon firing the same weight of shot, as well as more expensive and cumbersome. However, these disadvantages were offset by their relative "safety." Gunners found them far less prone to blow up in action. Guilmartin, *Gunpowder and Galleys,* pp. 284–91, has shown that the strength of the culverin casting derived from the pressure under which the molten metal was set. Long guns cast breech-downward in their molds had far stronger breeches than the shorter cannon. Thus, although the barrel length of the culverins gave no extra range with the primitive powder propellants available to sixteenth-century artillerymen, gunners were much more inclined to load the "long guns" with full charges. Hence, perhaps, their association with long-range fire.

cannon, the 10-pounder sakers, the 2- to 3-pounder falcons, and the heavy musket. This last item should not be confused with the infantry firearm making its appearance at this time. The *moschette* or *moschettone* of sixteenth-century Italian siege warfare was generally operated from a wall-mounted swivel, was frequently breech-loaded, and was always listed among the artillery.[18] These weapons were critical in defensive firepower. As can be seen from the table, the 265 moschetti, the 75 falcons, and the 73 sakers constituted fully two-thirds of the Florentine artillery. In over half of the ducal fortresses these light pieces were the only defensive armaments, and there is no reason to suppose that this situation was in any way atypical. Although no comparable survey exists for Siena, what information we have makes it clear that most Sienese artillery was relatively small like the moschettone.[19]

Only major cities, of course, could expect to match the heavy artillery of a siege train; but it would be wrong to suppose that the defenders of more lightly armed fortresses were placed in a helpless position. Smaller weapons could wreck battery emplacements, damage heavy guns, and kill gunners—a human resource that, like the guns they served, was in surprisingly short supply. Indeed, it was only when used against a massed human target—a square of pikes, a crowded breach, or a galley crammed with men—that heavy guns could inflict casualties commensurate with their weight of shot.

In siege warfare, moreover, speed of fire was important to both sides.[20] An effective bombardment—quite apart from its effect on morale—needed to suppress defensive fire and to breach the walls faster than the garrison could build secondary lines behind the target area. For the defenders it was vital to avoid periods of "safety" when their guns were being reloaded. And while attacks were being pressed home against breached or escaladed walls, it was essential to sustain rapid defensive fire for minutes at a time. Muzzle-loaders, of course, fired slowly. Between each round the barrel had to be carefully sponged to douse any smouldering grains of incompletely burned powder before the gunner could place another charge with his open ladle. Reloading itself was an exposed and hazardous task that demanded a particulary steady hand when loose gunpowder had to be placed in a reduced chamber at the end of a long barrel. A wad of hay or other material was then forced down the bore to contain the powder. The ball would then be rammed home, the touchhole primed, and the sighting checked before the gun was ready for another shot. Even when linen or paper cartridges containing a ball and a premeasured charge began to be introduced in the mid-sixteenth century,[21] accurate rapid fire could be expected only from the most expert gunners. The historian of military technology, John Francis Guilmartin, suggests that Venetian galley-gun crews could reload their forward-facing main armament in about two minutes, allowing them to fire once at the extreme accurate range of about 500 yards and to reload in time to get off another volley as the galleys rammed.[22] Two minutes perhaps represents the fastest possible performance for muzzle-loaders over a very short period. Ramming, after all, only permitted these two volleys before the boarding party stormed the enemy ship. Sustained rapid fire represented quite a different problem and, in the many bombardments studied in later chapters, we have found no heavy siege battery achieving rates of fire faster than six minutes per shot per gun.

Higher rates of fire could undoubtedly be achieved with the various types of breech-loader still found in the period. As many as two shots per minute could probably be delivered by guns using precharged chambers, usually shaped like beer mugs, which could be slipped quickly into the breech and secured by a wedge and a mallet stroke (fig. 7). Three or four such chamber pieces, plus the services of one or two reloading assistants, could probably keep a gunner fully occupied until the weapon became too hot to handle.[23] At close quarters the artillery could be supplemented by devices such as the *tromba di fuoco.* This was a homemade scattergun, fashioned from a reamed-out log and reinforced by leather, rope or metal bindings, which could be prepared for use in a crisis on a "once only" basis.[24] Finally, many early fortifications of the gunpowder era have embrasures evidently placed and dimensioned for hand-held weapons. Their contribution to defensive firepower is often overlooked. Yet the fifteenth-century *scioppetti* and the sixteenth-century *archibusi* and *moschetti* far outnumbered the available artillery pieces and were much better adapted to confined fortress interiors than the unwieldy crossbow of an earlier period.

Primitive handguns had been in use from the early fourteenth century but, until the end of the fifteenth century, were fired "in the French manner" by a slow match held in one hand while the other supported the gun itself against the center of the breastplate. It was not an arrangement conducive to accurate fire, and the shock of recoil against the chest meant that loads had to be limited in power. The development of the matchlock firing mechanism, however, greatly improved the effectiveness of handguns. This device consisted simply of a rotating arm, fitted with a notch or hole into which the length of smoldering match cord was fixed. By raising the other end of the "trigger" arm, the match was brought down into the flashpan and the weapon discharged. The matchlock allowed the sixteenth-century arquebus to be fired from the shoulder, steadied by both hands and sighted along the barrel, which not only improved accuracy—by allowing the soldier to look at the target rather than the touchhole—but enabled the average soldier to support a gun weighing up to ten pounds and firing a half-ounce lead ball.[25]

The later so-called Spanish musket was a heavier and more powerful weapon of the same kind. Weighing up to eighteen pounds—and in some cases even

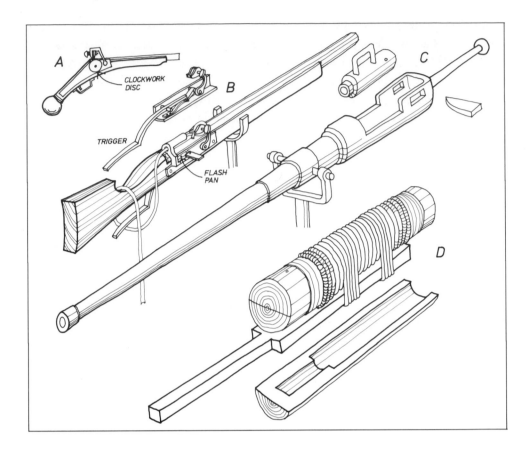

Fig. 7. Antipersonnel Weapons of the Six-teenth Century. **A:** Wheel lock pistol. The trigger releases a clockwork powered serrated disc which strikes sparks by spinning against the flint held in the screw jaws. It was an expensive device which explains why pistols were most often used by the cavalry.
B: Arquebus, showing forked rest and trigger mechanism. By raising the trigger arm the smoldering match cord is brought down to ignite the powder in the flash pan. The flame then passes through the "touch hole" to the charge in the breech. **C:** Moschettone, or swivel mounted rampart gun, with detachable chamber piece secured by a wedge. **D:** *Tromba di fuoco,* or wooden scatter gun, sectioned to show internal profile of the barrel.

more—it fired a two-ounce lead ball which could penetrate armor at more than a hundred paces and bring down a charging horse.[26] What today would be termed its "stopping power" was greatly valued by contemporaries such as the English captain, Sir Roger Williams, who stressed its importance in trench warfare as well as the open field and pointed out that the musket could be loaded with scattershot for fighting at close quarters.[27] Its only defect was weight. Strong men drawing extra pay were needed to carry muskets on the march. Even in the well-armed regular Spanish forces musketeers were outnumbered by arquebusiers. For any kind of accuracy in the field, the musket had to be fired from a forked rest. A fortress parapet or gunport, however, provided ideal firing conditions.

It is difficult to quantify the total numbers of small arms available to sixteenth-century armies. Unlike the artillery piece, the ordinary arquebus or the Spanish musket would never be the subject of a special survey, or a numbered item in arsenal records, still less a statistic quoted by the chronicler of a battle or siege. But there can be no doubt about their plentiful supply. As Siena prepared for war in the 1550s, arquebuses were purchased in lots of 500 at a time. Moreover, the proportion of shot to pike in regular Spanish infantry units increased steadily throughout the century; from perhaps 1 in 10 at the outset, to 1 in 3 by the 1570s and approximate parity at the close.[28] By the middle of the century, as we shall see, field fortifications were being constructed that must have relied almost entirely upon small arms fire for their local defense.

The other weapon often overlooked in artillery-centered accounts of Renaissance military architecture is the explosive mine. Whether mining represented a response to improvements in fortifications, deficiencies in artillery, lessons learned from gunpowder accidents, or merely a development from medieval siege tactics is impossible to say. Around the turn of the fifteenth and sixteenth centuries, however, gunpowder began to be employed in mines to spectacular effect. Credit for the first successful explosive mine has been given to Francesco di Giorgio Martini, a Sienese architect and the author of one of the earliest treatises on fortification design, who in November 1495 drove a shaft beneath the Castel Nuovo in Naples, packed it with barrels of powder, and brought down a section of the barbican in the ensuing explosion.[29] The shock of the new weapon rivaled that of the artillery bombardments of 1494–95. "Suddenly," wrote Paulo Giovio, "with a horrible crash the entire wall was uprooted from its foundations, with fearful slaughter of the French soldiers on the parapet, whose dismembered bodies littered the ground."[30] Although Giovio's account was probably somewhat exaggerated, the damage to the barbican was sufficient to cause its loss—together with the other ditchworks—and led directly to the fall of the castle. Further mine explosions were recorded at San Giorgio in Cephalonia (1500), Salses and again at Naples (1503), Padua (1509), and Thérouanne (1513). Indeed, mining was now being carried out defensively as well as offensively and was firmly established as a tactic of siege warfare which fortification designers ignored at their peril.[31]

The New Military Architecture

Architectural responses to the challenge of artillery took a wide variety of forms. Essentially passive measures included the thickening of walls and the massive "scarping" or "battering" of their bases.[32] Towers were lowered and reinforced with earth and timber to form stable gun platforms. Gunports would be pierced in medieval walls and towers: "keyholes" for weapons firing more or less along fixed lines, "letterboxes" in positions demanding a wider field of fire.[33] The bracketed machicoulis gallery and the *merlatura*—giving the distinctive crenellated profile of medieval works—were stripped off to remove features that were prone to splinter dangerously under cannon fire. Bales of wool, mattresses, and other absorbent materials were sometimes fixed to upper works in time of siege. A detailed account of this type of ad hoc scheme is to be found in the *Relazione* of Niccolò Machiavelli, who in 1526 acted as secretary to Pedro Navarra, the renegade Spanish engineer, then modifying the walls of Florence.[34]

The ditch, too, became an increasingly important element. According to Francesco di Giorgio it was "the principal member of any fortress that is not on a steep and high mountain . . . A fortress without a ditch is like an animal without one of its limbs."[35] Francesco's ditch served three functions; it forced miners to dig deep, it was the main obstacle to the approach of infantry, and it shielded the lower part of the walls from artillery fire. Itself quite invulnerable to bombardment, it would have had to be bridged or filled before the main walls could be reached. In new fortifications, moreover, all but the uppermost works could be concealed in the depth of the excavation. By the end of the fifteenth century, advanced fortresses such as Salses in Roussillon were already sunk into massive ditches and characterized by bare, curved, oblique surfaces on the exposed superstructure[36]—a clear step towards the simple geometry and low profile of the fully developed Early Modern system (fig. 8). Sarzanello is a similar example on the Italian peninsula.

However, it was the placing of defensive artillery that most clearly distinguished the different design solutions in new works. Amongst the very earliest purpose-built firearm fortifications were gun chambers set on the floors of dry ditches, often completely detached from the parent fortress (fig. 9). Francesco di Giorgio called these works *capannati*; to the French they were *caponiers*, to the English "casemates" or, more quaintly, "murthering houses." Today we would probably call them pillboxes. Location at the bottom of the ditch protected them from enemy guns and gave their defenders a fine field of horizontal fire along the foot of the main fortifications.[37] In Francesco's late fifteenth-century drawings they are often given half-a-dozen embrasures, sometimes more. Armed with small, rapid-firing guns, they would have been able to deliver a hot flanking fire. Indeed, Francesco illustrates some fortress projects where all of the flanking fire is delivered from low-level casemates (fig. 10).

Another early approach seems to have derived from the medieval system of concentric fortification, in which soldiers in advanced positions were supported

Fig. 8. The Fortress of Salses in the Roussillon, France. Although the towers themselves were round, the ditch, profile, and scarping of this unusual French fortress mark it as an important early work.

Fig. 9. Francesco di Giorgio's Fortress Project Showing Elaborate Ditch. Note that here and in Figure 10 the *capannati* are used as protected passageways across the ditches and as a means of delivering flanking fire.

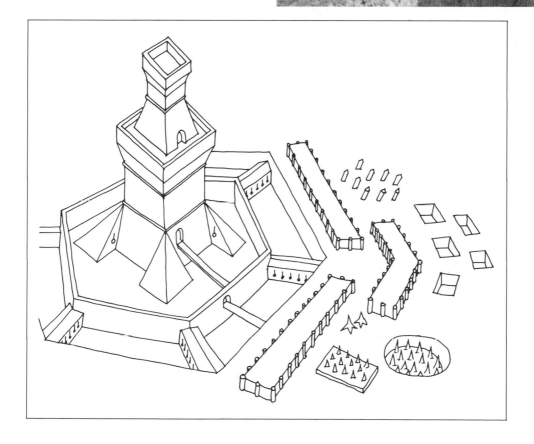

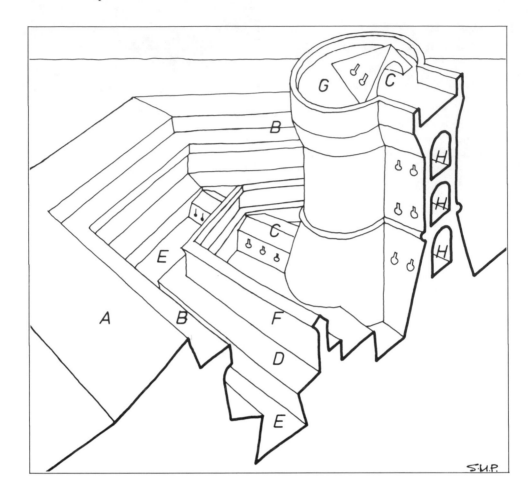

Fig. 10. Fortress Project (After Francesco di Giorgio) to Show Relation of Tower and Ditch. **A:** Ciglio. **B:** Covered Way. **C:** Capannati. **D:** Ditch. **E:** Lower Ditch. **F:** Mid-ditch wall. **G:** Gun platform. **H:** Flank batteries.

by others firing over them from inner walls.[38] In modernized fortifications a low-level gun platform would be laid out as a continuous gallery in front of the medieval wall. Heavy guns on the lower gallery would be supported by lighter pieces, handguns, and crossbows fired from the walls and towers behind. According to Eugène Viollet-le-Duc,[39] this was one of the most common French solutions of this period, the best surviving instance in Italy being the mid-fifteenth-century gun gallery around the base of the Castel Nuovo in Naples (fig. 11).[40] Concentric fortifications were also employed in one of the most successful modifications to medieval walls, the defense of Padua in 1509. Threatened by the advancing armies of the League of Cambrai, Venice had already modernized the walls of Treviso and Padua with a thickened rampart and a series of round and semicircular bastions designed by Fra Giocondo.[41] In the weeks immediately before the siege a dry ditch was excavated behind the front line, filled with stakes and other obstacles and swept by a number of low-level casemates. Behind was a second, higher rampart on which further guns were mounted. Guicciardini's

Fig. 11. Castel Nuovo, Naples: Two Views to Show the Development of the Concentric Fortification System. *Above:* The low-level artillery platform running around the landward faces of the Angevin Castle was added by the Aragonese in 1451–53. Note its fluted deco- rations. *Below:* Francisco de Holanda's view of 1540, showing a further concentric enceinte built mainly by the Spanish between 1503 and 1519 using circular gun towers. The triangular bastion was added in 1536.

description of the Paduan defenses adds that the advanced bastions were mined by their defenders.[42] In the fighting that followed, the League managed to capture one bastion, only to lose it and many lives when the retreating Venetians fired their charges. The inner lines were still intact when, after three weeks, the siege was raised.

Defensive artillery was also concentrated by stacking guns vertically in multistory structures. Francesco di Giorgio illustrates a scheme with three tiers of enclosed flanking casemates as well as an open gun gallery realized in exaggerated form in the six tiers of guns in the duke of Brittany's artillery towers at Fougères, begun in 1480 (fig. 12). Obvious difficulties were posed by the concussion and smoke in enclosed casemates, problems that led some designers to incorporate high ceilings and elaborate networks of smoke ventilators, while others planned their works open to the rear—a system praised by military men for if lost the work would be no use to the enemy. Despite these difficulties, the multilevel guntower was probably the most common early Northern European solution—particularly in Germany and Poland—and was developed theoretically as late as 1527 in the treatise of Albrecht Dürer.[43] Dürer's scheme had three tiers of guns in massive semicircular towers, flanked, as round towers must be, by isolated casemates in the ditch (fig. 13). Even guntowers were not unknown south of the Alps. The Venetians used them in the late fifteenth century for their Greek

Fig. 12. Fougères, on the Frontier of Brittany, France. Built around 1480, this multistory guntower uses artillery on an open gallery and within enclosed casemates on five lower levels. The lowest level is just visible above the water line of the ditch. A seventh tier could fire from the superstructure.

Fig. 13. Albrecht Dürer's *Etliche Underricht zur Befestigung der Stett, Schloss und Flecken* of 1527 shows an example of the small gun chambers built within a ditch before Regens-burg. Shaped like little truncated cones, these works seem to have been able to accommo-date two levels of artillery.

colonial fortresses at Coron and Nauplia; Michele dei Leoni employed them between 1518 and 1525 at Verona; and, as late as 1535, the fortress of Assisi was equipped with a free-standing circular barbican planned on similar lines.[44]

The barbican at Assisi seems to have been one of the last purpose-built Italian guntowers of the late Renaissance, but the principle of concentrating defensive artillery vertically informed the design of numerous early bastions. Vertical plan-ning, after all, was the most economical means of achieving rapid local defensive fire with the small weapons available in the early sixteenth century; indeed, it was not until the supply of heavy guns increased in the second half of the century that the larger bastions of the open gun-platform type became universal. Before then, only major powers could contemplate realistically the construction of works defended by large numbers of heavy weapons. Thus it was the aggressive papacy of Paul III that yielded what was almost certainly the most heavily armed example of mid-sixteenth century military architecture in the so-called double bastion of Antonio da Sangallo the Younger.[45] This work was built on Rome's southern wall in the years 1535–42. By doubling the number of flanks, by employing two tiers of guns on each flank, and by locating cavaliers or elevated gun platforms where they too could contribute flanking fire, Sangallo provided positions from which as many as twenty-four guns—sixteen of them heavy pieces—could sweep the ground in front of the curtain (fig. 14). The costs of this massive system were of course considerable, but its demands on defensive artillery were no less stunning. Fully to have armed this small section of Rome's enceinte would have required something like two-thirds of the heavy guns in the arsenal of Florence.

The double bastion also contained elaborate underground works devised to detect and frustrate enemy mining activity (fig. 15). At ditch floor level a passageway ran along the walls, serving small arms embrasures and sally ports: this was the now conventional countermine gallery, included in the improved fortifications constructed since the turn of the century. Here the gallery was enlarged at regular intervals to form oval lobbies, in the center of which a wooden hatch cover concealed the access to a lower chamber known as the *pozzo*, or well. Sangallo's pozzo consisted of a hexagonal security chamber, off which a dog-leg passage controlled by two doors led to the beginning of a horizontal shaft—the countermine itself. During siege operations, forward listening posts would be established in each shaft, the sentry being locked in with an ear trumpet, a drum with pebbles on it, and other acoustic instruments. Once a "fix" had

Fig. 14. Antonio da Sangallo the Younger, Bastions at Porta Ardeatina, Rome. The weight of flanking fire that could be supplied by these works was prodigious.

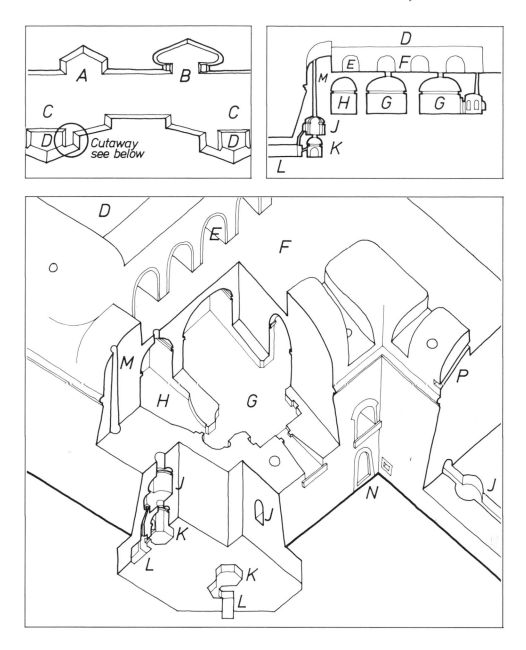

Fig. 15. Antonio da Sangallo the Younger, Bastion at Porta Ardeatina, Rome, 1542. *Top left:* Bastion and double bastion forms compared. *Top right:* Section through Ardeatine bastion. *Bottom:* Cut-away axonometric showing internal arrangements. **A:** Early sixteenth-century bastion with straight flanks. **B:** Later sixteenth-century bastion with *orecchioni,* or curved shoulders. **C:** Sangallo's double bastion, with integrated cavaliers. **D:** Cavaliers, raised gun platforms. **E:** Bombproof shelters. **F:** Open gun platforms. **G:** Casemates or enclosed gun positions. **H:** Magazine. **J:** Countermine gallery. **K:** *Pozzi* or well shafts. **L:** Countermine shaft. **M:** Ventilation flues. **N:** Sally port to ditch floor. **P:** Steeply angled embrasure for firing at ground close to the walls.

been obtained, the shaft could be extended toward the enemy mine, which could be broken into by a raiding party or destroyed by *camouflets*—"depth charges" laid ahead of it, sandbagged and fired by long fuses. The essential features of a modern countermine system were all present in Sangallo's scheme. The subterranean listening posts were well insulated by two doors and a hatch from any noise in the ground-level communication gallery. Once a countermine excavation had been started, moreover, the fortress itself was secure against any raiders who might break into the defensive works.[46]

Sangallo's double bastion was designed as the basic component of a new line of fortifications that was to have greatly reduced the 12 mile circuit of the Aurelian walls. By the time work started at the southern extremity of the Imperial wall, it was already clear that no shortcut could be agreed through the semideveloped "urban countryside" of Rome. Almost certainly this setback represented a victory for vested property interests, but one that enormously increased the total potential costs of what had always been an expensive scheme.[47] In the end, the double bastion at the Porta Ardeatina and another fragment on the Aventine were the only sections to be completed of what had promised to be one of the most sophisticated urban refortification projects of the late Renaissance.

Fully developed late sixteenth-century platform bastions, for all of their impressive size, were in many ways less attractive than their immediate predecessors. The fascinating three-dimensional arrangements of Antonio da Sangallo's designs were not to be encountered again until, at the end of the seventeenth century, Sébastien Le Prestre, marquis de Vauban, reintroduced heavily armed tower bastions and made extensive use of enclosed casemates as protection against explosive mortar bombs and "ricochet fire"—a technique invented by Vauban in which round shot was lobbed at low velocity into open bastions and bounced around, dismounting guns and mangling defenders. The only functional complexity in the platform bastion concerned the design of flanking batteries, which were often concealed behind a prominent curved shoulder (known to Italians as the *orecchione,* or big ear) and sometimes planned on two levels to increase their firepower.

Occasionally, flamboyant coats of arms enlivened the exteriors of modern fortifications (fig. 16). Gateways continued to be treated formally and were sometimes richly decorated. But the general architectural treatment of the late sixteenth-century fortress was a spare *stilo disornamentado,* which, at its best, achieved a functional clarity but hardly ever embodied the delight in form that had inspired Francesco di Giorgio, the older members of the Sangallo family, and the other military architects of the transitional period. Not only had the rules of orthodox fortification design become established, but the scale of fortress building and reconstruction had increased enormously; while idiosyncratic inventiveness might be highly prized on the small scale of the urban republic, in the context of larger bureaucracies of the later sixteenth century regular models and standards were deemed preferable. Inevitably, perhaps, this was to rob the later architecture of its appeal to all save the most tutored eyes. Bastioned fortification had become mass-produced architecture. The total extent of the sixteenth-century military construction program can best be appreciated by considering its three principal components: urban citadels, town walls, and frontier fortifications.

Citadels, Town Walls, and Frontier Forts

Italy was the first part of Europe to experience the new wave of postmedieval urban citadels. Pope Alexander VI (1492–1503) began the process at Castel Sant'Angelo, Rome, where Giuliano da Sangallo the Elder built new polygonal tower bastions around the late medieval curtain enclosing the great drum of Hadrian's mausoleum. Pope Paul III (1534–50) then refortified the Belvedere of the Vatican palace and the river front toward the Janiculum, employing a large team of architectural consultants that included Antonio da Sangallo the

Fig. 16. Papal Arms of Paul III (Farnese) on the Bastion at Porta Ardeatina, Rome.

Younger and his sometime rival, Michelangelo. Pius IV (1559–66) and his architect Francesco Laparelli completed the defenses of the Castel Sant'Angelo with an outer ring of three large bastions and two semibastions.[48] By then the Papal enclave on the north bank of the Tiber had become a formidable armed camp. Save for the fragments of Sangallo's earlier scheme, Rome itself remained not merely undefended but dominated by the adjacent Papal citadel.

Similar events were repeated elsewhere. Pisa, recently defeated by Florence, was held in submission by another of Giuliano da Sangallo's forts, begun in 1509.[49] By 1534, Antonio da Sangallo the Younger had begun the Fortezza da Basso in Florence, the first step in the Imperial and Medici program to secure the loyalty of that city.[50] In 1590 Bernardo Buontalenti completed the task for Grand Duke Ferdinand I with the construction of the Belvedere fortress. Paul III imposed fortresses in humiliating circumstances on the defeated rebel cities of Perugia and Ascoli.[51] In Naples the viceroy reconstructed the Fortezza Sant'Elmo on the highest point of the city, adding this modern stronghold to the two great medieval castles already in Spanish hands.[52]

The political implications of these all too tangible monuments to ruling authority were not wasted on Renaissance commentators. Alberti, writing in the mid-fifteenth century, drew a sharp distinction between the palace of a king and the castle—implicitly the fortified castle—of a tyrant.[53] Machiavelli advised against the use of urban citadels as both provocative and useless.[54] Bernardo Segni, himself a staunch republican, implicitly accepted their effectiveness when he complained of the Fortezza da Basso that the Medici were determined "to place on the necks of the Florentines a yoke of a kind never experienced before: a citadel, whereby the citizens lost all hope of ever living in freedom again."[55] Francesco de' Marchi, the military architect, expressed the opinion of most sixteenth-century treatise writers when he described fortresses as "like the bridle in the mouths of wild horses" and warned that "fortresses are dangerous to build in cities or places used to living free."[56] Events at Siena were amply to support these views.

Yet if progress in the construction of citadels was rapid, the refortification of city enceintes—despite early initiatives—proceeded at a very much slower pace. In 1509, Fra Giocondo had provided Treviso with extensive new ramparts and circular bastions. Biagio Rossetti built a similar round-bastioned fortification for Ercole d'Este's ambitious urban extension to Ferrara.[57] The year 1515 saw the first complete angle-bastioned enceinte built by Antonio da Sangallo the Younger at Civitavecchia, where, since the turn of the century, successive popes had fortified the papacy's most important harbor and naval base on the west coast.[58] Elsewhere, until the closing years of the century, only sections of the new system were built.

The costs of complete urban refortification were of course much greater than those demanded by citadel construction and, given the peculiarities of local topography, it was not always absolutely necessary to replace all of the medieval walls. The kind of planning difficulty that had circumscribed and probably killed Sangallo's proposals for the refortification of Rome were no doubt also significant in other cities. And in at least one well-documented case, that of Bologna, it was decided to rely upon the field forces that would be mobilized in defense of this key papal possession, rather than upon modern fixed architectural fortifications.[59] Bologna remained an open city. For all practical purposes, complete bastioned schemes were reserved for new urban foundations. The characteristic star-shaped pattern of fortifications surrounding Valletta, Palmanova, Sabbioneta and Castro, or Philippeville, Vitry-le-François, and Villefranche-sur-Meuse were by no means typical of sixteenth-century urbanism.[60] By the end of the century, none of the greatest cities of Europe could boast a completed and fully bastioned enceinte.

The siege studies presented in later chapters address themselves to the obvious and important question of how such incompletely fortified places were defended. But a partial explanation for the slow progress on urban refortification is provided by the activities of the European powers in the defense of their frontiers. Although many of the fortified outposts were small, poorly garrisoned, and underarmed, the total resources consumed by sixteenth-century border defenses were staggering. For not only did Europe's shifting dynastic frontiers demand fortification, but the eastern colonies of Venice and the entire Mediterranean coastlines of the Italian and Iberian peninsulas needed to be defended against Turkish raids—even, at times, invasions.

Spain provided the most energetic response to the Turkish threat. Between 1509 and 1511 a chain of forts, the *fronteras*, was established at half-a-dozen points on the North African coast by Ferdinand the Catholic. Major expeditions were launched by the Habsburgs against Tunis (1535), Djerba (1560), the Penon of Algiers (1564), Tunis again (1573), and Mostagenem (1585); and the reign of Philip II saw the extended *presidios* of Goletta and Oran ("Little Madrid," as it was later known) become substantial fortress cities. Venice built energetically in the Adriatic and the eastern Mediterranean. Despite this counteroffensive, all of the Italian coast remained in the front line against the Turks; and between the Christian naval defeat at Prevesa (1538) and their triumph at Lepanto (1571) the western Europeans were generally on the defensive. In these years the Spanish viceroy built no less than 313 watchtower-forts along the Neapolitan coast, while his counterpart in Sicily added a further 137.[61] Similar projects were undertaken by the viceroy of Sardinia, the Papal States, the republic of Genoa, and the duchy of Florence; the latter built Cosmopolis, present-day Portoferraio, to provide a strong point on the island of Elba. Indeed, during the 1540s nearly all of the limited fortress building resources of the republic of Siena were devoted to the construction and repair of town walls, forts, and watchtowers along its exposed Maremma coastline and its offshore islands of Mont'Argentario and Giglio.

The Sinews of War

Fortifications cost a great deal of money. Often the payments were so widely distributed and spread over such a long period that it becomes difficult to compute the total expenditure; but a few figures will convey their order of magnitude. Siena is said to have paid 2,000 scudi for the largest of the bastions built by Peruzzi between 1527 and 1532. Only a few years later Sangallo's very much larger double bastion in Rome—with an associated length of curtain—cost some 40,000 scudi, the total cost of the projected scheme for the refortification of Rome being estimated at 450,000 scudi.[62] The Fortress of Santa Barbara built in postwar Siena in the 1560s by the Medici cost 41,000 scudi. Over a period of some thirty years, the Spanish crown spent about 3,000,000 scudi on the fortifications and other military buildings of the *presidio* at Oran.[63]

Such building costs always seem staggering when compared to private incomes. Five or six scudi per annum would go to support a mid-sixteenth-century peasant family; 20 to 25 scudi was the yearly rate of pay for infantry pikemen in the Imperial army, who, when paid, were counted well off. The better-rewarded Italian architects could expect to receive 200 to 300 scudi. But the appropriate comparison is with other military expenditure. A naval galley with a complement of 150 oarsmen and another 150 soldiers, sailors, and officers cost between 6,000 and 7,000 scudi to build, rig, and arm, plus a further 6,000 to 7,000 scudi to maintain in pay and provisions each year. The full cost of paying, arming, and provisioning a Spanish *tercio* of 5,000 infantry came to over one million scudi for a single campaigning season.[64]

"War," observes Fernand Braudel, "is a waste of money." Yet within the wasteful economy of warfare, fortifications—despite their high cost—were relatively good value. Military theorists in the late Renaissance often discussed what they called the "Spartan Walls," the effective citizen army of the ancient military state which, it was said, allowed Sparta to avoid altogether the expense of permanent walls. Few of these classically minded theorists went along with the leaders of Bologna in recommending this approach for the Early Modern state for, as Francesco de'Marchi put it, "behind good walls a small force can defy a much greater host."[65] It was much cheaper in the long run to invest capital in a fortress and then to maintain within it a small garrison than to meet the crippling recurrent burden of large numbers of troops. Besides its appeal to repressive leaders, the fortress could be used as an arsenal for stockpiling munitions and as accommodation for troops who would otherwise prove an almost intolerable burden to the local community (which was sadly true whether or not soldiers and civilians were on the same side). Moreover, the fortress was there when it was needed. All too often at time of crisis, large bodies of troops proved useless or dangerously uncontrollable because of delays in pay.

Of course, these were the kinds of alternatives that rich states could contemplate with equanimity. For the smaller, even medium-sized powers, fortifications along with other military expenditure represented an onerous burden of public expenditure and private taxation, which contributed not a little to the destruction of independent states that had somehow—like Siena—survived into the mid-sixteenth century.[66] Some powers were insulated from the full cost of fortress construction. Florence, the Papal States, the Knights of Malta (and no doubt others) maintained thousands of galley slaves who, when not at sea, could be employed at little cost on public projects. Siena sent her own convicts to the emperor's galleys and, despite a failing economy and severe depopulation in some parts of the dominio, was compelled to carry out her own fortress construction program with citizen labor. As we shall see, her permanent works were generally modest in scale, relying for their effectiveness upon skillful siting and ingenious design. Many of them were planned quite explicitly for the use of light artillery and hand-held personal firearms. The much more extensive fortifications quickly erected in the immediate prelude to war were largely of temporary construction. Substantial parts of these works were built by enforced citizen labor, limited public funds being channeled into payments for small cadres of skilled craftsmen, materials, tools, carts, and refreshment for the unpaid *levée en masse*. By these means as many as sixteen provincial towns were fortified for the defense of the last Sienese republic, a figure that does not include works in the immediate vicinity of the capital, the coastal towers, or the dozens of privately fortified positions scattered throughout the dominio. This program represented the kind of effort that could only be extracted from a population under threat of invasion. It was Siena's particular misfortune that, having no sooner completed a massive extension to her medieval walls in the 1470s, she was soon afterward confronted by the threat of the new gunpowder artillery and the pressing need to rethink her approach to urban fortification.

2

BALDASSARRE PERUZZI AND THE MODERNIZATION OF SIENA'S MEDIEVAL WALLS, 1527–32

The Military Topography of Siena

MEDIEVAL Siena was built along three ridges, which come together to form an inverted Y-shaped plan, the arms of the Y corresponding to the *terzi*, the three administrative divisions of the city (fig. 17). The original nucleus, known as the terzo di Città, extended along the southwestern ridge from the Campo, the fan-shaped piazza at the center of the modern town. Subsequent development spread along the ridges which extended north and southeast from the Campo. Along their crest ran the via Francigena, the main pilgrimage route from France to Rome for much of the Middle Ages. Development on the northern ridge formed the terzo di Camollia and was enclosed by walls during the first half of the twelfth century. Later in the twelfth and thirteenth centuries the city walls were further extended to enclose more of Camollia and to fortify the southeastern arm of the city, the terzo di San Martino.[1]

Even after the completion of these extensions, considerable numbers of buildings remained outside the fortifications. Suburbs, or *borgi*, spread along the southwest and southeast radial roads, and the plan of the thirteenth-century city could well have been described in the terms used by Leon Battista Alberti of Perugia: "Like the fingers of a man's hand extending outward."[2] Undefended on their flanks, the narrow fronts of the borgi facing along the ridges were fortified by barbicans on the sites of the present-day Porta Laterina, Porta San Marco, Porta Romana, Porta San Viene, and Porta Busseto. Almost certainly it was the existence of these barbicans that determined the route of the last great fortification project of medieval Siena.

In the early fourteenth century, plans were laid for a new wall which was to enlarge greatly the space available to the terzo di Città and the terzo di San Martino and—on the northeast of the city—to enclose the church of San Fran-

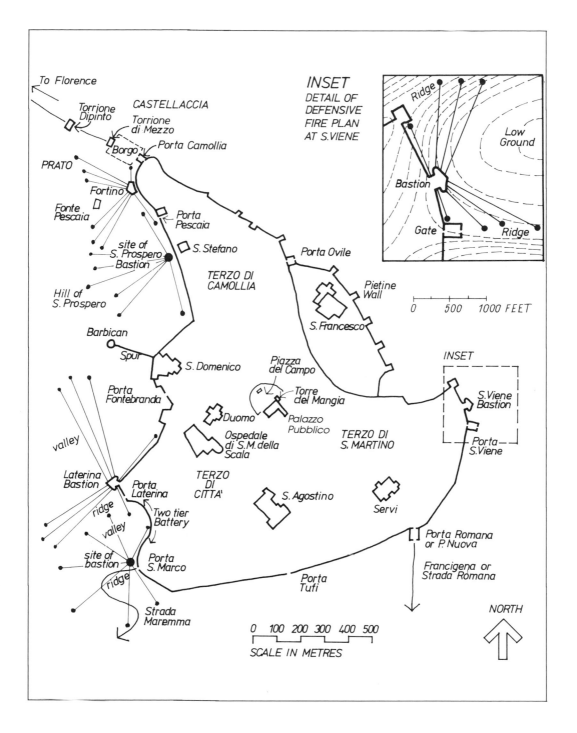

To Florence

CASTELLACCIA

Torrione
Dipinto

Torrione
di Mezzo

Porta Camollia

Borgo

PRATO

Fortino

Fonte
Pescaia

Porta
Pescaia

site of
S. Prospero
Bastion

S. Stefano

TERZO DI
CAMOLLIA

Hill of
S. Prospero

Porta Ovile

Pietine
Wall

Barbican

Spur

S. Domenico

Porta
Fontebranda

S. Francesco

Piazza
del Campo

Torre
del Mangia

valley

Duomo

Palazzo
Pubblico

Ospedale
di S.M. della
Scala

TERZO DI
S. MARTINO

Laterina
Bastion

Porta
Laterina

TERZO
DI
CITTA'

S. Agostino

Servi

Two tier
Battery

valley

site of
bastion

Porta
S. Marco

ridge

Strada
Maremma

Porta
Tufi

Porta Romana
or P. Nuova

Francigena or
Strada Romana

NORTH

0   100 200 300 400 500
SCALE IN METRES

INSET
DETAIL OF
DEFENSIVE
FIRE PLAN
AT S.VIENE

Ridge

Low
Ground

Bastion

Gate

Ridge

0   500   1000 FEET

INSET

S. Viene
Bastion

Porta
S. Viene

Fig. 17. Siena, circa 1535. The map shows
the defensive works of Baldassarre Peruzzi with
their hypothetical firing lines as well as the
major topographical and urbanistic features of
the city.

cesco and the Fonte di Fallonica. The vicissitudes of this grand scheme help explain the attitude of Sienese governments toward schemes of complete urban fortification in later centuries. Work on the new Porta Giustizia started in 1323, and, between 1326 and 1334, a new curtain was built between Porta Giustizia and Porta Romana. For the next thirty-three years the Sienese were compelled to concentrate their resources on the repair of their existing walls in the face of threats from *condottieri* companies. In 1367, work began again on the wall between Porta Fontebranda and Porta Laterina, but it was not until the 1460s that, under pressure from Pope Pius II and the Piccolomini family, the city walls were expanded for the last time by bringing San Francesco and the Piccolomini tombs within the enceinte. The circuit projected in the 1320s involved almost three miles of new wall and had taken nearly 150 years to complete.[3]

The walls themselves were not elaborate. For the most part they were simple curtains about 3½–5 feet thick and 20–30 feet high, built of rubble and mortar infill between two skins of the characteristic red Sienese bricks. In some parts of the wall, string courses of stone were incorporated. Although damage from the siege of 1554–55 and more recent repairs have removed all traces of the *merlatura*, sixteenth-century illustrations make it clear that much of the wall was originally equipped with *merli* (see fig. 66 below). The fourteenth- and fifteenth-century wall had few towers.[4] Indeed, the only part of it for which towers were planned as an important defensive component was the last to be completed, the mid-fifteenth century section enclosing San Francesco. Here there are five rectangular towers spaced at intervals of about 400 feet. Some of them appear to be equipped with keyhole gun embrasures, but it is impossible to say whether these formed part of the original design or were added later.

The gates were by far the most impressive parts of the structure. Above each of them was a high, battlemented tower containing guard rooms, armories, and winding gear for the portcullis. Outside the gate tower was a rectangular enclosure, the *ante porta* or barbican, with a further gate. The barbicans provided security for the inner gate and a space where troops could be mustered for sorties during a siege, and where duties were levied on entering merchandise in time of peace. On the three outer faces of each barbican there was a fighting gallery and *merlatura*: the barbican outside the Porta Camollia (destroyed in 1554) was reported to have been equipped with towers on its two outer corners. Well-preserved barbicans are still to be seen outside the Porta Ovile—the Porta San Viene and the Porta Romana (the last of these being particularly imposing; fig. 18).

By the end of the fifteenth century the only remaining "finger" pointed to the north, along the ridge outside the Porta Camollia. Here a wide open space, known as the Prato, was used as a livestock market and fairground and became

Fig. 18. Porta Romana, Siena, attributed to Agnolo di Ventura, ca. 1327. Entry gates such as this one are found at Porta Ovile, Porta San Viene, and Porta Laterina as well as the Porta Romana. The high back wall of these barbican gateways, common in Italy, facing out toward the countryside, were decorated with symbols of the city's rule. At a number of these barbican gates in Siena, images of the Virgin, Siena's protectress, were painted.

the nucleus for an extended colony of taverns, lodging houses, and ecclesiastical buildings catering for the pilgrims of the via Francigena; here, for example, was the Ospedale Santa Croce built to accommodate pilgrims. For some 500 feet north of the Porta Camollia the sides of the new borgo were protected by a curtain wall which made it effectively into a self-contained enclosure and gave the district the name of Castellaccia. A tall, fortified gate tower, known as the Torrazzo di Mezzo, opened onto the Prato from the Castellaccia. On the northern side of the Prato an outer borgo developed around a third gate tower, known for its religious fresco decorations as the Torrione Dipinto or the Torrione della Vergine, which served as the first obstacle to the approach along the Camollia ridge and as a formal entrance to the city.[5]

The Camollia ridge was of great military importance and figures in all of the fortification projects as well as the two sieges of the sixteenth century. The ridge slopes very gently upward from the city toward the Palazzo dei Diavoli, so called

Fig. 19. Giovanni di Lorenzo Cini, The Madonna Protects Siena During the Battle of Camollia (Siena, San Martino). One of many of the images of the Virgin painted after the "miraculous" victory of July 1526. In the foreground can be seen the Torrione Dipinto and the Torrazzo di Mezzo. Cini painted another version of the Battle of Camollia for the Biccherna, the financial ministry of Sienese government. The panel is located in the Archivio di Stato, Siena (Gabella di Biccherna, no. 49).

for its grotesque Saracen decoration, giving a slight height advantage to any force attacking from the north. To the north lay Florence, and when Pope Clement VII attacked Siena in 1526 with a powerful Papal and Florentine army, the weakness of the Camollia position became appallingly clear. Clement's army approached along the ridge and occupied the outer borgo, the Prato and the Torrione Dipinto, without difficulty. A battery of six heavy pieces of artillery was then established on a hillock beside the Torrione, and the bombardment of Siena's northern defenses began.

This was the first time that the city's fortifications had faced modern artillery and the description of its effects by the Sienese chronicler O. M. Orlandi recalls the shock of the chroniclers of 1494. "They broke, wounded, and destroyed everything, and each cannonball knocked another piece (of wall) to the ground." The Sienese predicament was made worse by the fact that they could not reply to the barrage. As Orlandi reports, "The city was not able in any way to [counter]attack from its high towers or from its walls."[6] It is a concise statement of the inadequacy of medieval fortifications: easily damaged themselves, they were unable to accommodate defensive artillery with which to engage enemy batteries.

On this occasion, however, desperate courage was to win the day for the Sienese. Following a brilliant inspirational speech from Gianmaria Pini, the republican militia sallied out of the Porta Fontebranda and the Porta della Pescaia, hidden from the enemy, and stormed the Papal-Florentine positions at Camollia before Clement's men could collect themselves to meet the attack. Their enemies fled in disorder, leaving many prisoners and all of the guns in Sienese hands. The events of 25 July 1526, in all important details, are depicted in Giovanni di Lorenzo Cini's painting of the following year in the church of San Martino (figs. 19 and 20).

Victory at Camollia, however, had not removed all danger from the city. The exiled Noveschi continued to threaten the regime and unsuccessfully attempted to capture the city in a coup de main. A large and semimutinous army moved through Sienese territory en route for the Sack of Rome in 1527 and, just over a year later, marched north again, skirting the dominio on its way to the Siege of Florence (1529–30). In short, the late 1520s were years of considerable peril to the republic. Its leaders, supported by their new Imperial allies, were determined to modernize their defenses, and in October 1527 Baldassarre Peruzzi was appointed to take charge of the project.

Baldassarre Peruzzi: City Architect

Baldassarre Peruzzi had spent much of his working career in Rome until 1527, when he had the misfortune to be captured by the mutinous troops of Charles V.

Fig. 20. Cini, The Madonna Protects Siena During the Battle of Camollia (detail). Here the cannon trained on the city walls can be seen. Some guns still point at the damaged Torrazzo di Mezzo, where a Sienese gun position was put out of action before the main bombardment could begin. Note also, in the foreground, hand-to-hand combat between the soldiers. To the right are the gabions behind which the Florentine gunners would have sheltered during their attack.

According to Giorgio Vasari he was badly mistreated by his captors and forced to leave on the payment of a large ransom, arriving in Siena wearing only his shirt![7] In fact, Sienese money advanced by one of the ambassadors to the republic in Rome had secured his release, and were it not for these circumstances it is doubtful that he would have contemplated leaving.[8] Rome offered work in abundance on major projects. Even though Adrian's parsimonious papacy (1524–25) and the Sack of 1527 had stopped work on St. Peter's, the construction of the suburban villa of the Sienese banker Agostino Chigi, the Farnesina (1508–11), had established Peruzzi as a major architectural figure. The resumption of work on St. Peter's and a commission for the Palazzo Massimo (1534) was later to tempt him back.[9]

Peruzzi arrived in Siena in late June 1527; on 10 July he was officially appointed Architect to the Republic of Siena with a salary of sixty scudi a year.[10] For the next seven years, until early 1533, he was active on behalf of the Sienese government in a variety of ways: as inspector of the city's works, as a hydraulic engineer, as a specialist in metallurgy, and as architect responsible for the fortification of the *contado* towns.[11] On 24 October 1527, Peruzzi was given what was to be his major assignment when he was elected to the committee to oversee the walls and defenses of his native city.[12] With the specific authority of this post Peruzzi was responsible for the planning and implementation of the largest civic building project since the walls themselves had been enlarged almost a century earlier: the construction of a series of new fortifications for Siena.

The terms of reference for the defense of the city are contained in a note in the archive of the Concistoro, now in the Archivio di Stato, where it is reported that Peruzzi was to make "bastions at all the gates" and to do work at "other necessary places." In addition, he was to make provisions so that it would be possible to "run around the walls while remaining under cover."[13] Although some work was done to facilitate protected movement along the walls, the main work was the construction of five bastions: one each beside the Porta San Viene, the Porta Laterina, the Porta San Marco, and, on the northern front of the city, near the Porta Camollia and the Sportello di San Prospero. From this group, three remain standing today, at San Viene, Laterina, and Camollia.[14] Analysis of each of these bastions reveals Peruzzi's careful site planning and the skillfully inventive nature of his architectural defense.

The Fortifications near Porta San Viene

The finest and best preserved of Peruzzi's bastions is that built near the Porta San Viene on the east of the city. It is sited some 230 feet from the gate of San

Fig. 21. Baldassarre Peruzzi, View of the Bastion at Porta San Viene. The photograph is taken from just in front of the barbican gateway of Porta San Viene. Although the bastion was restored around 1840 and some seams have been discovered, notably in the faces and domical roof, it seems to be in relatively good condition. The basis for most of the restoration of the vault is clear; only the oculus may be fanciful.

Viene at a point where the curtain wall changes direction (fig. 21). The trace, or ground plan, is of a common early-sixteenth-century type; two straight faces meet at the front in an obtuse angle and are connected by rounded orecchioni to a straight neck (the "gorge"), which joins it to the city wall (fig. 22). However, its height and internal arrangements are somewhat surprising. At a time when many Italian bastions were beginning to be planned as squat gun platforms, low and wide in their proportions and with the principal gun emplacements uncovered above, Peruzzi's San Viene bastion has three stories, with the casemates open only to the rear and its upper level covered by a vaulted roof with an oculus at its center (figs. 23 and 24). Thus, the proportions of the work resemble more closely those of a medieval tower than of an Early Modern bastion. Moreover the external ground level, in front of Peruzzi's bastion, may have been slightly raised when the peripheral road was built during the nineteenth century. During the sixteenth century, therefore, the impression of height would probably have been even more pronounced.

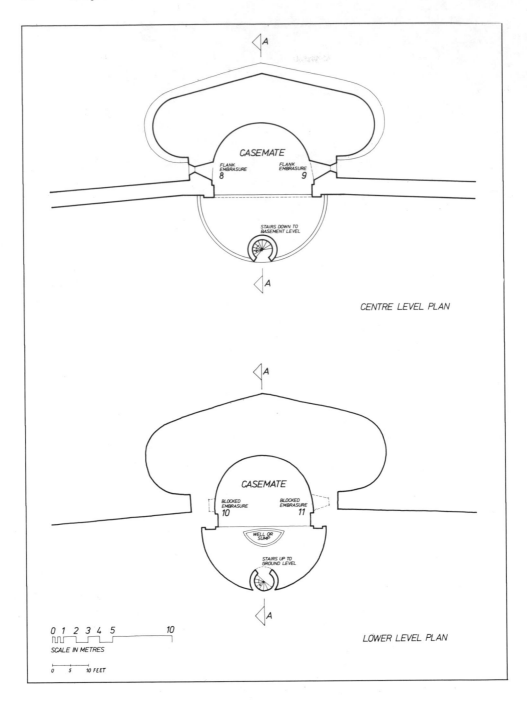

CENTRE LEVEL PLAN

LOWER LEVEL PLAN

Fig. 22. Baldassarre Peruzzi, Plans of Lower and Center Levels of the Bastion at Porta San Viene. The trace of the bastion is relatively conventional. Note the location of the sump or well so that defenders on the upper levels can haul up buckets of water for sponging down the guns. All drawings of the San Viene bastion are drawn to the same scale.

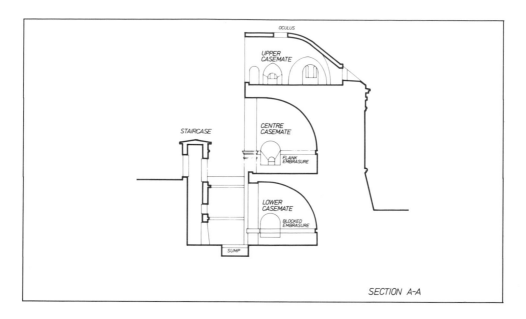

Fig. 23. Section through the Bastion at Porta San Viene. Note how the lower casemate is below grade at the rear of the bastion.

Fig. 24. Rear (West) Elevation of the Bastion at Porta San Viene. Access to the top story was originally up a set of crampons placed in the wall; they are still in place just to the right of a modern staircase. In the face of the center level are a pair of crampons that were probably part of a light wooden drawbridge system. Peruzzi's bastion enjoyed high security. Note also the use of nonfunctional "medieval" machicolation for decorative purposes.

The lowest tier of gun embrasures in the front is now below ground level. At the back, the basement floor was always some twelve feet below ground and reached by a spiral staircase enclosed in a turret. Here there is a sump or well, which may have been intended to drain the basement area after rain and was probably also used to supply water for damping powder or sponging down the guns. Such wells were common in Renaissance fortifications. A pair of crampons remains fixed on the face of the floor of the top story, which probably held a pin swivel for the arm of a hoist or pulley used to raise up the buckets of water (and possibly the much heavier gun barrels). Ammunition was probably stored at basement level, where it was well protected from enemy fire and the risk of accidental ignition from lighted tapers and sparks when the cannon in the upper casemates were in action.

On the lower two levels the casemates are semicircular in plan, open at the rear for light and ventilation and protected to the front by at least twelve feet of solid masonry. The flank embrasures, although somewhat cramped, are particularly well shielded from enemy fire by the prominently projecting orecchioni. At the third-story level, Peruzzi created a space of considerable geometric complexity (fig. 25). In plan it reads as a rectangle, off which lie a number of complicated trapezoidal spaces. Visual coherence is provided by a vault which covers the entire casemate, springing from seven subsidiary vaults and providing a dazzling display of differently angled surfaces (fig. 26). Seven gun positions are provided at this level. Those for the heaviest weapons (positions 2–6 on the plan) are located over the solid front walls and orecchioni but, despite their advanced position, are well protected against incoming fire by the small size of the embrasures and the thickness of the lower parts of the vault. Except from a distance, indeed, it is very difficult to see the openings in the protective vault, which sits—like a giant tortoiseshell—over the gunners (figs. 27 and 28).

Although finished almost entirely in brick, a remarkable feature of the San Viene bastion is its ornamental character. The prominent roll molding, or cordon, dividing the vertical wall from the scarped basement is reflected by a second cordon just below the junction of the upper and central casemates. An elegant brick and molded terracotta frieze marks the top of the vertical external wall (figs. 29 and 30). At the back of the bastion, where ostentation of any kind would not be expected, Peruzzi surprises us with a pair of giant pilasters and a corbel table clearly intended to give visual unity to the multilevel rear elevation (fig. 31). Inside the casemates themselves, a flat horizontal molding marks the transition between the vertical wall of the semicircular vault. Even the spiral staircase leading down to the basement is treated as a roofed turret splayed at the bottom, and the moldings from this turret are continued around the retaining

Fig. 25. Bastion at Porta San Viene, Upper-Level Plan. The bastion is connected to the wall by a short set of stairs. These would have allowed entry onto the walls to the medieval tower in one direction and the barbican of Porta San Viene in the other. Peruzzi's project was to have allowed protected passage all the way around the walls.

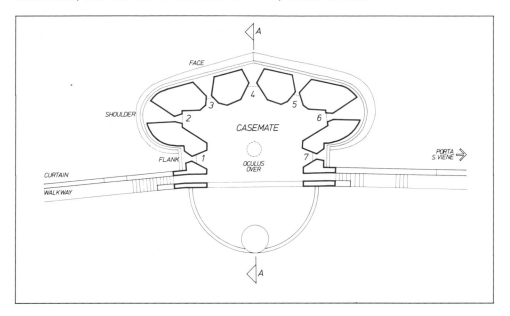

Fig. 26. Bastion at Porta San Viene, Upper Level. The openings illustrated are gun embrasures 6 and 7 from figure 25 and, on the right, the door leading to the curtain-wall gallery. These doors could probably have been sealed to obstruct an enemy that had captured the curtain. The oculus in the center of the vault is just visible at the top.

Fig. 27. Bastion at Porta San Viene, View up the Flank and Orecchione. This startling view shows how defenseless most bastions were against an attacker at close range. Once bastions had lost their machicolations, they had to rely upon the flanking fire of their neighbors. In this case, the anteportal of the adjacent gate of San Viene provided local defense.

Fig. 28. Bastion at Porta San Viene, Detail of an Embrasure. Even close up, the embrasure is remarkably well hidden. Its design had to provide a good field of fire (plenty of sideways movement, or traverse), while avoiding a large opening that might funnel-in enemy shot. Some early embrasures were built with a stepped splay to prevent funnel action (a feature that could still be seen in permanent fortifications as late as World War II).

wall of the basement area, enlivening what would otherwise be a bland surface (figs. 31 and 32).

This much ornament is rarely encountered in fortifications. In the fifteenth century Alberti had argued that the walls of a city should be built in such a manner "that the enemy at the bare sight of them may be struck with terror, and be sent away with a distrust of his own forces,"[15] advice which was generally understood in the sixteenth century to mean plain, undecorated surfaces.[16] Technical factors—such as the dangerous fragmentation of unnecessary projecting or applied decoration under the impact of cannon balls—also militated in favor of a severe architecture, enlivened only at a decorated gateway or with an occasional flamboyant coat of arms. Yet both back and front of the bastion are decorated, using a vocabulary used also by Peruzzi on contemporary civil buildings (fig. 33). Indeed, the very attractiveness of the San Viene bastion has served to mark it as old-fashioned and, implicitly, to devalue it as a functional fortification. Its elegant proportions, plastic quality, and rich decorations place it, in the eyes of one authority, in "a line of picturesque experimental solutions that reaches back to the mid-fifteenth century."[17]

Francesco di Giorgio Martini is an obvious fifteenth-century source for some of the arrangements of the San Viene bastion. His treatise illustrates numerous high-profile works with three or more tiers of casemated flank embrasures; while on top of Francesco's towers are to be found bombproof shelters not unlike the vaulted roof in Peruzzi's bastion (fig. 34).[18] The tightly curved orecchioni, narrow flanks, and decorative cornice of San Viene also bear a striking resemblance to those of Giuliano da Sangallo's coastal fort at Nettuno (1501–2; see fig. 4).[19] These are certainly turn-of-the-century features. However, the use of enclosed casemates persisted well into the sixteenth century, appearing in the Veronese schemes of Leone (1520s) and Michele Sanmicheli (1530s)[20] and in Antonio da Sangallo the Younger's fortifications (fig. 14) at Rome (1534) and Perugia (1540–43).[21] In Northern Europe, moreover, the stacking of guns in tiers of enclosed casemates—best known from Albrecht Dürer's treatise designs (fig. 13)—was sufficiently widespread to constitute an alternative tradition in Early Modern military architecture.[22] In short, some but by no means all of San Viene's features were old-fashioned; and the resulting fortification certainly does not fit easily into the standard history of the evolution of the Italian gun-platform bastion. To evaluate Peruzzi's design, however, it is necessary to ask if any of the *retardataire* or unconventional features detracted from its military effectiveness. Did the bastion work?

The main function of the bastion was to cover the approach to Siena along the road that climbed up to the San Viene portal and its air-lock security system (fig. 17). Guns in the south flank of Peruzzi's bastion would sweep the front of

Figs. 29 and 30. The Dentil Frieze and Corbel Molding on the Bastion at Porta San Viene. The corbels are marked alternately with a grooved and feathered pattern. The embrasures, shielded behind the frieze, can just be seen. The extraordinary decoration of this bastion suggests that the bastion was endowed with the same symbolic authority as the walls themselves. Peruzzi has translated the Gothic decoration of the medieval walls into a classical idiom.

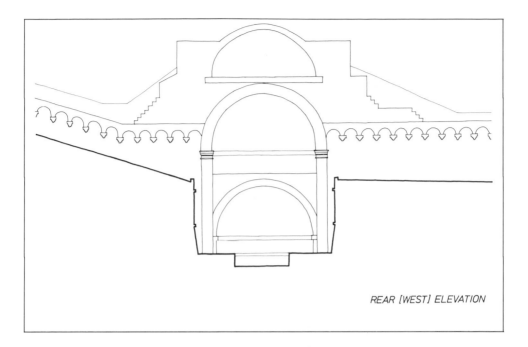

REAR [WEST] ELEVATION

Fig. 31. Rear Elevation, Bastion at Porta San Viene. In this drawing the stair turret has been removed in order to show the relief paneling along the inner face of the bastion.

Fig. 32. Spiral Staircase and Basement Retaining Wall, Bastion at Porta San Viene. The staircase tower seems almost a miniature version of the bastion itself; like the bastion, it is divided into three sections with a scarped base, corbeled molding, and embrasure.

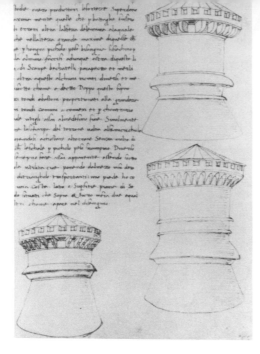

Fig. 33. Baldassarre Peruzzi, Palazzo Neri-Pollini, Siena, ca. 1530. Traditionally attributed to his period as Architect to the Republic of Siena, this palace with its scarped base and dentil and corbel frieze recalls Peruzzi's fortifications.

Fig. 34. Francesco di Giorgio's Vaulted Towers. These designs recall Francesco di Giorgio's work in the Marche for the duke of Urbino. Whether Peruzzi knew these works in the original, or exclusively through the treatise, is not known.

the gate as well as the curtain between the bastion and the gate. Guns in the north face of the barbican (where traces of a number of sixteenth-century gun embrasures are to be found) would sweep the front of the bastion. Since the ranges were no more than 350 feet, the pieces used would probably have been relatively light, possibly of the rapid-firing type that used a number of precharge-able breech sections.[23]

The artillery in the front part of the upper casemate of Peruzzi's bastion had two targets. Guns firing from positions 4, 5 and 6 (fig. 25) could be brought to bear on the approaches to the Porta San Viene, in particular the area of level ground along the present-day via Sant'Eugenia (fig. 35). (These weapons would probably have been heavier than the flankers but, like the other guns, would almost certainly have been breechloaders. There would have been insufficient space in the upper casemate for more than one or two guns to be run in for muzzle loading.) From positions 2 and 3, fire could be directed to the ridge of the present-day via Vivaldi and via Cozzarelli. Although less accessible to enemy gunners than the Sant'Eugenia positions, nonetheless the Vivaldi-Cozzarelli ridge was very dangerous because it looked down on both bastion and gate, giving gunners on the high ground a strong advantage. One of the few towers on the wall of 1240 had been built to dominate the Vivaldi-Cozzarelli ridge, and Peruzzi's new bastion provided extra gun positions covering this area. No doubt one reason for the height of Peruzzi's bastion was to afford a level trajectory for fire in this direction. Certainly the high ground explains the provision of a vaulted roof for the upper casemate: without it, the defenders would have been dangerously exposed to fire from the north.

Peruzzi's works, therefore, formed part of a mutually supporting system of fortifications on the southeast corner of the city, a system which incorporated the gate and its barbican, the new bastion, and the old thirteenth-century tower. The addition of a single tall bastion considerably aided the security of this area, the topography of which goes far toward explaining the unusual form of the design.

From Porta Laterina to Porta San Marco

To fortify the southwest approaches to Siena, Peruzzi built bastions outside both the Porta San Marco and the Porta Laterina. Only the latter now remains, albeit in poor condition. Like San Viene it is built of brick and is in three stories with a scarped lower level and a vertical middle section, the two being separated by a prominent cordon (fig. 36). Because of its location on a corner of the main wall, the Laterina bastion is more sharply pointed in plan, the two faces making

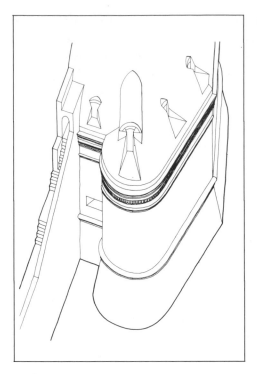

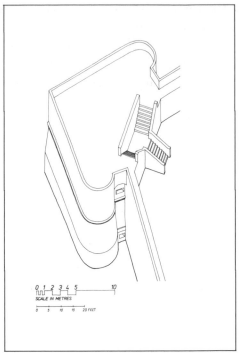

Fig. 35. Axonometric View of the Bastion at Porta San Viene. The relation between the upper level embrasure and the plan is of special interest, for though the orecchione is oriented in line with the barbican of San Viene, the embrasure is canted outward so as to direct fire toward the road from Arezzo.

Fig. 36. Peruzzi's Bastion near the Porta Laterina. Though the plan is similar to that of the Porta San Viene, it seems not to have been vaulted like San Viene. The axonometric shows the embrasures that faced the gate at Porta Laterina; similar embrasures faced along the wall of the enceinte toward the city. In so acutely angled a bastion there was little space for maneuvering the guns.

a right angle at the salient. Unfortunately the gun platform has been completely altered by the landscaping of the hospital gardens into which the back of the bastion opens, and the casemates appear to be blocked. However, embrasures can be seen at two levels on each flank: one pair sweeping the wall toward the Porta Laterina, the other flanking the curtain toward Fontebranda. The size and spacing of these embrasures suggests internal arrangements similar to those at San Viene.

Cannon would also have been mounted on the roof, although in the absence of embrasures it is possible only to generalize about their size and the direction they would have been intended to fire.[24] One battery faced the Laterina ridge, covering the approach to the gate from the Maremma road; the other was capable of delivering long-range fire toward the hill of San Prospero on the other side of the valley (fig. 17). As we shall see, San Prospero represented a potential jumping-off point for attacks on the northern front, so that a gun position that covered this hill from the flank was a useful addition to the defensive fire plan. It is impossible to say whether or not these upper batteries were protected by a roof. There is no obvious military necessity for a roof since the bastion is not overlooked. But, it is clear that the upper levels of the bastion have been considerably modified; even an open battery would have been equipped with a more substantial parapet than the existing sixteen inches of brickwork. Moreover, it is inconceivable that the architect who designed the elegant brick and terracotta frieze for San Viene would have been content with the crude detailing of the Laterina parapet.

No trace of the work at San Marco now exists, and early views present conflicting evidence of its form. They do agree that the bastion was sited to the north of the San Marco gate (toward Porta Laterina), where the slope of the site suggests that it was probably much closer to the gate than either the Laterina or San Viene bastions, perhaps as close as eighty feet. The primary task of the Porta San Marco bastion would have been the defense of the gate and the road leading up to it. But the San Marco bastion would have also covered the ground to the north, where one further modification to the walls should be recorded. At the head of the valley between San Marco and Laterina, the curtain was pierced by numerous gun embrasures at two levels. The lower level could be served from the ground; above is a firing gallery corbeled out in brickwork from the main wall. Only hand-held guns could have been used from the upper gallery, but the lower embrasures could have been used either for handguns or light artillery pieces mounted on fixed timber frameworks, a common enough mounting in early sixteenth-century fortresses. This series of embrasures would have delivered a heavy weight of fire down the valley which, because of its relatively gentle gradient, was one of the more practicable approaches to the medieval wall. Although there is no hard evidence that these embrasures were built by Peruzzi, they must have formed part of his scheme. And in their provision of double tiers of small gunports they show a marked similarity with the last of Peruzzi's surviving designs.

The Northern Front

The zone that presented Peruzzi with the most urgent problem was that along the northern front of the city, toward Florence. As we have already seen, the Camollia ridge provided a level approach to the Prato, site of the present-day

Piazza Giovanni Amendola, from where the Florentine batteries had bombarded the walls in 1526. There was no question but that after the Battle of Camollia this northern front was exceptionally vulnerable and in urgent need of new defenses.

Peruzzi built two works in this zone, one near the Porta Camollia, the other at the so-called Sportello di San Prospero. Of this latter bastion, nothing can now be seen, although it is reputed to have been one of Peruzzi's most impressive structures. The chronicler Agnolo Bardi recorded that "that of San Prospero cost two thousand scudi, it was so handsome and solid."[25] The gate of San Prospero was almost certainly located at the end of the present-day Vicolo dello Sportello (fig. 17). The bastion, as Peruzzi's other works, would not have been far from this gate; in all probability, it was in the vicinity of the church of Santo Stefano and thus could flank both the Porta San Prospero and the Porta della Pescaia. Its primary function, however, would have been to fire across the Lizza saddle toward the hill of San Prospero, the area of greatest potential danger. As the only one of Peruzzi's bastions to be singled out for special mention by Bardi, it was clearly both architecturally impressive and defensively significant.

The fortino near the Porta Camollia today survives in a semiruined state on a bank of earth that leads out from the foot of the old wall (figs. 37 and 38). In plan, the work at Camollia employs the most common sixteenth-century bastion trace: two angled faces, with two straight flanks connecting them to the curtain (although in this case the work is detached from the main enceinte by the sloping bank). Once again Peruzzi has used a common plan type for a most unusual fortification. All that remains are two stories, one partly below ground level and the second, once vaulted, above it.

Local tradition claims that access to the work was by means of a tunnel or tunnels, now blocked, leading back into the city. However, a recent cleaning out of the fortino stopped well short of the excavation that would have been needed to determine the access arrangements, or to discover if there are any further defensive works beneath the surviving lower story. Nothing is known about the superstructure, which has been entirely lost.

Both surviving stories of the fortino comprise a vaulted corridor about five feet wide and six feet high, set back about six feet from the face of the work. At regular intervals along these corridors small gun-chambers are distributed, each with a narrow front opening but a wide rear, allowing a certain amount of traverse for the gun. The floor of these gun chambers is flat, but the vaulted ceiling gives about five feet of headroom at the rear, an arrangment permitting fire on a more-or-less level trajectory and for the breech of a gun to be raised to shoot downwards. Peruzzi's fortino may very well have included an upper gun platform housing bigger guns capable of engaging targets on the Prato: but in

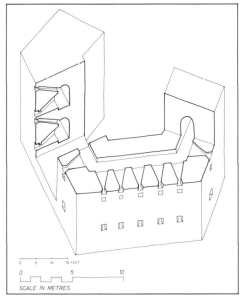

Fig. 37. Peruzzi's Fortino at Porta Camollia. View from the front, showing the lower row of face embrasures and the bank behind leading up to the medieval wall.

Fig. 38. Axonometric of the Fortino at Camollia. Despite its ruined state, it is still possible to read the major elements of the plan and the location of the embrasures. The casemates are alarmingly small and during battle would have been filled with chokingly dense smoke.

the absence of physical remains or documentary sources we can only speculate on this point. We can be quite certain about the function of the smaller gun positions. Evidently these were designed to furnish emplacements delivering horizontal or plunging fire into the valley between the Prato and Porta Camollia, as well as sweeping the approaches to the gates in this sector. Three embrasures are visible in the flank pointing north to the Porta Camollia, but a modern structure built into the hillside obscures the full original dimensions on this side. The south flank, sweeping the approaches to the Porta Pescaia, contains four embrasures. It is clear, however, that the primary objective of the fortino was to deliver a heavy weight of shot to its front. With no less than twenty face embrasures—ten on each face and ten on each level—the work offered a staggering concentration of firepower.

This was in many ways Peruzzi's most unusual work. Fifteenth-century Italy offers a number of examples of small advanced works, such as Baccio Pontelli's ravelin outside the gate of the fortress of Ostia (fig. 39), Giuliano da Sangallo's circular pillbox at Colle Val d'Elsa (fig. 40) and the capannati, which provided flanking fire in the ditches of fortresses illustrated in Francesco di Giorgio's treatise.[26] The use of capannati rather than bastions continued well into the sixteenth century, as we have seen in the preceding chapter. In Antonio da Sangallo the Younger's designs for Castro and in Pietro Cataneo's drawing for a small coastal fort defending one end of the boom across the harbor entrance at Orbetello, we see schemes employing capannati as surface fortifications—without a ditch—much like Peruzzi's fortino. None of these examples, however, rival the firepower of Peruzzi's fortino.

How effective the fortino would have proved in practice is problematical. Conditions inside the confined corridor and casemates would have been intolerable from concussion and fumes, and after the first volley it would have been difficult, if not impossible, to aim through the smoke. One can only conclude that Peruzzi relied upon a heavy weight of fire from small-caliber but rapid-firing guns, trained on fixed lines at an area target. Possible models could have been earlier Renaissance designs for multibarreled guns or carts mounting a battery of light artillery pieces on a fixed framework (fig. 6).[27] Peruzzi's fortino at Camollia appears to translate such ideas into architectural form.

The Building Program

Construction of Peruzzi's bastions for Siena seems to have taken place between November 1527, following his appointment to the committee to oversee the walls, and some time early in 1532, when references become scarce in the archives and seem to suggest termination. The first explicit notice that we have been able

Fig. 39. Baccio Pontelli's Fortress at Ostia, 1483–86. Within the ditch before the fortress, Baccio Pontelli placed this small ravelin. Keyhole gunports are visible at the bottom of the work, and letterbox embrasures can be seen at the upper level.

Fig. 40. Giuliano da Sangallo, Pillbox along the Walls at Colle Val d'Elsa, ca. 1485. Now isolated, since the curtain wall that once linked it to the rest of the defensive perimeter has been demolished, this work probably had two tiers of artillery positions.

to find concerning Peruzzi's intervention in the defensive strategy of the city concerns the bastion—reputed the largest—that he designed for the Sportello di San Prospero. The notice of the deliberation of the Balìa is dated 1 November 1527, just a week after he was appointed to the committee. In it, Peruzzi points out the need for further defense in the zone recently ravaged by the Florentines: "that our city may be invulnerable to these easy assaults." The architect warns that the site is notably weak and liable to attack and proposes a bastion be built there; an inexpensive project, he assures the government. The proposal is accepted, and priors are elected to supply "provisions, and lime, brick, rubble, and other necessary things."[28]

For no other bastion is there documentation which provides both a date for the beginning of work and a reason, albeit in general terms, for its construction. At the Porta San Viene site, 35,600 bricks were received in October 1528, and in December 1528 the bastion is referred to as "nuovamente facto."[29] At San Marco there is a report that a group headed by Peruzzi intends to visit the site in January 1528 to view what are probably still proposals for the zone.[30] Nearby at Porta Laterina, in March 1528, permission from the religious authorities is needed for the construction of the bastion there.[31] But for Camollia it is impossible to separate the payments made for the repair of the advanced tower gates—the Torrione Dipinto and Torrazzo di Mezzo—from those made for work on the new bastion. Nonetheless, in July 1529 a certain Cristoforo Cenni declared money received from the government for the construction of a "torrazio" near San Pietro alla Magione, approximately the site of the Camollia fortino.[32] In short, it is likely that by early 1529 work was underway at all locations around the walls.

Progress was sufficiently advanced by the middle of 1528 for foreigners to sit up and take notice. The Sienese ambassador in Florence wrote to report Florentine reaction to the Sienese defensive plans: "The provisions made for the security of our territory and also of the city are very suitable and commended by all who hear of them . . . [They will] serve not only for the honor and use of our republic but for the security and strength of this state [Florence]."[33] Later still in 1528, Antonio de Leyva, the Imperial commander and governor of Milan, asked to see a set of measured drawings of the work that Peruzzi was doing. Fortunato Vecchi, the Sienese ambassador in Milan, writes that the Spaniard had heard "that Your Magnificent Lordships are strongly fortifying their city with *torazzi* and *baluardi*, and had said that he would much like to see a drawing both of the city site and of the new walls. It would be good if [Your Lordships] would have a little sketch made under the supervision of Master Baldassarre, containing the form and measurements with the circumference, thickness, and height of the aforesaid *torazzi* and enclose it in a letter, sending it to me as soon as possible."[34] No trace of the drawing has been found, and a more unlikely request to make and a more unlikely request to accede to one cannot imagine. Nonetheless, from these letters we can sense something of how the defense of Siena by a major architect helped alter, however slightly, the balance of power on the peninsula. Clearly, Peruzzi's work was respected by contemporaries.

It is also clear that the project imposed severe strains on Siena's economic resources. During late 1529, plans were laid in Siena for a festive entry by Charles, soon to be crowned Holy Roman Emperor. It was expected that he would go to Rome for the coronation and would pass through the city. The city had to be decorated for the occasion, but it soon became apparent that the costs of providing decorations for the emperor as well as new bastions for the city walls could not be borne by the government at the same time. In a series of governmental provisions beginning 10 December 1529, it was decided that all money intended for the defenses would be transferred to the decorations. On 21 January 1530 this provision was renewed, and a similar decision was taken as late as 7 March 1530. Peruzzi himself was active in the civic decorations, and it was not until April 1530 that work began again on the fortifications.[35] Charles, ironically, was crowned in Bologna and came to the city only in 1536.[36] His surrogate received the master's welcome that had so slowed the construction of the defenses of the city.

The date for the completion of the bastions is difficult to establish. One clue concerns an incentive bonus that Peruzzi was to receive for the completion of each bastion. The incentive was first offered a year after the beginning of work, in November 1528, when Peruzzi's stipend had just been doubled and he was offered an additional twenty-five ducats for each torazzo completed. When his stipend was again increased in October 1531, the offer was renewed.[37] Sadly, we have been unable to find a record that confirms that Peruzzi was ever presented with his reward.

Yet there is circumstantial evidence for the completion of part of the work around the beginning of 1532. On 26 October 1531, permission was given to the workers on the new church of San Jacomo e Cristofano—which was being built to celebrate the Camollia victory—to remove bricks from the area of the Sportello di San Prospero.[38] If building material was no longer needed on the largest fortification site, we may surmise that work was probably winding down elsewhere. The complete absence of documents referring to the various works after 1532 suggests final completion during that year. It should be borne in mind that, although complex and numerous, most of Peruzzi's bastions were not large-scale works. Making allowance for the delay brought about by the preparations for the emperor's expected visit, a four-year construction program—from late 1527 to early 1532—was more than sufficient. By the standards of the later wartime projects, it was rather slow.

3

THE SPANISH CITADEL

PERUZZI'S fortifications strengthened Siena's walls against external enemies. When construction began in 1527, the most immediate threat to the republic had been from the exiled Noveschi, at that time allied with Florence and the papacy. Yet before the completion of these defenses, Sienese politics—indeed, the political map of central Italy—had been transformed. In 1530 the Imperial negotiators of Charles V brought together Siena's rival factions, including the leaders of the Nove at the *grancia* of Cuna, where a treaty was signed readmitting the exiles.[1] It was an enforced reconciliation, backed by Spanish troops, who remained in the city to maintain order and the vital supply of munitions, food, and laborers from Siena to the Imperial troops then besieging Florence.[2] When the last Florentine republic surrendered later in the same year, it must have seemed that the Pax Hispanica was at last secure. The papacy had been humbled. Although disappointed in her hope of territorial gains at the expense of defeated Florence, Siena's independence was now guaranteed by the emperor. Florentine Tuscany was ruled by an Imperial duke, Alessandro de' Medici, with power firmly in the hands of the emperor's creatures. Florence herself was soon to be dominated by the Spanish troops garrisoned in the newly constructed Fortezza da Basso.

The equilibrium negotiated in 1530 was not to remain undisturbed for long. Duke Alessandro was assassinated in 1537, to be replaced on the ducal throne of Florence by Cosimo de' Medici, a distant relative and an apparently malleable eighteen-year-old. At Montemurlo in 1539 his troops routed a force of anti-Medici patricians headed by the Strozzi family, a victory which not only rid him of dangerous enemies but gained him a measure of freedom from his Imperial sponsors. Energy, administrative efficiency, and a pervasive system of intelligence brought the young duke total command of Florence, allowing him to demand the withdrawal of Spanish garrisons from the Fortezza da Basso and other Tuscan fortresses. Although always loyal to the emperor, Cosimo ruthlessly played off Spain, France, and the papacy against each other in his lifetime's task of building an independent Medici state.[3]

While Cosimo's successes inevitably caused some diminution of Spanish power in Tuscany, Siena's instability represented a real threat to peace. Throughout the 1530s and 1540s, Siena was subject to outbreaks of factional violence resulting, in part, from economic hardship. In addition, the subversive activities of Florentine exiles provided numerous occasions for intervention by the resident Spanish representatives, whose general incompetence did much to alienate the populace, even among those who were the emperor's potential allies. Charles's agents increasingly resembled military governors. In 1540, Charles V, whose antipathy to the Renaissance city-state was pronounced, intervened to decree the adoption of a reformed constitution designed to ensure an equitable distribution of public offices among the squabbling monti. The Sienese were disarmed, taxes raised, and forced loans ordered without the consent of the Balìa. The garrison was progressively enlarged. In 1547 it was proposed to curtail the growing number of violent incidents between the citizens and the troops billeted in their houses by quartering troops in isolated barracks. By 1549 the plan for barracks had been overtaken by proposals for a fortress proper, a citadel with internal security as its prime function.[4]

The Citadel Project

The Spaniards, of course, maintained that a citadel was needed to defend Siena from French aggression as well as to control the lawlessness which prevented the exercise of Sienese liberties. It was certainly true that the project was supported by some of the Sienese, most notably by the persecuted noveschi.[5] Charles was, if nothing else, persistent. He may also have noted, as a later Sienese historian conceded, that once the fortresses of Pisa and Florence had been yielded to Cosimo, the emperor had no central Italian strong points of his own, while the French enjoyed the use of Castro and Ronciglione in the Papal States as well as Pitigliano, an independant feud in southern Tuscany.[6] Charles's representatives even suggested that a citadel with a much reduced garrison represented a long-term economic solution for the Sienese. Here as elsewhere in the empire, Charles expected his troops' hosts to pay for their own protection.[7] Neither realpolitik nor special economic pleading, however, made any impression on the Sienese populace, already exercised over the political violations of the Imperialists. Opposition to the Spanish coalesced around the issue of the citadel as an intolerable affront to their ancient liberties, a permanent and highly visible symbol of oppression.

There was, indeed, little room for doubt about the repressive function of the proposed citadel. Money to pay for it was to be raised by a special local tax, forced loans, and the cynical misappropriation of public monies intended for coastal fortifications against the Turks. Sleight-of-hand accounting techniques were also employed, and economical building material was provided by the demolition of the noble families' towers.[8] Moreover, three of the sites suggested for the citadel implied the sort of punitive demolitions more appropriate to a defeated enemy than to the loyal ally Siena felt herself to be.

In September 1550, under the heavy-handed guidance of Don Diego Hurtado de Mendoza, the Spanish minister responsible for Siena, the city was visited by a group of experts headed by Giangiacomo de'Medici, marquis of Marignano ("capitani pratichissimi e sperti nelle fortificationi, e buoni ingegneri" as the chronicler Agnolo Bardi describes them). Charged with determining a location for the citadel, the group was divided in its choice: the zone outside Porta Camollia was favored by some, the areas of Campansi and the Poggio dei Servi by others. The land occupied by the Convent of Sant'Agostino was favored by Don Diego himself, but was opposed by the others because it was overlooked by the Monte di Castelvecchio and by the Poggio dei Servi. A fortress at Sant'Agostino, moreover, would have entailed extensive and highly provocative clearances in one of the oldest parts of the city. The potential cost—economic and political—eventually weighed against the Sant'Agostino site as well as the other potential inner city locations, the Poggio dei Campansi and the Poggio dei Servi. Two other sites in the poorer districts of the Castellaccia and the Prato did not present problems of clearance, but both were too far from the center of town for Spanish purposes. The marquis of Marignano—who a few years later was to command the Imperial forces at the siege of Siena—eventually headed the consensus view in support of San Prospero, a relatively undeveloped hill commanding an excellent field of fire into the terzo di Città and Camollia.[9] A certain Giovambattista Romano was commissioned to make a model of the city and its fortifications, which, together with the site analyses, was carried to the emperor for a decision.[10] Charles personally confirmed the San Prospero site, and construction began in November 1550.[11]

The Protest against the Citadel

In the summer of 1550 the campaign to block the project got underway; a special Committee of Eight with two representatives per monte was instituted to coordinate efforts. This body recommended an embassy and set out the arguments to be employed by the orators.[12] The citizen body was disarmed, they argued. A reliable Captain of Justice had been appointed, and Spanish troops were now stationed in the city. The Eight recognized the continuing need for these troops but questioned whether a fortress represented a truly economic solution.

The embassy, headed by Girolamo Tolomei, was received at the Imperial court in September, but its petition was rejected.[13] When news of Tolomei's failure reached Siena, it provoked more public forms of protest. Already in July public prayers had been offered in the Duomo, and now in November, after an impressive procession through the city, Claudio Zuccantini, prior of the Concistoro, made an oration which introduced in dramatic terms the central issues of civic honor, dignity, and liberty.[14] The oration took the form of a prayer to the Virgin Mary, who had saved her city at Montaperti and Camollia in the past. These crises had never been equaled until today, when Siena's "benefactor and protector Charles V is seeking to build a castle, which she is neither able nor willing to resist by means other than your own prayers to your beloved Son . . . For pity's sake remove such a fatal thought, unfitting to our sincere faith and carrying with it the destruction of honor, dignity, and our sweet liberty, preserved until today under your guardianship and protection."[15]

Claudio Zuccantini's oration was followed by another *memoriale*, which was signed by one thousand citizens and presented to the emperor by a further embassy headed by Orlando Malavolti, the chronicler. It stressed the same issues of honor, dignity, and liberty. The city of Siena realizes that the emperor, in his great love as a merciful father, is moved to provide for her liberty and peace in the way that seems to him most suitable. Even so, she hopes and trusts that, in order to cure her, he will not use "so sharp a medicine that it destroys the body and consumes life, as without any doubt would be the result of the castle . . . In its foundations—together with liberty—would be buried for eternity the reputation, honor, and glory of our name. Dishonored and reviled, we must be considered by all the world suspect and unfaithful to our Idol."[16]

The *memoriale* mixes almost blasphemous compliments with dark hints. His Imperial Majesty is reminded of past services which lead the signatories to expect a place "at the table of his happy fortune." Instead, they are forced to throw themselves on his mercy, for the fortress "opens the gate to our desolation and ruin."[17] As the walls of the citadel began to rise on the hill of San Prospero, polemic gave way to direct action. Brandano, known as the "Sienese Prophet," demonstrated in front of the works and, as he was arrested, cried out: "Oh Spaniards who have betrayed Siena . . . God will call you to account for your crimes!"[18]

There was now no way to avoid confrontation. For better or worse, Charles felt he had to make a stand,[19] and the Sienese minor factions, naturally his political allies, felt outraged and betrayed. Indeed, the French, as ever, were waiting in the wings. The result was precisely that which the emperor had wished to avoid.

The Expulsion of the Spaniards

The revolt began on 27 July 1552. Mendoza was in Rome, raising money for the fortress, where he inadvertently assisted the conspiracy by informing Don Francesco d'Avalos, his deputy, that the latest intelligence from French councils indicated the postponement of hostile action against both Milan and Siena in favor of support for Turkish attacks on Naples. Acting on this misleading report, Don Francesco reduced the garrison in the city. Despite numerous last-minute warnings of the plot, he delayed calling for Florentine assistance and imposing a curfew and "state of siege" until 26 July,[20] when the sentry on the Mangia (the tall campanile of the Palazzo Pubblico) spotted insurgents under the command of Aeneas Piccolomini delle Papesse approaching from the south, and gave the alarm. Hundreds of young men broke curfew and poured out of their houses to join the rebels, shouting, "Liberty, Liberty," "Victory, Victory," and, what is more, "France, France."[21] A Spanish company defended the Porta Romana: but the Porta Tufi was opened by the citizens. At the same time two Florentine companies entered the city by the Porta Camollia and joined the Spaniards in the defense of the Campo. The Imperial troops at the center, however, far from taking control of the city, found themselves quickly surrounded. During the night they moved to less confined positions at San Domenico and San Prospero, where they prepared to defend themselves.

By the afternoon of 28 July the first regular French troops had arrived from Ottavio Farnese's state of Castro to the south, which, since the Franco-Papal treaty of Parma (1552), had become the main French base in central Italy. An immediate attack on the incomplete fortifications was postponed because of the casualties certain to be suffered. It was believed that the Imperialists were short of food and ammunition and, given time, could be talked out of their positions. So it proved. On 3 August, a surrender treaty was signed which allowed the garrision to march out of the city with full honors of war, leaving only its artillery behind.[22] As the Spanish commander made his farewells to personal friends, he expressed admiration for the spirit of the Sienese but commented: "This time you have offended too great a man."[23]

For a short time immediately following the uprising there was a small possibility of a negotiated settlement. The members of the Balìa, who had all been appointed by the Spaniards, were not replaced when they were found to be as compliant to the wishes of the revolutionaries as they had been to those of the governor. On 28 July, while the Spanish garrison was still holding out in the monastery and citadel, the Balìa sent an ambassador to the pope to make an act of homage. Another went to Cosimo de' Medici begging him not to intervene in his neighbors' attempts to rid themselves of the tyranny of Don Diego and assuring him of their continued devotion to the imperial cause.[24]

Duke Cosimo's attitude to the revolt was at first ambiguous. Florentine claims to Piombino had recently been rejected by the emperor in favor of Genoa. Cosimo's resentment at this setback was, however, checked by his awareness of the activities of the French and Florentine exiles in south Tuscany, and by his realization of the Imperial need for a secure position in central Italy. For Medici purposes a Spanish presence in Siena was preferable to the obvious alternative, a base on Florentine territory. Cosimo was therefore torn between his personal grudges against the chief Imperial officials in Italy, his fears of French intrigues, and his hopes of turning the situation to his own advantage, particularly vis-à-vis Piombino. The duke of Florence needed to be seen to act on behalf of the emperor but not to get involved in a war on his own.

Word was immediately sent to the imperial admiral, Andrea Doria, who was embarking German infantry at La Spezia for passage to Naples, advising him to take them instead to Livorno or Piombino to assist the emperor. Florentine troops were ordered from Pisa to the Sienese border. Cosimo then felt free to send "observers" to Siena to report on the developing situation. The observers arrived in time to see the Spaniards from San Domenico taking shelter in the citadel. They visited the citadel under truce and found that the garrison was in no shape for prolonged resistance. They then returned to Florence, bringing with them yet further Sienese pledges of loyalty to the emperor. However, just as it seemed that Cosimo could safely pretend to view the situation at Siena as a dispute between loyal Imperialists and their misguided governor, the French played their hand. A strongly worded ultimatum arrived in Florence in which the French claimed responsibility for the liberation of Siena and promised to take a serious view of any interference in the affairs of that state.[25] Lansach, the French ambassador in Rome, had already appeared in Siena where he announced the protection of the king of France and received the applause of the crowd, which was becoming daily more hostile to the Imperialists. When the treaty for the surrender of the citadel was signed, it was Lansach who received the keys from the Spaniards and who then handed them over to the republic in the name of Henry II of France.

The ceremony of surrender took place 3 August 1552. The formal transfer of the citadel's sovereignty from Spain to France and then to the Sienese republic became an event scarcely less significant than the victory at Camollia in 1526. Its protocol was described carefully by Alessandro Sozzini.

> After the departure [of the Spaniards] the Most Illustrious Monsieur de Lansach went into the fortress, and at the Sixteenth Hour the clergy entered in procession with the Lords and the Captain of the People; and there the

Most Illustrious Ambassador of the Most Christian King of France consigned the fortress to the city with these words: "Most Illustrious Lords, my Sire, having heard that the tyranny of Charles V had subjected you, has sent me to liberate you, and because this place was the cause of holding you in servitude, he returns to you Liberty, and hands over to you the said place: in return for which my King wants nothing from you besides that you acknowledge the gift from the hand of Blessed God, and be mindful of him who has struggled for your Liberty," And, the notary being summoned, he declared: "Notary, record that my King makes a gift to the City of Siena of all that she has to spend in his service." And, these words being spoken, he departed and left in the fortress the said most Illustrious Lords, who gave one turn inside, and with their own hands began to demolish and level it; and afterwards, with great jubiliation and cheerfulness, they returned to the Palace [the Town Hall].[26]

Reconstruction of the Spanish Citadel

In view of the many thousands of words generated by the detested citadel, it is surprising that no coherent description survives. Even the site is problematical. Since virtually nothing now remains above ground, for purposes of reconstruction, we are forced to rely upon pictorial sources and plans of varying quality. This task is further complicated by the fact that the citadel site has been much changed since the sixteenth century, when the hill of San Prospero was joined to Camollia by a somewhat lower saddle running beneath the modern Lizza gardens. On all other sides the hill rose steeply from the surrounding valleys. This is still clear enough to the north and west, but the valley between San Prospero and San Domenico was considerably built up when the Stadio Comunale was constructed in 1937, and the saddle was both raised and leveled when the Lizza was landscaped in the eighteenth century.[27]

The easternmost works almost closed the gap between San Prospero and the Camollia wall. This is shown by the *tavolette* of the Biccherna of 1552, which depict the happy event of that year: the destruction of the citadel (figs. 41 and 42). The artist was Maestro Giorgio di Giovanni, an architect intimately involved in the demolition and reconstruction works of the fall of 1552, who later served with distinction as a fortification designer during the campaigns of 1553–55.[28] He could therefore be expected to take a well-informed personal interest in the subject matter of the painting. Indeed, despite its small size, the painting is remarkably specific in its topographical and architectural detail. In the foreground can be seen the small gate in the Camollia wall: this must be the Sportello di San Prospero, which stood near the church of Santo Stefano on the Lizza and

Fig. 41. Maestro Giorgio di Giovanni, Destruction of the Spanish Citadel. One of the series of painted covers commissioned by the Biccherna for their registers. The panel shows the Sienese citizenry exiting from the old city walls armed with pickaxes, mattocks, and spades. Beyond the citadel can be seen the Prato and the Castellaccia, the zone from which the Florentine-Papal force had caused so much trouble in 1526. The counterforts, or internal masonry buttresses of the rampart, can be seen exposed to the right of the Spanish works.

the present-day Vicolo dello Sportello. The medieval wall is shown to descend—presumably to the concealed Porta di Pescaia—before ascending again toward Camollia. Part of Peruzzi's fortino can be seen in the middle distance. On the horizon are the Torrazzo di Mezzo and the hillock on the south side of the Prato, where Clement's guns had been located in 1526. Its western limits were approximately those of the present-day Medici fortress dedicated to Santa Barbara.

A drawing in the Biblioteca Comunale, Siena, confirms the essential points of Maestro Giorgio's representation (fig. 43).[29] The sheet is an unusual plan made of the city during the siege of Siena. It shows the underground aqueduct system of the city, its walls and the significant locations within the walls. In all major particulars it has proved itself an accurate representation of Siena.[30] The hand-

Fig. 42. Maestro Giorgio di Giovanni, Destruction of the Spanish Citadel. The second of the panels painted by Maestro Giorgio for the Biccherna shows a similar scene from a closer viewpoint. Although dated after December, rather than August 1552 as fig. 41, this view appears to show a much earlier phase in the dismantling of the inner works of the citadel. The walls are here almost full height and have been equipped with *puntoni*, the triangular footing of the curved salient that removes its blind spot. Similar *puntoni* are to be found on the extant Medici fortress of Baldassarre Lanci (see below, fig. 50).

writing on the sheet has been identified as that of Cosimo I's military architect Giovanni Battista Belluzzi, known as I1 Sanmarino, and the sheet can be dated to February 1554, when secret Florentine efforts were being made to cut off the water supply to Siena.[31] In addition to the many particulars of the city, the plan shows a remarkably detailed plan of the Spanish citadel: a five-bastioned fortress with the southern curtain—which faced the city—cranked to provide a protective recess for the gate. The two easternmost works are not full bastions but demi-bastions, together forming a hornwork stretched across the saddle leading out to the Poggio San Prospero. Another sheet by an unknown hand, a simple line drawing without annotation, date, or scale seems to suggest that the citadel was planned in two parts: an upper rectangular fort on the San Prospero hill to the east on much the same site as the present-day Medici fortress, and a separate lower hornwork extending across the Lizza towards Camollia (fig. 44). The Belluzzi plan too, by color coding in red for stone or brick construction and in brown for earth construction without the benefit of permanent covering, confirms some difference between the sections.[32] In this arrangment the upper fort would have commanded a wide field of fire both into the city and onto the Prato. The hornwork would then have secured the Lizza saddle, the best direction for an attack on the hill of San Prospero itself. Together the two works would have presented a modern rampart front to any attack that might be launched from the Prato across the Valle di Pescaia—a threat which had been identified by Peruzzi twenty years earlier when he had built two works in that area.

Three further drawings confirm the essential elements of Maestro Giorgio's

Fig. 43. Plan of Underground Siena and its Aqueduct System. In all probability this plan was made as a survey of Siena's water supply by the Florentines. Attributed to the Florentine engineer Giovanni Battista Belluzzi, the drawing is probably based on intelligence missions carried out by him during the early months of 1554. Besides the aqueducts (blue in the original but shown on right as a broken line) the surveyor has recorded the fortifications (red in the original, thin line at right) with the recent earthworks marked in sepia (shown on right as a heavy line). The only omission appears to be Peruzzi's bastion at Porta Laterina, where a gap has been left in the wall. The sheet is approximately 31 × 20 inches.

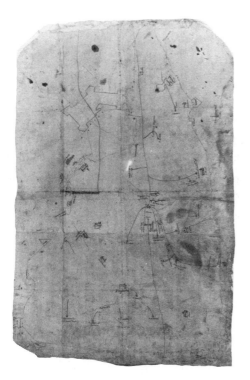
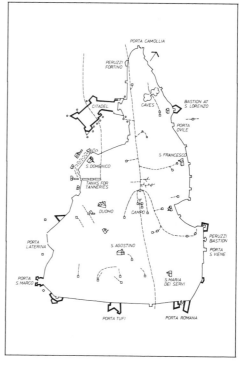

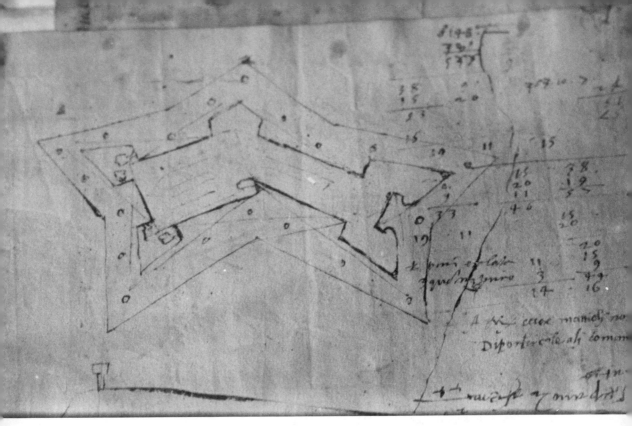

Fig. 44. Anonymous Author, Plan of the Spanish Citadel, 1552–55. One of the features of the citadel brought out clearly on this plan is the series of small circular works all the way round the ditch. Some of these can be seen in other views. They may be wells to drain the site or, possibly, pillboxes or entrances to a countermine system. Their purpose remains a mystery. They are visible on other later representations; see, for example, Maestro Giorgio's panel (fig. 42).

tavolette and the Belluzzi plan. One, attributed to Francesco di' Marchi (fig. 45), shows a remarkable degree of detail concerning the staircase circulation, internal barracks, and the like, as well as what appears to be the remains of the bastion at the Sportello di San Prospero of Baldassarre Peruzzi at the edge of the old enceinte. A recently published but unattributed drawing from the Uffizi, Florence (fig. 46), shows the main components of Siena's fortifications during the siege of 1554–55.[33] Certain inaccuracies in the arrangement of streets and major civic buildings suggest that the plan may well have been prepared by a foreigner unable to approach the city very closely. However, the significant features of the trace—five bastions, irregular cranked plan—are consistent with the other plans and painted views. Finally, the postwar sketch plan of Francesco Laparelli (see fig. 52 below), although fragmentary, shows the same proportions, dimensions, and locations as the other pictorial sources.

What is abundantly clear about the Spanish fortress is its size. It was approaching twice the size of the extant Medici fortress with a northern front somewhere between 1300 and 1600 feet long. Its total perimeter must have measured in the region of 3,200 feet. When the destruction of the inner curtain had been completed in the autumn of 1552, and the northern curtain joined to the main Camollia wall in early 1553, these formerly Spanish works formed the most up-to-date, perhaps the only truly up-to-date, sector of Siena's main enceinte.

Of what was the citadel made? In the absence of Spanish building records we can only answer this question by consulting the documents of the body generally considered to have been responsible for the total destruction of the citadel. Sienese public opinion demanded the demolition of the Spanish fortress. Military necessity dictated that at least the outer face of the works be retained and completed as part of the enceinte.[34] The solution devised by the government was to carry out both activities—that is to say, some demolition and a great deal more construction—under the guise of a body ostensibly dedicated solely to demolition, the "Quattro sopra il guasto della Cittadella."[35]

The Spanish surrendered the citadel on 3 August 1552. On 7 August the Committee of Four on the Destruction of the Citadel held its first meeting. A

Fig. 45. Francesco de' Marchi, The Spanish Citadel. One of a series of drawings attributed to Francesco de' Marchi, this plan reveals something of the citadel's interior. Cavaliers reached by circular stairs are located at the east and west ends. The gate is particularly well concealed. Francesco's drawing also shows the location and plan of the Peruzzi bastion at the Sportello di San Prospero: evidently it was very similar to that at San Viene.

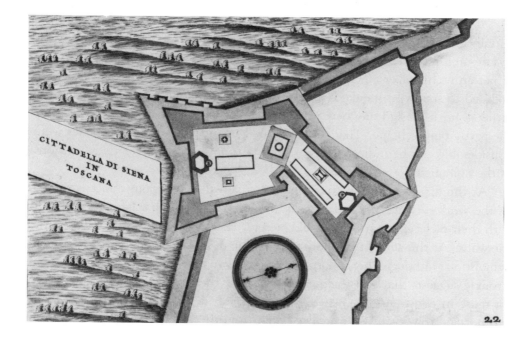

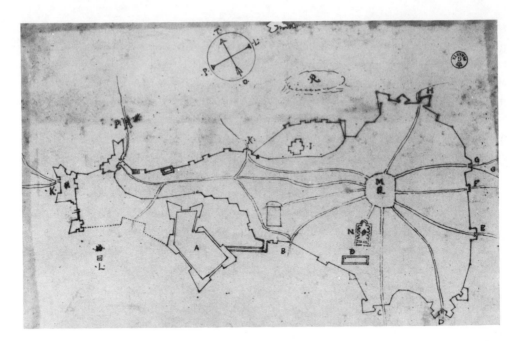

Fig. 46. Anonymous Author, Plan of the City of Siena During the Siege (1554–55). Evidently keyed to a list of locations in the city, this sheet shows the major components of the defenses: Camollia outworks, portal defenses, and the citadel, which appears to have been connected to the city along a passageway up to the church of San Domenico. "R," to the east, indicates the hill of Ravacciano, which, as we shall see, figured prominently in one of the major Imperial attacks.

certain Claudio Bartolucci was appointed commissioner general, to be assisted by the architect Maestro Giorgio di Giovanni, and Maestro Sabbino, who was either an architect or a builder.[36] It seems likely that Giorgio and Sabbino were engaged to supervise standards and to coordinate the many building tradesmen rather than to design any new works. After all, the design already existed for the partly built scheme. That the site management problems and logistics were considerable can be indicated by a selection from some of the early resolutions of the committee.

At the first meeting, instructions were given to the various trades involved in the work. All *maestri* and *manuali* (masters and skilled workmen) together with their picks and mattocks should present themselves at the site to dismantle the walls. At this stage, the emphasis in public pronouncements was entirely on demolition; although the importance attached to the presence of skilled men strongly suggests that construction (or, at least, the careful salvage of materials for reuse in construction) was already very much in mind. The guild of bakers was notified that each was to collect grain from the citadel with which to bake bread for the labor force. Blacksmiths were ordered to bring all their stocks of iron for the manufacture of pick and mattock heads. Carpenters were instructed to send two of their *maestri* to the Palazzo Pubblico to make handles for picks and mattocks. Penalties were fixed for those who did not do their share of the work.[37] On 8 August, orders were placed for fifty barrows; baskets were requisitioned from shopkeepers; anyone wishing to offer catering services on the citadel site was free to do so without tax. On 9 August a commissioner was appointed to recruit men from the dominio.[38] On 10 August an order was placed for 1,000 pick and mattock handles—which may give some indication of the size of the labor force that was envisaged.[39]

All the elements of project administration are here. Workers, skilled and unskilled, had to be drafted from the city of Siena and the dominio. Both men and women appear in the lists of workers paid; and the draft included all able-bodied men between the ages of fifteen and fifty-five years. There appear to have been two basic kinds of employment. Skilled tradesmen, their apprentices, and regular building laborers were hired at a daily rate of pay, but were required to work on the fortifications under pain of fines, loss of pay, and corporal punishment.[40] By January 1553, when all works on the San Prospero site were clearly directed toward the completion of the outward facing sections, there were special musters of the entire able-bodied population to work unpaid on the citadel for a single day.[41] During the siege of 1554–55, these general musters became more frequent and often lasted for two or three days.

Tools and building equipment were major preoccupations of the Committee of Four. The pick and the mattock seem to have been the most important iron-headed tools, and until mid-September 1552 the documents contain numerous records of orders placed and payments made for new deliveries as well as efforts to recover stolen items (often, it seems, removed from the site by drafted laborers on their return home). The next most commonly mentioned item of equipment was the *corbello*, presumably the same heavy-duty split-twig basket that can still be seen in use on southern European building sites to contain earth and rubble. These were being purchased in bulk as late as December 1552 for use on the citadel, while *corbellai* (basket makers) remained on the payroll for other fortification projects in 1553.

When it was captured in August 1552, the incomplete citadel was faced with a brick revetment with a dressed stone base. The brown-colored, evenly spaced horizontal coursing of the brickwork and the gray stone dressings are to be seen in Maestro Giorgio's *tavoletta* painting of the destruction (fig. 42), and it is what one would expect of a major building in Siena. For the postwar Medici fortress the same combination of facing materials was used. However, there is no surviving record of brick purchases by the committee during 1552–53. Does the absence of brick purchases mean that construction of the citadel continued exclusively in earth? If not, from where were the bricks obtained?

There was, of course, a very large number of bricks already on site. Maestro Giorgio's *tavoletta* suggests that by August 1552 the ramparts were already quite tall and apparently of equal height on both inward and outward facing sides. When scaled against the human figures in the picture, the Spanish ramparts seem to have been at least sixteen feet high, possibly more than twenty feet tall, given the tendency of most artists to exaggerate the height of the human body in topographical pictures. Since the inner walls were to be dismantled, there would have been a vast number of salvageable bricks already on site and suitable for reuse on the outward-facing sections that still needed to be completed. This may well explain why there is no record of the committee ordering further supplies, although on 28 August some builders' houses were searched for bricks said to have been removed from the citadel works.[42]

The records of the committee, however, do show the purchase of materials used in earthwork construction: *legname* (timber), *stipa* (brushwood), and *fascine* (faggots). Timber, of course, is used for many purposes in building, including the scaffolding and boardwalks indicated in Maestro Giorgio's paintings, and the floor and roof structures of conventional buildings such as those built at the citadel for the accommodation of the drafted laborers. *Stipa* and *fascine*, on the other hand, are bound to be associated with earthwork construction.

Another clue to the nature of the construction is the type of worker employed. From August to December the workforce at the citadel comprised *muratori* from Siena and *guastatori* drafted from the dominio. The *guastatori* were unskilled laborers. The term *muratori*—literally "wallers"—describes the masons who built walls in stone or brick and were engaged in a variety of heavy construction activity, often leading gangs of laborers and apprentices.[43] Between August and December, therefore, a labor force of *guastatori* and *muratori* probably indicates that the building work was concentrated on traditional masonry construction for the completion of the buttresses and the external brick skin of the outward-facing rampart. After the major deliveries of *legname, stipa,* and *fascine* in December and January the nature of the workforce also changed. A number of other specialist trades appear on the site: *segatori di tavole* (sawyers of planks), *gratticiai* (hurdle makers) and *corbellai* (basket makers).[44] Moreover, on 4 January and again on 23 January, orders were given for all able-bodied residents of Siena to present themselves for work.[45] This kind of muster would have put thousands of workers onto the site, as opposed to the hundreds who had worked there regularly before Christmas. It is the kind of mass unskilled labor force normally associated with large-scale earth movement.

Our analysis of employment patterns and the acquisition of building materials for the citadel suggests that, at different stages of the building program, masonry and earthwork construction were both used. It is by no means improbable that both systems of construction were used on the same sections of the project; but to make sense of this point something needs to be said about the two most common methods of construction employed in sixteenth-century fortifications.

A masonry rampart was not made of solid stone or brick. It comprised a front retaining wall, usually made of two skins of brick or stone, with a thick layer of dry rubble, or rubble and mortar, sandwiched between them. The lower part of the wall was usually scarped, that is to say, thickened out at the base: this thickening being designed to increase the stability of the structure as a retaining wall, to increase its ability to resist artillery fire, and to provide space for various low-level chambers, in particular the countermine passage that ran around the base of many fortifications giving access to the lower handgun embrasures, sally ports, and the countermine shafts that ran out beneath the ditch. Strong as this front wall may have been, it was no stronger than the walls of many medieval towns and castles that had been brought down relatively quickly by artillery bombardment when the new weapons began to be used during the fifteenth century. The mechanical strength of the rampart turned upon its being backed by a large mass of earth and supported by internal buttresses known by the Italians as *contraforti*.[46] The contraforti could do much to keep the rampart in existence even after the front wall had been shot away. The contraforti themselves presented a narrow face to the front and were very difficult to destroy by gunfire.

Earthworks varied considerably between temporary field fortifications and permanent works. The most primitive earthworks took the form of a ditch with the spoil heaped up on one side into a self-retaining slope. Renaissance warfare gives us numerous examples of this kind of work, sometimes built on a gigantic scale as field fortifications or as walls of circumvallation; that is, works built by the besiegers to enclose a town, preventing both a breakout and a relief.[47] With stakes and brushwood or thorn entanglements they made an effective obstacle to infantry and cavalry, but would have to be well covered with defensive fire. Given the resources of an army or city, such works could be thrown up surprisingly quickly. But they did not last under the heavy rains of winter and spring, and they often made poor platforms for mounting heavy artillery.

Permanent or, at least, semipermanent earthworks could be also built. One of the best descriptions of mid-sixteenth-century earthwork technology is to be found in the treatise of Giovanni Battista Belluzzi himself (fig. 47). Belluzzi describes a composite timber, brushwood, and earth structure built in the following manner.[48] First a framework of heavy timber uprights, crosspieces, and diagonals would be constructed. Fascines—faggots of long twigs bound together—

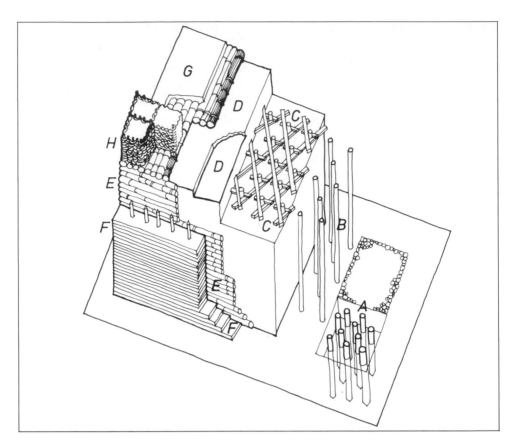

Fig. 47. Earthwork Construction: Cut-away Axonometric of a Rampart Based on the Account in Belluzzi's Treatise. **A:** Foundations formed by piles, driven to leave the heads exposed and then packed with rubble. **B:** Heavy timber uprights, planted on five-foot grid. **C:** The chain, or *catena*, of lateral timber reinforcements, which is laid out at three- to six-feet vertical intervals. The chain must be free to settle under the weight of the rampart. The tips of the chain that face outward are sharpened to deflect enemy shot. **D:** Earth and twig infill, to be laid in two- to three-inch layers and well rammed. The earth would be sieved to remove stones, which would become secondary missiles when struck by cannonballs. **E:** Containment of earth infill by a wall of fascines tied back to the heavy timber internal structure. **F:** External lining of turfs, laid like bricks, secured by twig reinforcements running along the courses and by vertical pegs. **G:** Deck formed by rammed clay or mud. **H:** Parapet and gun emplacements formed by gabions.

would be laid in layers across the rampart and built up into front and rear retaining walls. Earth would then be mixed with brushwood and consolidated between the fascines, the brushwood acting as a kind of reinforcing mesh (fig. 48). Layers of clay would be introduced from time to time to form dampproof courses. Finally the whole structure would be protected from the weather by a layer of turfs, well pegged into the sloping surfaces.

A rampart of this kind was stable enough to support heavy artillery and was capable of absorbing a great deal of punishment from enemy shot.[49] With regular maintenance and provision for drainage on the land-drain principle, it could last for many years. Indeed, there was a minority school of thought in northern Europe which held that well-made earthworks were better than masonry fortifications.

Sometimes the two systems were combined. In this solution the lower half or perhaps two-thirds of the rampart was constructed on the masonry system, which meant that it was possible to incorporate a wet ditch. The upper works would be built of reinforced earth, which gave a rather more adaptable and shot-resistant area from which to attempt to outshoot the enemy batteries. In this case the guns would be housed behind temporary parapets made of gabions, enormous baskets filled with earth which provided a good deal of protection against all but the heaviest shot (fig. 49). *Grati*, or hurdle screens, would be installed on the upper works to obscure the enemy snipers' view. It is probably significant that the documents record the installation of both gabions and *grati* in the final stages of the citadel works.[50]

Drawing all of these threads together, we may reconstruct the citadel as

Fig. 48. Bernardo Puccini, Drawing of the Network of Timber Used within an Earthwork Construction. Puccini's treatise on fortifications borrowed heavily from that of Giovanni Battista Belluzzi. In this drawing Puccini shows in plan how the network of branches can hold the earth together. A masonry cladding is shown at the lower edge of the plan.

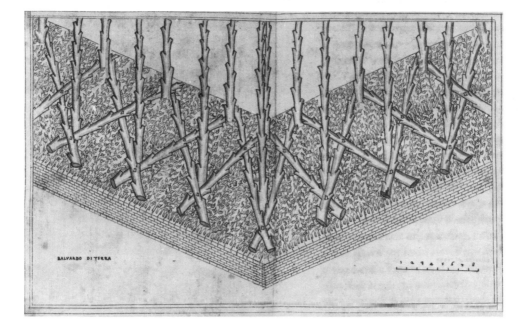

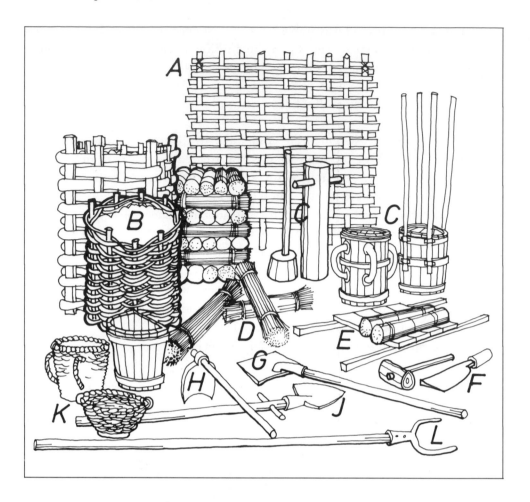

Fig. 49. Earthworks: The Tools of the Trade.
A: Blinds: wicker screen used to conceal the sappers or gunners from aimed enemy fire.
B: Gabions: wicker baskets filled with earth to protect gun emplacements. Square, circular, or triangular gabions were common. **C:** Rams for consolidating earth and pile driving.
D: Fascines: bundles of twigs used to reinforce earthworks and, sometimes, to construct lightweight gabions. **E:** Tray for moving bundles of fascines. **F:** Fascine cutter and turf trimmer. **G:** Turf lifter. **H:** Mattock. **J:** Spade with foot piece. **K:** Baskets and panier barrels for earth shifting; note shoulder straps.
L: Forked prop for erecting and supporting heavy timber reinforcing members.

follows. It was a long, narrow work of five bastions covering a site that extended from close to the Camollia wall in the east to occupy the highest parts of the Poggio di San Prospero to the west. The plan was cranked to fit onto the hill and, as such, well illustrates the willingness of sixteenth-century architects to adapt geometrical systems to the exigencies of local topography; the plan had little connection to the regular polygonal geometry associated with mid-century treatises on military architecture.

Probably the citadel was planned in two parts, with a lower hornwork over the present-day Lizza. Certainly the works on the saddle were much lower than the works on the hill. At the time of the uprising in 1552, the Sienese were able to build a platform on the Poggio dei Malavolti from which they could shoot down into the positions occupied by the Spaniards on the saddle. There can be

Fig. 50. Baldassarre Lanci, Fortress of Santa Barbara, Siena. The *puntone* keeps sappers away from the salient as well as providing a sharp, forceful angle for the fortress.

little doubt that completion of the Spanish design would have involved the construction of works tall enough to forestall this kind of overlooking. Francesco de' Marchi's plan (fig. 45) has a cavalier or raised platform located in mid-curtain on the eastern end of the citadel, which would have provided a high point overlooking the Camollia approaches. There was at least one such cavalier in the works completed by the Sienese after the expulsion of the Spaniards. In all likelihood it formed part of the outward facing works on the northern ramparts, from which it would have had a good field of fire onto the Prato as well as down into the Valle di Pescaia. The Sienese cavalier was completed early in 1553, when a stonemason was paid for dressing the marble edges to its gun embrasures, a high degree of finish which strongly suggests that the entire original platform was constructed in permanent masonry.

The construction of the rest of the citadel—in its completed form—was probably a mixture of masonry and earthwork; with the lower half or two-thirds of the ramparts and bastions in masonry finished in brick revetments and stone dressings. Maestro Giorgio's *tavolette* paintings provide the best visual evidence for the state of the works after their capture in August 1552. At this time they were between sixteen and twenty feet high with a molded stone base and a *puntone* at the salient of the southeast bastion, a detail that was used again in the postwar Medici fortress (fig. 50). In one of the Biccherna panels, masonry *contraforti* were exposed by the demolition of the inner curtain (fig. 42). What seems to have happened is that during the autumn of 1552 the bricklayers and masons, aided by relatively small numbers of laborers from the dominio, built up the outer ramparts using materials salvaged from the inner works. This would explain the fact that no new bricks seem to have been purchased. Later, in the early weeks of 1553, tradesmen associated with timber-reinforced earthworks make their appearance in the records of the project. Finally, the upper earthworks, noted by Belluzzi, were completed by thousands of Siena's inhabitants drafted onto the site to work like pack animals carrying earth in late January 1553. The finishing touches to the modified citadel took place in the spring of 1553. It was then that the embrasures of the cavalier were dressed, the winding gear fitted to the drawbridge, and the *corpi di guardia* built for the garrison.

4

OUTWORKS AND FRONTIER FORTIFICATIONS, 1552–53

T HE incorporation of the Spanish citadel into the Sienese walls gave the city a new and powerful defensive position (fig. 51). Artillery, which had so threatened the city in 1526 from the Prato, could now be matched with guns in the excellent positions in the rebuilt citadel on the Poggio San Prospero. Yet as valuable as this new defensive wing was, it remained a passive strategy; that is, the republic might sit behind its walls and await attack. There is some irony in this judgment, for what had always distinguished Renaissance thinking in fortification design was the active response. The angle bastion itself had evolved to meet the need for a device which would provide both enfilading fire from the flanks and, all too often forgotten, a very large number of gun positions along the two faces, capable of countering, in some cases even outshooting, the batteries of an enemy. A logical extension of the idea of an active response was to place advanced positions well in front of the walls, from which the enemy could be engaged before coming within range of the city. An enemy would have to fight one action, and possibly more, before coming to grips with the principal defenses. As we move into the 1550s, this was the strategy that Siena adopted.

As Siena and her new French allies prepared to meet the Spanish counter-attack during the winter of 1552–53, a group of substantial outworks was constructed on the northwest approaches to the city, designed to prevent—or at least to postpone—the occupation of the Prato and the Camollia ridge. The forts at Camollia became the first components of a system of outlying fortifications, eventually extending some miles beyond the main circuit of walls, which was to perform a vital role in the defense of the capital.

The Forts at Camollia

The decision to build an outwork at Camollia is credited to Paul de La Barthe, sieur de Thermes, a celebrated light cavalry leader and future Marshal of France, who had arrived in Siena in the autumn of 1552 to command the royal forces.[1] For the first weeks, Thermes spent much of his life on horseback, surveying the

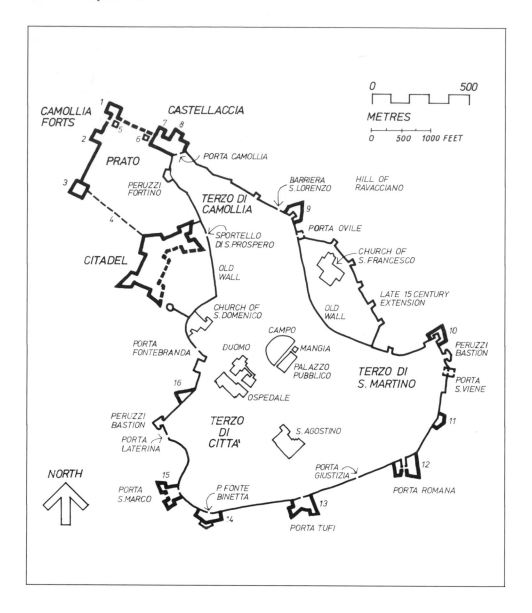

Fig. 51. Siena's Fortifications in the Mid-sixteenth Century. The plan shows an outline of the walls with the fortifications pre-1550 (thin line); the fortifications of 1550–55 (thick line); works not completed during 1550–55 (broken line). The numbers on the plan refer to significant locations around the walls: **1, 2, 3:** Forts built at Camollia during the spring of 1553. **4:** Curtain linking the Camollia forts to the Citadel, begun in the summer of 1553 but incomplete at the time of the siege. **5:** Torrione Dipinto (medieval tower gate and barbican). **6:** Torrazzo in Mezzo (medieval tower gate and barbican). **7, 8:** Batteries constructed in spring 1554. **9–16:** Earthworks built 1553–54 in form indicated on contemporary plan attributed to Giovanni Battista Belluzzi (fig. 43).

fortifications of the republic's extensive dominio and taking rapid and sometimes unpopular decisions on the defensibility of towns. Just before Christmas 1552 he returned to Siena and gave orders for the clearance of buildings along the Camollia ridge and the construction of a fort on the Prato.[2] Its design was placed in the hands of Giovambattista Peloro, who had recently been recalled from the Medici court and appointed Architect to the Republic at the high salary of 150 scudi per annum.[3] Born in 1483 and a contemporary of Peruzzi, Peloro was the most distinguished and most experienced native architect the Sienese could have hoped to engage, though his treatment by some overpatriotic historians has been somewhat colored by his close personal association with Cosimo I and an unwelcome and unsubstantiated attribution as a designer of the Spanish citadel. However, he gave sterling wartime service to the republic at Siena and half-a-dozen provincial sites.[4] Not only in his salary but in all official documents concerning his affairs, he seems to have been treated with the greatest respect.

The Camollia fortifications of Thermes and Peloro were built north of the Torrione Dipinto astride the road to Florence. They were conceived as three independent forts (fig. 51, nos. 1, 2, 3), later to be linked by curtains, rather than as a single major fortress with fully integrated curtains and bastions. There can be little doubt that the construction of smaller separate works—in modern terminology, redoubts—represented an intelligent approach to the topography. Two forts just in front of the Torrione Dipinto would prevent an enemy from moving directly along the ridge from the north on to the Prato. A third fort on the western extremity of the Prato plateau would impede any attack from the low ground. This explanation suggests, moreover, that the decision to build three independent forts was motivated by the urgent need to get some defenses constructed quickly in this area. Time permitting, the works could later be joined by a frontal curtain and linked to the main defensive perimeter.

The most accurate surviving plan of the Camollia forts was drawn just after the war by Francesco Laparelli, a Cortonese architect who worked extensively for Cosimo I and the Papacy and is perhaps best known as the designer of the new city and fortifications of Valletta following the siege of Malta in 1565 (fig. 52).[5] Laparelli shows two forts (marked 1 and 2 on fig. 51) north of the Torrione Dipinto or, as he calls it, the "Porta della Vergine." Their north faces are angled to allow mutual flanking fire across the fronts. Fort 1 was located close to the eastern edge of the ridge and could fire into the Ravacciano Valley as well as southward to flank the Castellaccia. Fort 2, besides firing northward along the Florence road, gave a heavy weight of flanking fire across the fronts of the other forts. The third fort was somewhat isolated from the others, located about a thousand feet to the west. This last work had to provide its own flanking fire on the south and west faces; this was achieved by very small bastions in the three outer corners—so small, in fact, that they were probably designed to accommodate infantrymen armed with muskets or wall-mounted swivel pieces rather than artillery proper. Once again, the main battery of this fort was along the north face, toward the likely direction of attack.

All three forts were surrounded by ditches, and the second and third were apparently joined by a communication trench. They were largely of earth construction, although, as with the works on San Prospero, gates and other key parts such as corners and embrasures were executed in masonry.[6] Earthwork construction was speedy and time was now running short.

Fig. 52. Francesco Laparelli, The Camollia Forts. One of a series of drawings made by Laparelli in 1562 during his trip through central Italy. Although he made the drawings some years after the siege, Laparelli was able to discern the incomplete trenchwork linking San Prospero with the western Camollia fort: "Traversa cominciata dai Francesi per chiudere dal forte alla fortezza." In addition to his work as a military architect in Malta and elsewhere, Laparelli was active as a civil architect in Cortona.

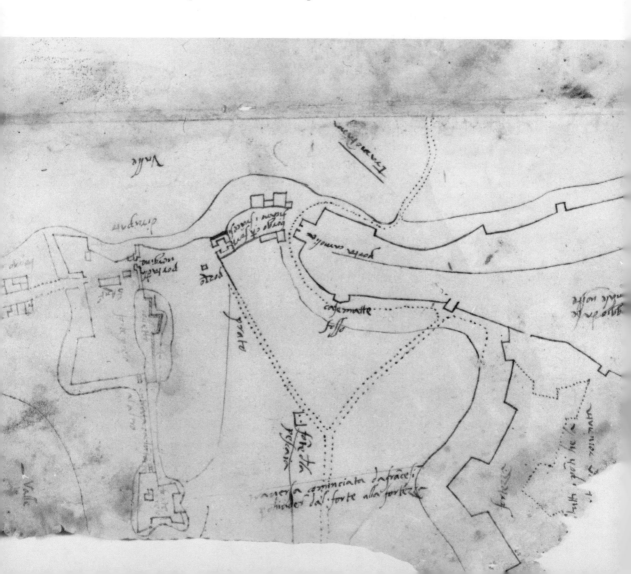

On New Year's Day 1553, a Spanish force of 14,000 men had marched north from Naples. It passed Rome on 15 January and concentrated in the flat lands between Lago Trasimeno and Cortona toward the end of the month. There it was joined by 5,000 Italian foot and, most importantly, some heavy artillery sent from Florence by Cosimo. Another body of 2,500 Spanish infantry sailed from Naples on 5 January, put in at Civitavecchia on 8 January, and disembarked on 10 January at Livorno. Florence was to remain technically neutral throughout the first year of the war, a fiction that enabled Cosimo to support the emperor's forces with food, transport, weapons, and reinforcements while continuing both to trade with Siena and to lodge diplomatic protests whenever Florentine property was damaged in the fighting. The quarrel was between the emperor and his rebellious subjects.[7] Siena expected to be attacked soon and increased the pace of her defensive preparations.

Work at Camollia began to be recorded on 21 January 1553, when the Committee of Four extended their activities once again to include the construction of the forts.[8] The entire civilian labor force of Siena, which had already been twice pressed into service on the citadel during January, was mobilized for continuous work on the forts. Each terzo was assigned a fort. Led by Ippolito d'Este, cardinal of Ferrara, the French king's lieutenant in central Italy, the people threw themselves into the task in what was described as a "holiday spirit."

> The whole city [reported the chronicler Agnolo Bardi] worked with such willingness that citizens, shopkeepers, the old, the young, and women too came with quite amazing frequency to labor all day or to go making fascines. The *contrade* [small administrative districts] came in formation with their standards, and often the cardinal worked carrying fascines with all of his court, as did the archbishop of Siena with his entire clergy of priests and friars with the white banner painted with the Assumption of Our Lady. To witness the construction of these fortifications was a pleasure, a triumph, a festival.[9]

It was even recorded that the cardinal sent his own musician to the site where he "played on the flute so sweetly that everyone stayed to listen to it as a thing most rare."[10]

Here, once again, patriotic memories can be deceptive. As with the works to the citadel, initial public enthusiasm and participation was high; but the completion of the fortifications demanded penal sanctions and constant pressure from the leaders of the republic. The records of one of the terzi, the terzo di Camollia, allow us to monitor the laborious administrative process required for this urgent communal enterprise of fort building.

Administration: The Terzo di Camollia

A general meeting of the 150 heads of households was held on 4 February in the church of San Cristoforo, under the presidency of Andrea Marchi, captain general of the terzo. Four *provveditori* (purveyors) were elected by the congregation from a shortlist of twenty-four politically reliable citizens, and a general tax of six lire was approved; one hundred and fifty in favor, none opposed.[11] Next day the four provveditori and the captain general held their first business meeting; they fixed regular meetings for Sundays, Tuesdays, and Fridays, agreed on a system of eight-day rotating chairmanships, and appointed tax collectors and a treasurer to whom monies were to be paid within eight days. An organizer, or *capo,* was nominated for each parish, each of whom was to produce eight men daily to work on the fort. Nine *capi* were named, implying a regular labor force of fifty-six unskilled men and women from the terzo.[12] This arrangement only lasted a week, however. At the meeting of provveditori on 12 February it was decided that everyone in a parish, or group of small parishes, should work on the fort for one day a week, with the parishes taking turns.[13] A cadre of building professionals—masters and laborers—was assigned to each of the three forts from the main citadel site, and a site architect was appointed to supervise the Camollia works.[14]

Absenteeism quickly became a problem. On 17 February the provveditori announced that because of the particularly poor attendance by the parishioners of San Pietro a Ovile, the site would be visited hourly and absentees fined. On 19 February, half-day shifts were introduced. This reduction in hours certainly did not reflect the near-completion of the works, because at the same meeting it was announced that permission had been obtained from the colonel-general of the republican militia for soldiers to help with the building.[15] Presumably the six *contrade* companies contained the youngest and fittest members of the terzo, whose efforts were needed on the fort. In any event, this combination of civilians working half a day a week—drawn from all able-bodied souls in the parishes below the age of sixty—and the young militiamen taking a day a week from their military exercises, seems at last to have proved satisfactory.

The other main difficulty concerned the collection of the taxes. A second contribution of six lire had been voted at a general congregation on 11 February, but by this time the provveditori were already beginning to threaten that those who had not yet paid the first would be "given to the bailiffs."[16] On 25 February the first list of defaulters was published. Ten further lists were published between 28 February and 13 June. By May, all but a few had been pressured into parting with their twelve lire, and the final list on 13 June recorded the goods collected by the bailiffs in lieu of payment. A price was put against each item and, unless the money was paid by "Sunday next," the property would be sold.[17]

Curtains and Trenchwork

Despite the administrative problems encountered by the leaders of the terzo di Camollia, the forts appear to have been completed with remarkable speed. Work began in the third week of January 1553, and by the beginning of February, the terzi were beginning to play their part. By April the city was still not under attack, which encouraged the government to proceed with the second phase: the construction of curtains linking the three forts and a trenchwork connecting the fort of the terzo di Città to the works on San Prospero. On 12 April yet another committee of four citizens was appointed to raise money for these works by means of taxes levied on the professional, commercial, and trade institutions of the city. This body held its first meeting on 13 April, when it was stated in the preamble to their terms of reference that the "three terzi of the city had assumed the task and already in large part completed at their own expense the construction of the three forts at Camollia."[18] Three months—from mid-January to mid-April—had seen the three forts "in large part completed."

It was now necessary and important, continued the terms of reference, to meet the cost of the trench that was to be built from the fort made by the terzo di Città to the hill of San Prospero. The committee was urged to approach this task with "a hot zeal for the public welfare." The Committee of Four seems to have been zealous enough in the raising of monies. It met regularly until 28 July and taxed no less than forty-four city institutions. After 28 July, however, the notarial record ceases. Had the trench been completed? The two most reliable contemporary plans of the city's fortifications both mark the trench running between the Prato and San Prospero. Both, however, indicate that it was incomplete. The Uffizi plan (fig. 46) marks it in a broken line and gives it a bastioned trace. Laparelli's plan (fig. 52) indicates a straight line but annotates it "traverse begun by the French to join the fort to the fortress." Begun but not apparently completed: evidently "hot zeal" was not enough.

The Defense of the Dominio

The shortcomings of the Camollia outworks should not be allowed to convey the impression that the republic remained supine before the gathering storm.

This would hardly have been possible, for the government was constantly deluged with all manner of intelligence on Imperial troop movements and intentions. Letters were received from as far away as Rome urging the fortification of other sectors of Siena's walls believed to be the objective of Spanish plans. By the end of March the Imperialists had taken Monticchiello and laid siege to Montalcino, the latter only some twenty miles to the south of Siena. During April, therefore, the Sienese diverted some of their own efforts toward the construction of further forts on the approaches to the Porta San Viene, Porta Romana, and Porta Tufi— all on the southern side of the city.[19] Attempts also had to be made to satisfy the often desperate pleas for help from provincial towns threatened by enemy troops already across the republic's frontiers. Long-term resistance rested almost as much upon the defenses of the frontiers, ports, and the towns of the agricultural hinterland as upon those of the capital. For political reasons, too, the Sienese were obliged to make scarce resources available for the defense of communities who remained loyal in the reasonable expectation of aid.[20]

Some of this aid took the form of soldiers, guns, and ammunition; and in a score of places fortifications demanded immediate repairs or substantial additions. As with Siena itself, most of the labor for construction was recruited locally in circumstances often made difficult by shortages of rural manpower and by the many conflicting demands made upon it. For besides fortification building, the republic attempted at this time to gather and store food supplies and livestock,[21] to billet their own soldiers,[22] to rebuild strategic roads and bridges,[23] to establish law and order in a state infamous for banditry,[24] and to upgrade the ferryboat and courier systems essential to efficient communications.[25] It was a task that strained Sienese administrative skills and financial resources to breaking point.

The government of the republic was highly centralized. As we have seen, special committees were set up from time to time on an ad hoc basis to handle major projects; but most public administration was managed by the appointment of politically reliable commissioners with Letters Patent giving either general powers in a certain place or special responsibilities over a wide geographical area. It was a system whose inevitable product was conflict. The commissioner with authority to collect draft oxen clashed with men using oxen to haul food or building materials. Laborers found themselves pressed into different public projects, paid by neither commissioner and reluctant to leave their families unprotected in homes where yet another official had billeted troops. In an attempt to coordinate defensive preparation, commissioners general were appointed with regional authority, but the position of these senior officials remained unclear vis-à-vis the military, many of whom held their commissions from the king of France.

The leading Sienese military advisers—Thermes, Cornelio Bentivoglio, Piero

Pieri—attempted to ensure that efforts were concentrated on strategically significant and defensible sites. Despite this expert advice the government of the republic found it impossible to pursue a strictly military policy in the face of political pressure from traditionally loyal communities, or even influential families. The town of Pienza near the eastern border provides an excellent case in point. A relatively unimportant village in the early fifteenth century, the birthplace of Enea Silvio Piccolomini, who became Pope Pius II, Pienza had been raised by him to a bishopric and adorned with a monumental civic core (1459–64). Yet Pienza's medieval fortifications, despite modernization during the reign of Pius II, could be easily approached on two sides from level ground and offered no obstacle to a modern army. Despite its indefensibility, the Piccolomini family persuaded the *Otto della Guerra* (the War Committee of Eight, charged with supreme authority in the emergency) to reverse its first decision to abandon the place. Hurried and expensive last-minute attempts to fortify and arm Pienza came to nothing when the town surrendered without a proper defense.[26] Subsequently it changed hands at frequent intervals throughout the war.

The final resolution of this conflict came in February 1554 with the declaration of a clear regional defense policy.[27] Sixteen provincial towns would be defended, garrisoned, and fortified (see frontispiece). Civilians were directed to bring their livestock and stores into these towns or risk confiscation or destruction without compensation. This was the general authority for what outside the defended towns amounted to a scorched-earth policy. The proclamation of February 1554, however, merely formalized a strategy that had been formulated a year earlier. By January 1553, indeed, enemy intelligence reports to the duke of Florence correctly listed the sixteen towns that were to be defended by the Sienese.[28]

Massa Marittima, Monterotondo, Montepescali, and Gavorrano guarded the northern approaches to the Sienese Maremma.[29] Monteriggioni and Casole overlooked the shortest direct routes to Siena from the Florentine border fortresses of Poggio Imperiale and Colle di Val d'Elsa. The Val di Chiana frontier and the Florentine-held salient of Montepulciano was defended by Lucignano, Monticchiello, and Chiusi. The three last-named fortresses might seem a quite insufficient obstacle to incursions from the east, but the long Val di Chiana frontier was much less exposed to attack in the sixteenth century than would be the case today. Much of it was then marshy, and, as Leonardo da Vinci's well-known map (fig. 53) indicates, a large part was permanently inundated.[30]

Chiusi also played a role in the defense of the southern frontier with the Papal States. Although technically neutral, the Papal States were to be used throughout the war as a transit zone for Imperial reinforcements from Naples.

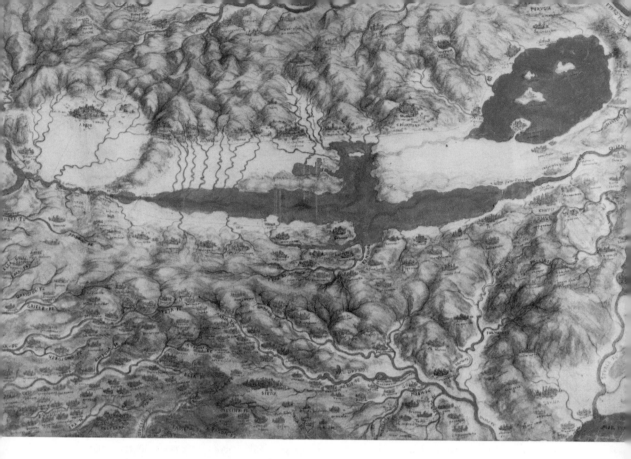

Fig. 53. Leonardo da Vinci, The Val di Chiana. Leonardo's bird's-eye pictorial map looks from west to east, with Siena in the central foreground and Arezzo and Cortona on the far side of the Chiana. Even in this black-and-white reproduction the extensive area of inundated ground separating Sienese from Florentine territory is clearly visible. The causeway linking Ponte a Valiano (on the east) with Montepulciano (Florence's toehold on the Sienese side) can also be seen. The drainage and canalization of the valley was to engage the attention of generations of engineers; their dream was to create a central Italian canal running from Florence to Rome. This sheet was probably intended as a military map for Cesare Borgia.

To guard this border the Sienese planned to defend Sarteano, Radicofani,[31] Sorano, and Caparbia, the last a tiny village overlooking the coast road and the southern entrance to the coastal plain of the Maremma.

Flat, swampy, and malarial along the coast, the Maremma provided Siena's outlets to the sea. Grosseto was the main town and strong point of the area, possessing one of the few completely bastioned fortification systems of Sienese Tuscany. By the early months of 1553, six new bastions and their connecting curtains were nearing completion. No original drawings of the scheme have survived, but from the detailed description in one of the commissioner's progress reports it seems likely that the wartime layout was somewhat similar to that adopted later by the Medici architects, beginning with Baldassarre Lanci (1510–71), when they modernized the walls in the 1560s and 1570s.[32] Since then, however, the surrounding topography has been radically changed. In the sixteenth century, Grosseto was a port on the shallow but well-sheltered lagoon. Unfortunately for the Sienese, the entrance to the lagoon was too close to the Imperial naval bases of Piombino and Elba for Grosseto to serve as the principal supply port in time of war.

The military port of Sienese Tuscany was Orbetello, built on a peninsula projecting into a shallow lagoon behind the offshore volcanic mass of Monte Argentario. Surrounded on three sides by water, Orbetello was also the strongest defensive position in the region, as was demonstrated by the ability of a small Spanish garrison—resupplied by sea—to sustain itself there from the rebellion of July 1552 until the Imperial reconquest of the Maremma later in the summer of 1555. With Orbetello denied them, the Franco-Sienese allies were obliged to make use of the smaller and more exposed harbor facilities of Port'Ércole, located on Monte Argentario itself, as their main naval and supply base. During the war, the allies carried out their largest fortification project at Port'Ércole, where by the summer of 1555 no less than seven forts had been built on the precipitous hills surrounding the harbor.

The most important provincial fortification scheme of the winter of 1552–53 was at Montalcino. Unlike the other defended towns, Montalcino was located neither on the coast nor on the frontiers but in the mountainous heartland of the republic. However, its military importance derived only in part from its hilltop defenses which, as we shall see, suffered from both natural and man-made defects. The nearest substantial town to the south of Siena, it was the obvious center of support for a capital that lay precariously close to an unfriendly border. Moreover, Montalcino enjoyed excellent communications. Roads through the mountains linked it with both Grosseto and Port'Ércole. Montalcino also overlooked the *strada romana,* the vital main road from Siena to the south. Its pivotal position made it an obvious choice as the French command center during the siege of Siena and, following the loss of the capital in 1555, as the seat of the republic-in-exile. All these qualities, of course, made Montalcino one of the obvious potential objectives for the Imperial army. Between October 1552 and the opening of siege operations in March 1553, two separate lines of defensive works were constructed on the exposed southern side of the town, and at the

Fig. 54. (See following pages.) Maggi and Castriotto, Monticchiello under Siege. The bastion is located almost along the seam of the volume. The city walls still retain their *merli,* and with the exception of this single modern bastion in the center, the towers are in traditional medieval form.

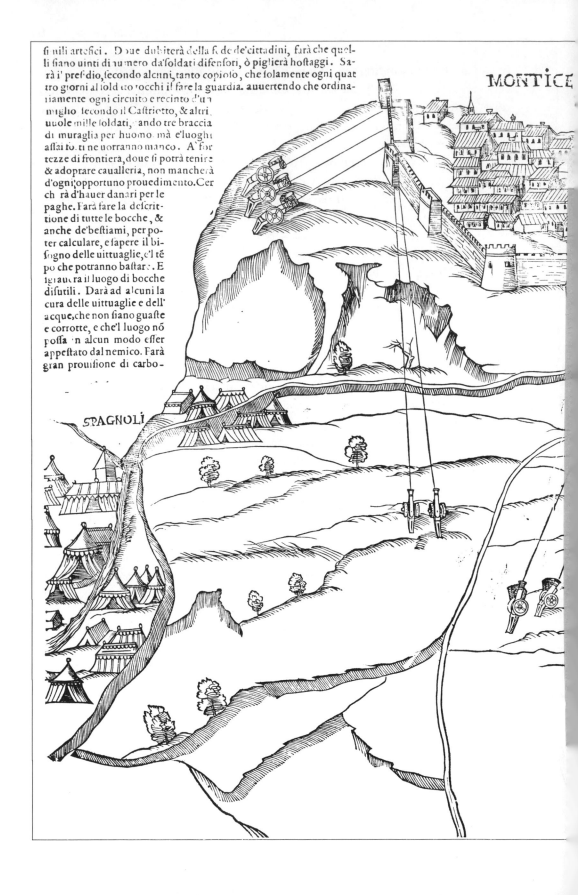

fi mili artefici . Doue dubiterà della fede de'cittadini, farà che quelli fiano uinti di numero da'foldati difenfori, ò piglierà hoftaggi. Sa-
rà i' prefidio, fecondo alcuni, tanto copiofo, che folamente ogni quat
tro giorni al foldato tocchi il fare la guardia. auuertendo che ordina-
riamente ogni circuito e recinto d'un
miglio fecondo il Caftrietto, & altri,
uuole mille foldati, dando tre braccia
di muraglia per huomo, mà e'luoghi
affai forti ne uorranno manco. A' for
tezze di frontiera, doue fi potrà tenire
& adoprare caualleria, non mancherà
d'ogni opportuno prouedimento. Cer
ch rà d'hauer danari per le
paghe. Farà fare la defcrit-
tione di tutte le bocche , &
anche de'beftiami, per poter calculare, e fapere il bifogno delle uittuaglie, e'l tê
po che potranno baftare. E
igrauera il luogo di bocche
difutili. Darà ad alcuni la
cura delle uittuaglie e dell'
acque, che non fiano guafte
e corrotte, e che'l luogo nõ
poffa in alcun modo effer
appeftato dal nemico. Farà
gran prouifione di carbo-

MONTICE

SPAGNOLI

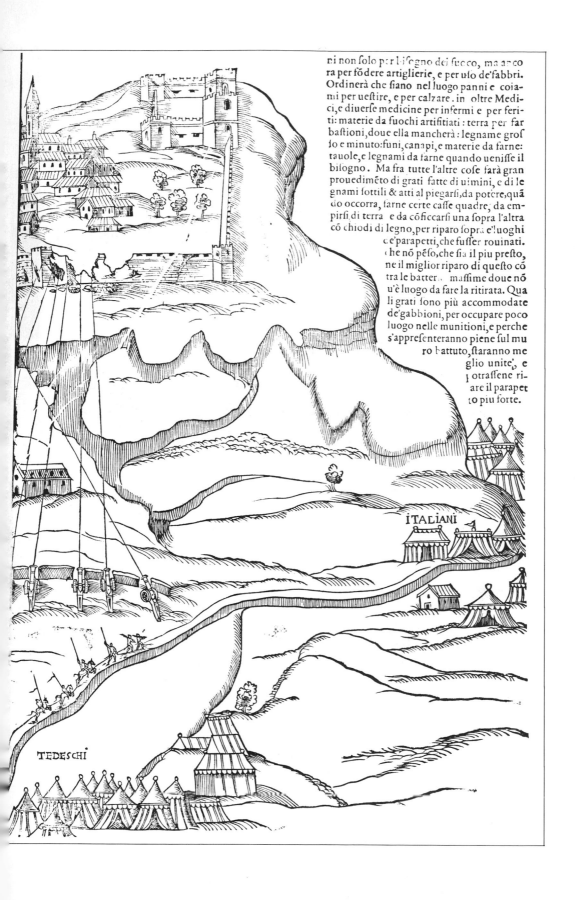

ri non folo per bifogno del fuoco, ma anco
ra per fōdere artiglierie, e per ufo de'fabbri.
Ordinerà che fiano nel luogo panni e coia-
mi per ueftire, e per calzare. in oltre Medici, e diuerfe medicine per infermi e per feri-
ti: materie da fuochi artifitiati : terra per far
baftioni, doue ella mancherà: legname grof
fo e minuto: funi, canapi, e materie da farne:
tauole, e legnami da farne quando ueniffe il
bifogno. Ma fra tutte l'altre cofe farà gran
prouedimēto di grati fatte di uimini, e di le
gnami fottili & atti al piegarfi, da potere, quā
do occorra, farne certe caffe quadre, da em-
pirfi di terra e da cōficcarfi una fopra l'altra
cō chiodi di legno, per riparo fopra e'luoghi
c e'parapetti, che fuffer rouinati.
c he nō pēfo, che fia il piu prefto,
ne il miglior riparo di quefto cō
tra le batter⋯ maffime doue nō
u'è luogo da fare la ritirata. Qua
li grati fono più accommodate
de'gabbioni, per occupare poco
luogo nelle munitioni, e perche
s'apprefenteranno piene ful mu
ro battuto, ftaranno me
glio unite', e
ı otraffene ri
are il parapet
to piu forte.

ITALIANI

TEDESCHI

Fig. 55. Monticchiello Today. This view and the road leading to the village marks the main axis of the Spanish attack. It confirms the major elements of Maggi and Castriotto's topography. On this axis the Sienese placed their only substantial defensive work. To the right and behind the village the slope is far too steep to allow an approach.

busiest period as many as seven hundred and fifty laborers worked on the project. Although not completely finished by the beginning of the three-month siege, Montalcino's fortifications were successfully defended in what became the key military operation of 1553.

Before turning to these events, however, we should examine the effectiveness of Thermes's strategy for regional defense. Could the smaller frontier forts be successfully defended against a modern army? As with many military questions, the answer was to be found as much in the fighting spirit and skill of the combatants as in the relative strengths of their forces, fortifications, and weapons. Lucignano, Siena's northern position in the Val di Chiana, was lost without a fight to a small Imperial force amid disgraceful scenes of confusion. The defense of Monticchiello was a very different story. Although eventually captured, Monticchiello showed the kind of stubborn and effective resistance that could be offered by the newly defended frontier forts.

The Siege of Monticchiello

Monticchiello represented the first serious obstacle to Don Garcia's invasion force, which arrived before it on 28 February 1553 (figs. 54 and 55). The village was held by Adriano Baglioni and about four hundred soldiers, supported by a civilian population numbering perhaps five hundred men, women, and children. Like many of the other Sienese frontier fortresses it was built on a spur of high ground, surrounded on three sides by steep slopes. The fourth side formed a more gentle slope away from the walls to the east. Here a single, centrally located bastion had been built in front on the medieval walls, giving flanking fire in both directions across the front.[33] The east front was overlooked by higher ground to the southeast and to the north, but both of these potential battery sites were at the extreme range for accurate artillery fire. Although Monticchiello's fortifications were modest, the combination of a difficult site and partially modernized walls gave the determined garrison a defensible position.

Possibly the Imperialists expected no serious resistance for, without any prior bombardment, an infantry assault was launched against the east front on 2 March, only to be repulsed with heavy losses. Further attacks went in on 5 and 7 March, incurring yet more casualties. By 8 March the main Florentine siege train had reached the camp, after which a general bombardment of the city began. The difficulties of hauling artillery into position on the high ground proved formidable: it was not until 15 March that two batteries, comprising eighteen guns in all, had been established in positions commanding the principal defensive works. The next day fire was concentrated on the central bastion, and in the evening of 16 March, Spanish infantry gained a foothold in this advanced work. Baglioni then asked for terms. Don Garcia de Toledo, the Spanish commander, held Baglioni and his two senior captains as prisoners of war. Deifebo and Virgilio Zuccantini, the two civilian commissioners, were ransomed—although the latter was shortly afterward recaptured and hanged for a breach of parole. The other troops, after swearing to take no further part in the campaign, were released with full honors of war and, to the disgust of Cosimo de' Medici, were permitted to march out of the town with their colors flying.[34] Both sides claimed Monticchiello as a victory.

The operation demonstrated for the first time in this campaign the practical limitations on the use of artillery. In a month of heavy rain and snow it had proved extraordinarily difficult and slow work to move the guns to Monticchiello and, once there, onto high ground.[35] In action, moreover, the guns proved less than adequate. Following a single day of shooting on 16 March, Cosimo's chief gunner reported that three of his eighteen guns were unfit for further service.[36] After all this, it seems that it was shortage of ammunition rather than fear of further bombardment that forced the defenders to sue for terms. Large quantities of small arms ammunition had been expended against the attacking Imperial infantry. Although casualties among the Spaniards had been heavy, it was reported that most of the wounds received in the capture of the bastion had been inflicted by stones hurled from the walls behind.[37] In the absence of artillery, much of the siege had been an infantry battle, so that Baglioni's garrison, while its ammunition lasted, had been well able to hold the relatively unsophisticated defenses of the east front against repeated assaults. After the bloodletting at Monticchiello, Don Garcia's regular Spanish infantryman—reputedly the best fighters in Europe—were not used again in daylight against unbreached Sienese walls.

Monticchiello's eighteen days of resistance was a classic frontier action. Such places were not expected to hold indefinitely without relief, though a stubborn defense could significantly delay the passage of an invader compelled to reduce positions that would otherwise threaten lines of communication. Because of Siena's scorched-earth policy, the Imperialists had to rely to a large extent upon supplies transported from the Florentine territory. Montepulciano, on the western or Sienese side of the Val di Chiana, was the advanced Imperial supply base, but a new fort had recently been built by the Florentines at Valiano to protect the bridgehead of the causeway that led across the marsh lands of the valley from Arezzo and Cortona.[38] After the fall of Monticchiello, Don Garcia was advised of the need to capture and garrison another dozen small villages and castles simply to protect the Imperial army's line of communications to San Quirico, which was to serve as its forward base for the attack on Montalcino.[39] The siege of Monticchiello and the capture of these flanking positions together consumed one month of the campaign, a month that was to prove critical to the outcome at Montalcino.

5

THE DEFENSE OF MONTALCINO

The Fortifications

MONTALCINO occupies the eastern slope of a hill which juts out from a range of high country into the Val d'Orcia. On three sides the ground falls away steeply from the walls, rendering these approaches secure from artillery bombardment. To the south, however, Montalcino is joined to the range of higher hills by a saddle offering a relatively level approach. An impressive Rocca (castle with a keep) had been built here in the fourteenth century to dominate the saddle,[1] while the rest of the southern perimeter was protected from the assault of medieval siege engines by a gulley, known as the Fossatello, separating the city from its parent range of hills (fig. 56). By the mid-sixteenth century, this curtain was well within the range of guns emplaced 500 feet away on the southern heights. Indeed, nearly all of the southern perimeter was vulnerable to modern artillery, and it was along this front that new fortifications were constructed during the winter of 1552–53.

The principal new work was known as the bastion of San Martino. It was located on the edge of the saddle, between the Rocca and the Porta Cerbaia, on a site that has been much altered by earth moving and leveling for the construction of the present-day Stadio Comunale (fig. 57). Guns in this position could fire westward across the saddle and the front of the Rocca, as well as eastward across the Porta Cerbaia. Although evidently built well in front of the medieval enceinte, the San Martino bastion was not a detached work. An illustration of the siege works by their principal architect, Maestro Giorgio di Giovanni, shows a conventional triangular bastion attached to the wall by its flanks (fig. 58). A somewhat smaller work known as the Porta al Cassero bastion was built in front of the Rocca and the gate of that name, probably on part of the site now occupied by the postwar Medici bastion. Guns in this position could fire northward along the town wall and eastward to sweep one face of San Martino in the classic Italian manner. The medieval wall across the saddle was reinforced by a rampart added to its inside face, more than doubling its original thickness.[2] A third bastion, located outside the Porta Cerbaia, was to have flanked the other

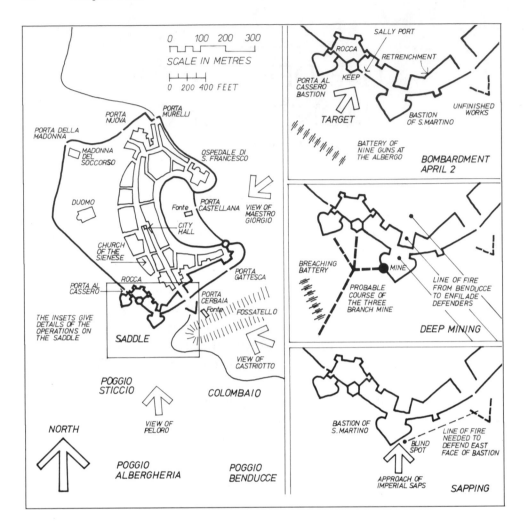

Fig. 56. Map of Montalcino with Inset Views of the Major Actions of the Siege

face of San Martino as well as the lower parts of the southern town wall.[3] However, this work was incomplete at the beginning of the siege, leaving (as we shall see) a potentially disastrous gap in the defensive fire plan.

Inside the medieval enceinte two retrenchments were built to contain any advance through a breach in the southern perimeter. These were substantial works consisting of an earth and timber rampart behind a ditch; the retrenchment itself being cranked to form bastions or demibastions. One can be seen clearly in Maestro Giorgio's view running from just inside the Porta Cerbaia to a junction with the eastern town wall. The other retrenchment was built close behind the curtain from the Porta Cerbaia to San Martino.[4]

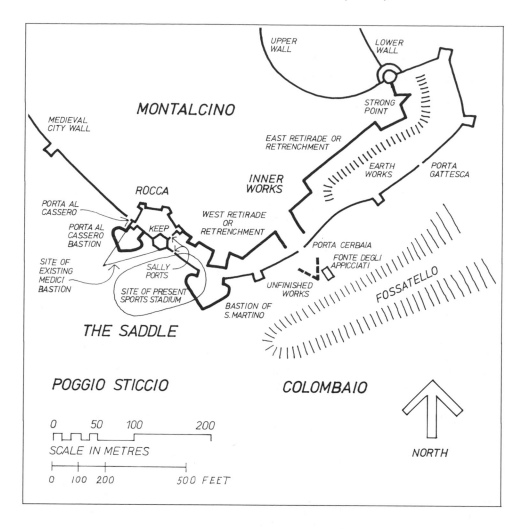

Fig. 57. The Southern Defenses of Montalcino

To a patriotic Sienese observer the fortifications of Montalcino seemed most impressive. Alessandro Sozzini, the diarist, proudly recorded the great size of the principal bastion, the bales of wool that protected the medieval keep, the two retrenchments, and the completion of all these works before the arrival of the enemy.[5] Giovanni Battista Belluzzi, Cosimo's military engineer, described the same works two days after the opening of siege operations in rather different terms. All of the wall, he reported, was in bad condition and dangerously overlooked from the hills. Not trusting in their wall, the Sienese had built a retrenchment which seemed to have been well made with fine bastions. However, the other bastions—those of the outer line—were small, while those of the fortress

Fig. 58. Maestro Giorgio di Giovanni, The Siegeworks at Montalcino. Another of the painted book covers of the Biccherna, this view is taken from the east and provides the most complete visual record of the fortifications and the Imperial positions. Note the depth of the *fossatello* in front of the southern curtain. The outline drawing (opposite) shows the details of the view.

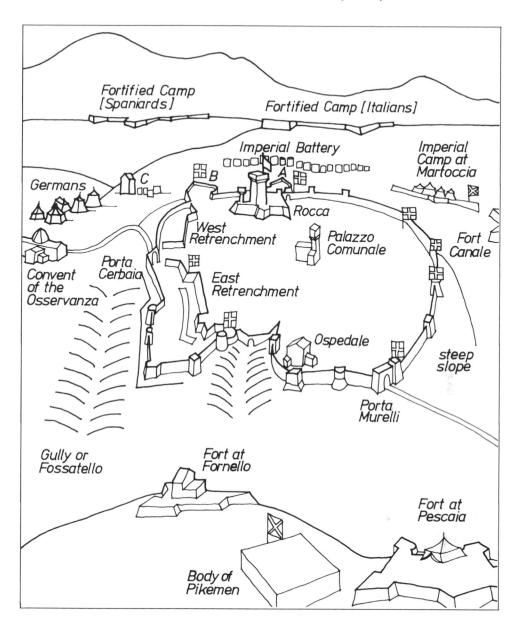

Fortified Camp [Spaniards]

Fortified Camp [Italians]

Imperial Battery

Imperial Camp at Martoccia

Germans

C

B

A

Rocca

West Retrenchment

Palazzo Comunale

Fort Canale

Porta Cerbaia

East Retrenchment

Convent of the Osservanza

Ospedale

steep slope

Porta Murelli

Gully or Fossatello

Fort at Fornello

Fort at Pescaia

Body of Pikemen

were so dominated from the Imperial positions that their defenders had to remain constantly under cover. Men and women, he observed, could be seen laboring energetically on the incomplete works.[6]

Because of Montalcino's successful resistance and the natural biases of Sienese historians, the uncritical views of Sozzini have taken precedence over the professional judgment of Belluzzi. Yet Belluzzi's critical observations are generally confirmed by the surviving records of the Sienese building campaign. When

Montalcino was surveyed in October 1552, the walls were found to be dangerously weak.[7] Colonel Giovanni da Torino, who commanded Montalcino's garrison during the winter of 1552–53, believed the place to be indefensible against artillery.[8] These views were evidently shared with the civil population of the city who, as Belluzzi seems to have heard, showed enthusiasm only for the construction of the retrenchments. Giovanni da Torino and Maestro Giorgio, however, were agreed that all the available resources of an increasingly demoralized, impoverished, and exhausted population had to be concentrated on the outer perimeter, in particular on the critical zone of the saddle.[9]

Colonel and architect, supported by successive Sienese commissioners, maintained this policy throughout the early winter months. Works on the saddle began in earnest at the end of November. Early February saw the completion of the main structures of the San Martino and Porta al Cassero bastions as well as the reinforced wall that joined them to the Rocca across the saddle. The third bastion at the Porta Cerbaia had been marked out late in December, but since then had advanced very little. However, when large numbers of troops, volunteers, and paid laborers poured into the city during January, February, and March, efforts were unaccountably diverted from the outstanding work on the external perimeter to the construction of the retrenchments, amounting to a practically separate inner line of fortifications.[10] By the end of March 1553, a new commander, Giordano Orsini, with his garrison of 1,000 soldiers and the 2,000 men, women, and children of Montalcino faced a Spanish army 14,000 strong from behind fortifications which, although very extensive, were by no means a model of the fully flanked Italian bastion system.

The Beginning of the Siege

The leading elements of Don Garcia's army arrived outside the city on 27 March 1553 and, after some fierce skirmishing, occupied defensive positions on the southern heights (fig. 59). Three camps were established on national lines. The Germans stationed themselves around the monastery of the Osservanza, the Spanish camped on the Poggio delle Benducce, while the Italian contingent occupied the Poggio dell'Albergheria immediately above the saddle.[11] Despite patrolling by the Imperial cavalry, Montalcino remained open to the north for some weeks after fighting began, which permitted some of the deficiencies in Franco-Sienese preparations to be repaired. A munition convoy entered the city while the initial skirmishing on the Albergheria was in progress[12] and, throughout the early part of the siege, ammunition, provisions, and money entered Montalcino at frequent intervals. Indeed, Imperial control in some parts of the approaches was so poor that a small garrison in the nearby fortress of the Romitorio managed to sustain itself throughout the siege.[13]

Other shortcomings in the defenders' preparations were not to be remedied so easily. Against all the rules of siege warfare, buildings had been left standing dangerously close to the walls. On 27 March the Imperialists took possession of the Fonte degli Appicciati, just outside the Porta Cerbaia, from where a sniper killed a Sienese officer reconnoitering a house "which our people had not had time to demolish during the day." Next day the defenders' fears were realized when the enemy occupied this house and installed in it snipers armed with *archibusi apposta* (heavy-caliber swivel-mounted arquebuses) who commenced a hot short-range fire against the city "so that one could not stand in the San Martino bastion without very great danger." Two small guns were installed in the house of a certain Camillo Landi, from which position they too fired on San Martino. Moreover, last-minute attempts to burn the Albergo on the saddle had left a substantial ruin which the Imperialists willingly incorporated into their main battery when the heavy artillery arrived at the end of the month.[14]

Estimates of the total Imperial artillery strength at Montalcino vary widely because of different reporters' failure to distinguish clearly between the heaviest pieces (full cannon) used in the main siege batteries, the field pieces (half-cannon, culverins, and sakers) employed in a supporting role, and the much larger number of heavy arquebuses and swivel guns that served as antipersonnel weapons. It seems certain, however, that the principal siege artillery comprised the dozen or so pieces of heavy cannon already on loan to Don Garcia from the "neutral" Duke of Florence. During the night of 31 March, nine guns were installed at the Albergo battery facing the Rocca, with three more in a battery on Monte Sticcio.[15]

The Bombardment

Just after dawn on 2 April the battery at the Albergo opened fire (fig. 60). The target was the medieval Rocca, which towered over the other fortifications on the saddle and which evidently accommodated most of the defenders' light artillery. It may well be that some fire was directed here in an attempt to silence the Rocca's guns. The more precise descriptions, however, tell us that the Imperialists concentrated their fire on a section of the curtain near the Porta del Soccorso which they had been told contained an internal passageway leading to a cistern in one of the towers. With its hollow interior, this part of the wall was much weaker than the solid sections, and because of the defenders' wish to keep the Porta del Soccorso free for sorties it had not been backed by an earth ramp.[16]

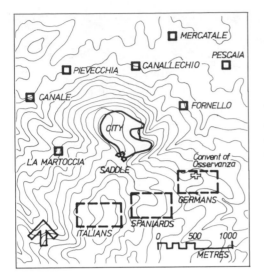

Fig. 59. The Imperial Positions at Montalcino. As a matter of prudence, camps were
divided on national lines following outbreaks
of fighting between the Italian and German
contingents in Don Garca's Imperial army.

As soon as the establishment of the enemy battery made it clear where the
bombardment was to be expected, Giordano Orsini and Maestro Giorgio "made
a fine and very strong work so as not to lose the entrance into the bastion." This
would have been another retrenchment, close behind the curtain. Given the
short time available, however, it was probably neither as fine nor as strong as
the account would have us believe. Indeed, at the height of the bombardment
the Montalcinesi were leaving nothing to chance; helped by the soldiers, they
carried barrels, tubs, doors, shutters, and beams from their own houses to the
emergency works. A number of soldiers distinguished themselves by removing
the stones falling from the wall, so as to keep the gateway clear.[17]

The bombardment ended at dusk with results that gave great encouragement
to the defenders. A breach only about two meters wide had been made in the
wall beside the Porta del Soccorso, and a small number of casualties had been
inflicted—among them Orsini, who was slightly wounded in the arm when a
ball smashed a stone into fragments. Over 500 shots had been fired—estimates
vary from 514 to 532—during the day. By the standards of later centuries a
breaching battery of 500 rounds per day was not particularly noteworthy. It must,
however, be regarded as a striking exhibition of firepower for the mid-sixteenth
century, and some explanation of its trifling effects is demanded.[18]

Part of the answer is probably to be found in the rate of fire. Accepting the
high shot-count of 532 rounds and assuming a lengthy, ten-hour bombardment,
we have rate of fire of 52 rounds an hour; that is, 5.7 rounds per gun per hour
(or 10 minutes per shot) assuming only the nine guns on the Albergo were firing,

or 4.4 rounds per gun per hour (13.6 minutes for each shot) if we include the three pieces on the Sticcio. Both figures represent relatively fast shooting when sustained over a whole day; possibly it was too fast for accuracy. It seems that the Imperialists were attempting a kind of bombardment that demanded a high degree of precision. Against medieval curtain walls it was long-established practice to begin by shooting away the *merlatura* and then to breach the wall, starting at the top and working down. This practice had evolved in the days of the bombards that fired heavy stone balls at low velocity. Such projectiles could drop sizable chunks of a thin wall, but it is easy to see that a technique of "chipping away" needed precise gun laying and excellent fire control. Volleys were used as a fire-control device as well as a means of concentrating the destructive impact of the cannonballs, many of which were still of stone as late as the mid-sixteenth century.[19] A new technique had been developed for use against earth-filled ramparts. Here the guns were laid to strike a horizontal line about one-third of the way up the face. A deep cut was scored into the rampart for the width of the breach required, so that the masonry skin collapsed from above, allowing the earth to spill out forming a slope through the breach that could easily be mounted by the attackers. "Cutting" required a strong and dense projectile that would penetrate the rampart rather than disintegrate on impact: it demanded iron cannonballs. Accuracy was needed too; but fire control was much less of a problem when each gun in a large battery could be allocated its own length of the cut.

At Montalcino the Imperialists apparently employed the older chipping-away technique and fired in volleys.[20] As we have seen, chipping caused much of the debris to go with the shot, to fall on the inside of the wall, where brave men could indeed work *sotto la batteria,* removing stones blocking the gate. The narrow width of the breach also suggests a chipping rather than a cutting bombardment.

Finally, it is more than likely that the weapons used against Montalcino were in poor condition, badly served, and short of ammunition. As already mentioned, the artillery for the Imperial army had been supplied by Cosimo from fortresses in Florence, Arezzo, and Montepulciano. It had been assembled for the bombardment of Monticchiello, the Sienese border fortress, where a single day of shooting on 16 March had ruined three of the eighteen guns in the Imperial batteries and provoked a letter of protest to Cosimo from a Florentine official outraged at Spanish misuse of the duke's artillery.[21] The Spanish retorted that the guns were in bad condition. Most of the pieces that survived the Monticchiello bombardment were then hauled to Montalcino, where they were installed in the batteries under conditions of such chaos that the Florentine official in charge of the draft oxen complained both to Don Garcia and to the duke of Florence.[22] One week before the bombardment of Montalcino, Don Garcia's artillery train contained eight full-cannon with 800 rounds: at that time the

Spaniard hoped to receive another six cannon and 1,200 rounds from Cosimo, but these did not arrive until much later in the siege.[23] The bombardment of 2 April, therefore, must have consumed more than half of the available heavy-caliber artillery rounds. Shortage of ammunition helps explain why the bombardment was not resumed the following day.

Sapping and Mining

The poor results of the bombardment of 2 April brought a change in Imperial strategy. Shots continued to be fired at the parties working on retrenchments behind the San Martino bastion and further large-scale bombardments are recorded on 19 April and 5 May, the last being regarded by the defenders as more destructive than all of its predecessors together. Don Garcia's immediate response to the gunners' poor performance was to initiate sapping operations, with the mining of San Martino and the Rocca as the prime objectives.

On the night of 3 April a group of Imperial soldiers dug themselves into a little gulley close to San Martino. By morning the position was fortified with gabions, which served as the sandbags of early modern warfare and gave some protection to the men who were advancing a zigzag trench across the ditch toward the fortifications.[24] After a week of sapping, the defenders struck back. On the night of 11 April, as the trench approached the foot of San Martino, incendiary devices were suspended over the bastion.[25] Snipers on the keep of the Rocca then opened fire on the sappers, while the defenders of the bastion—unable to bring their weapons to bear on the foot of the wall—dropped heavy stones into the ditch. The sappers were forced to withdraw, leaving a number of dead behind them.[26]

Next night the garrison sortied out to raid the Imperial works. A small patrol left from the San Martino sally port and surprised the Spanish pickets in the saps, where they proceeded to wreck the works. A much stronger force of fifty arquebusiers left the Porta al Cassero to support the raid. This force overran the forward Imperial positions and temporarily occupied the Colombaio, where they succeeded in spiking some guns in a subsidiary battery and, in their fighting withdrawal, wounded Ascanio della Cornia, one of Don Garcia's senior officers.[27]

After these events the mine went underground. Belluzzi was evidently closely involved in this complex operation, for the Florentine engineer corresponded regularly with Cosimo about the slow progress of the excavation and the dispatch of professional tunnelers from the mines of Northern Tuscany.[28] Underground mining was, of course, a much more lengthy operation than surface sapping, and another six weeks were to pass before this latest Imperial enterprise bore fruit. In the meantime, Don Garcia's officers chafed at the delays in the siege. Camillo

Colonna complained in a letter to the emperor that he had never yet "seen a city of importance taken by force of pick and shovel."[29] We can detect further traces of Colonna's frustration at Don Garcia's failure to use his considerable superiority in troops to full advantage in the treatise of Maggi and Castriotto. Castriotto (the military mind of the pair), who had been an imperial officer at the siege, remarks dryly on the need to close with an enemy if you want to conquer him.[30]

After almost a month of unsuccessful siege operations, Montalcino had not yet been sealed off from the outside world. Almost daily the defenders sortied out to raid the Imperialists, to collect building materials for the defenses and to escort messengers and supplies from Siena. The initiative at this stage of the siege rested so firmly with the Sienese that one of the diarists records for 15 and 16 April that "no one loses time bringing in timber and fascines through the Murelli and Castellana gates, which stand continually open."[31] This situation was shortly to change.

The Blockade

On 17 April a large part of the Italian infantry moved from its camp on the Albergheria and entrenched itself at Il Canale, on the plain to the northwest of Montalcino. Around the new camp they established a number of *corpi di guardia,* small fortified outposts. Three days later five *insegne* (platoons) of the Florentine militia arrived, bringing with them 500 pioneers who immediately began to cut down vines, olives, and other trees in order to construct a fort at Pievecchia, due north of the city. These were joined on 22 April by yet another five *insegne* of Florentines, who began to fortify a camp at Fornello, to the east, which by then was the only completely open approach to Montalcino. Finally, on 27 April, a large body of German reinforcements arrived and fortified themselves at La Martoccia, between the Albergheria and Il Canale.[32] The encirclement of Montalcino was virtually complete (fig. 60).

Nonetheless, though it was now difficult, it was by no means impossible to penetrate the Imperial blockade. A Neopolitan in the service of Thermes simply

Fig. 60. (See following pages.) Maggi and Castriotto, The Siege of Montalcino from *Della fortificatione.* Castriotto served in the Imperial army at the siege, probably arriving in mid-April following the fall of Rocca d'Orcia. The three original camps are correctly located. Nine guns are shown on the Poggio Sticcio, where a building—possibly the Albergo—has been incorporated into the battery. The other battery in front of the Porta Cerbaia indicates a later gun position and its field of fire into the city. The bastion of San Martino is the only new work shown on the outer perimeter from this viewpoint. The low walls outside the Porta Cerbaia may represent the incomplete third bastion.

Ritratto di Monte Alcino in quel di Siena, cõ l'affedio, e batteria. CAP. XXII.
IAC. CASTR.

ELL' anno predetto, ritrouandomi all'imprefa di Mont'Alcino, & hauendo da o-
gni banda confiderato la difficultà del fito, & il buon principio fatto per la difefa
di tal luogo, come fanno tutti quegli Illuftrifsimi Signori, che ui fi trouarono;
difsi, che uolendo conquiftarlo, non era da perder tempo, ma da far fubita rifolu-
tione di combatterlo; e che fi douefse uoltar tutto il difegno inuerfo quei gabbioni, che
erano piantati uerfo la porta, prima che fuſſero ſtati infieme con le cafe terrapienati: e con
quattro pezzi d'artiglieria battere tanta cortina, che la gente poteſſe entrar dentro à quello

ITALIANI
Piazza

SPAGNOLI
Piazza

S.or Camillo Colõna

Confe fanta fiore

S.r Napol

Ciò fatto, porre il refto dell'artiglieria nel luogo dimoftrato per le lettere. O. e battere tutte le cafe per fianco : per che quelli di dentro fareb
lati sforzati abbandonarle, e leuarfi dalla difefa: e cofi fi farebbe fatto qualche buono effetto: altrimenti auuertiffero i detti Signori, che fi fareb
duto il tempo, fenza acquifto alcuno .   104

GIROLAMO MAGGI.

A' fi può dire, che quanto feguì, fuffe per effaltatione dello Illuftfsimo Signore, gràn maftro di guerra il Signor Giordano Vrfino, q ra-
le oltra l'hauer prima nella fua piu uerde età in Fiandra, in Africa, & in altri luoghi dato gran fegni del fuo fommo ualore; in quefto
luogo fece ueder chiaro al mondo, che'l fapere, unito con l'animofità, e col ualor militare, può facilmente faluare le Città, e gli ftati .
Come anche fece in San Fiorenzo di Corfica. Donde oltre à'grandi honori che per tali proue egli meritò appreffo al Rè Chriftianifsim o; fu
rere di molti Prencipi, e Signori ftimato degno di ftatue, e di fopranome contrario à quello del Rè Demetrio detto Efpugnatore delle Città,
do quefto gran Signore conferuatore di quelle.

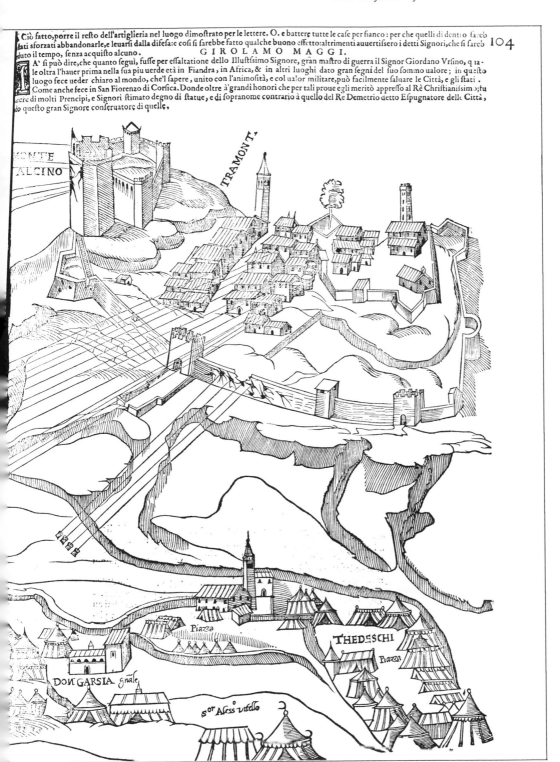

pitched his tent among those of his conationals and, spotting an opportunity, slipped into the town bringing money for the troops. On 22 April, when the blockade was almost complete, a local peasant named Tiranfallo Guidi took thirty of his fellows loaded with ammunition and money through the screen of sentries. On 29 April the count of Gaiazzo and his Sienese company were ambushed at La Campana but, in the confusion of the action, the peasants they were escorting managed to enter Montalcino with their provisions.[33] Despite these exploits, it became increasingly difficult to get bulk items into the city and, by the second week in May, severe food shortages were being lamented by Montalcino's chroniclers. However, it was always possible to communicate with the mother city, either by signal fires which could be seen on a clear night or by means of letters smuggled through the blockade. Altogether thirty-five letters dating from the siege of Montalcino are still to be found in the Archivio di Stato, Siena, while a further six were acknowledged to have been received but are now lost. No less than fourteen of these letters are known to have been received from Montalcino during May and the first half of June.[34] Tiranfallo Guidi earned great distinction by successfully undertaking twenty-two return trips between Siena and Montalcino during this siege. At no stage, therefore, could the city be described as totally isolated.

The absence of a continuous trenchwork, or even double trenchwork, around the city obviously assisted the defenders to penetrate the Imperial blockade. Yet Don Garcia's decision to patrol the approaches from the forts and the smaller *corpi di guardia* represented up-to-date practice in mid-sixteenth-century siege warfare, a technique which is discussed at length and with approval in Maggi and Castriotto's treatise. Vast numbers of men were needed to build and garrison the continuous lines of circumvallation of ancient warfare, and with the advent of long-range artillery the scale of such works would be greatly increased. Maggi and Castriotto argued that isolated forts represented an economic solution by providing secure positions for much smaller bodies of troops. Although conceding that it was always possible to penetrate a ring of forts by night, they cite the sieges of Mirandola (1552) and Siena (1554–55) as proof that a blockade was sufficiently effective for this not to alter significantly the eventual outcome.[35] A woodcut of the double ring of forts at Mirandola reproduced in their treatise (fig. 61) shows works very similar to those that can be seen clustered around Montalcino in Maestro Giorgio's painting (fig. 58).

There remains one point where the practice of Don Garcia diverges from the theory of Maggi and Castriotto. In theory the besiegers are protected from the sorties of the besieged "as in a walled castle." It seems clear from Maestro Giorgio's painting, however, as well as from numerous accounts of raids on the Imperial encampments, that a high proportion of Don Garcia's forces were in

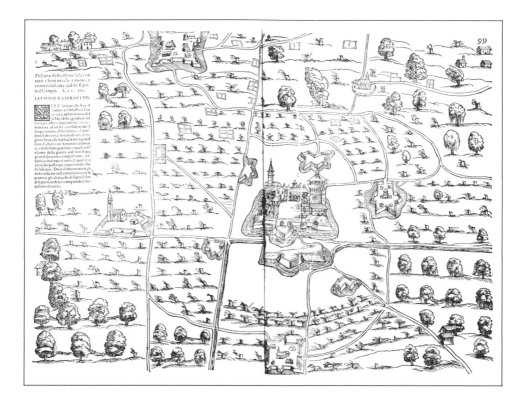

Fig. 61. Maggi and Castriotto, The Fortifications at Mirandola from *Della fortificatione*

fact encamped outside the forts. Indeed, Giulio Landi's account draws a distinction between the seven camps and the nine forts around the city.[36] With the Florentine and German reinforcements, the original 14,000 troops in Don Garcia's army had swollen to about 20,000. Allowing for roughly the same number of pioneers, *vivandieri,* and general camp followers, we can reasonably estimate an Imperial host of some 40,000; far too many to be accommodated in the forts.[37] Not only were the emperor's subjects continuously exposed to harassment from the garrison, but the siege "lines" were crowded with noncombatants, which must have proved no small advantage to Tiranfallo and his fellow blockade-runners.

The Underground Siege

The underground mine started in mid-April was no secret, although news of its progress sometimes reached the defenders by roundabout routes. In Rome an

Imperial officer from Montalcino talked too loudly in the presence of a Sienese agent, whose report to the ambassador was passed back to Siena for inclusion in a regular dispatch into Montalcino. By 12 May, Giordano Orsini received word of the mine's position at the beginning of the same month: "almost beneath the scarp between our two cavaliers of San Martino and the Porta al Cassero, where they were beginning three branches, two in the direction of the aforesaid cavaliers and the third to the keep of our castle."[38] The governor reported back to Siena that defensive measures were already in hand.

Countermines had been excavated in April to discover the whereabouts of Imperial miners. Two or three such listening posts could "get a fix" on the enemy mine and plot its course. A countermine shaft could then be advanced, enabling the defenders to break into the enemy works and engage their miners in hand-to-hand combat: a hellish fight in the dark with pistols, knives, and digging tools. Alternatively a tunnel could be dug to a position ahead of the enemy and a gunpowder charge prepared, fused, and sealed into the shaft to be detonated when the enemy approached. It was also possible to prepare the walls and their foundations to resist the explosion of a mine, a technique known as "ventilation." Francesco de' Marchi in his treatise written in the 1560s expounded on the construction of new walls containing a network of interconnected internal air passages, through which the expanding gases of an exploding mine could exhaust themselves.[39] Existing walls could be modified to achieve much the same effect by excavating chambers under the threatened section of the wall and shoring them firmly to prevent collapse. The initial shock of the explosion would be absorbed by the volume of air in the chamber and, as in de' Marchi's scheme, the gas pressure would be released through a system of vent shafts to the surface. This seems to have been the technique adopted by Maestro Giorgio, who began "with all speed and diligence to make a spacious countermine beneath each of the aforesaid bastions."[40] Another account mentions "certain other vent shafts."[41] About eighty men worked night and day on the excavation, and "it was a marvelous thing to see rocks of immeasurable size taken out."[42]

By 26 May the mine was ready. Before dawn, the Germans took their position on the Poggio dello Sticcio: they were to be the shock troops that would storm the breach immediately after the mine had been sprung. The Italians were drawn up behind the Germans on the heights of the Albergheria, while the Spaniards massed in battle order on the Poggio delle Benducce. It was noticed in the city that most of the Imperial artillery was now concentrated toward the Benducce, while seven heavy pieces were emplaced directly in front of San Martino.[43] The guns close to the bastion were evidently to assist in opening the breach. Those on the Benducce, while much farther away, were in a good position to support an assault by enfilading the defenders at the western end of the retirade.

As dawn began to lift, a general assault appeared imminent, and for the first time since the arrival of the Imperialists the bell of the Palazzo Comunale was sounded, calling the people to arms. The first enemy movements began about half an hour before full daylight, when the Florentine militia demonstrated on the northeast sector. These movements were so obviously diversionary that only a small force of forty men sortied out from the Porta della Madonna to put the Florentines to flight. At full light the artillery opened fire at San Martino. The mine beneath the bastion was then sprung:

> Immediately there was an enormous earthquake . . . shaking the entire city with such horrendous and frightful thunder, accompanied by such pestilential smoke, that it seemed that hell had burst open; neither could one see the sky for earth and great stones. It would have struck terror into the stoutest heart . . . And in this we saw clearly the special bounty of God, and the protection his most holy Mother—defender of this unhappy city—has for us; for with her power she diverted all the debris away from us and toward the enemy, a great number of them being buried and killed. When the smoke cleared, we saw with gratitude only a small opening of one palm (width).[44]

Even allowing for exaggeration on the part of the anonymous author of the so-called *Giornale,* it seems clear from other accounts that the bang was enormous but damage to the bastion slight. Giulio Landi reports merely that "the bastion opened a little but remained on its feet."[45] The anonymous author of the *Verissima descrizione,* a chronicle of the siege, tells us that "the mined cavalier raised itself somewhat and in some places cracked, only then to drop for half a braccia (just under a foot), and to detach itself from the wall on the Cerbaia side by as much."[46]

The last account also furnishes what could be the explanation for the failure of the mine. The explosion, it says, was heard underground "in a ditch at the foot of this cavalier, a very weak place, being almost full both now and for a long time with artificial soil [i.e., it was filled ground] which together with very many stones . . . went flying into the air to seek out and strike our enemies in fine style."[47] This description of the explosion strongly suggests that the defenders owed their escape less to the countermine excavations—whose effect would have been to absorb the blast—than to the miners' failure to dig far enough under the bastion. An explosion that seemed to come from under the ditch and that threw large quantities of ditch debris on to the troops waiting to storm the breach was certainly spectacular, but much less effective than a charge—not necessarily very big—placed well under the bastion so that the explosion would push the front retaining wall outward into the ditch, allowing the loose fill to spill out forming a slope.[48] Precise underground navigation and accurate placing was as important as the size of a mine. After six weeks of digging, it may be that the mine was a few feet short?

The East Face of San Martino

Three days after the failure of the mine, the Imperialists began what was to prove their final attempt on the bastion of San Martino. On 29 May the footings were reconnoitered, and on the next day a party of sappers began work in a trench equipped with a timber superstructure to provide cover from above.[49] Despite the superstructure, some Imperial casualties were caused by heavy stones—seven to ten pounds in weight—hurled from slings known as *mazzafrusti*. And a number of men were hit by snipers as they withdrew from the base of the wall. While working at the foot of the bastion, however, the Imperial sappers were safe from all but the stones. As the *Giornale* explained: "Nor could our men defend the bastion with weapons other than stones, because it had not been possible to finish a fortification started at the Porta Cerbaia which should have overlooked that side."[50]

The Imperialists had at last shifted their attack to the blind face of San Martino. They could hardly have been unaware that the defenders had begun the construction of yet another cavalier behind the threatened area and were busy cutting a new, inner ditch to isolate the salient.[51] However, once San Martino had been taken and its flanking fire silenced, the whole of the southern perimeter east of the saddle would be open to breaching and storm. The final two weeks of the siege saw the hardest fighting, a bitter hand-to-hand struggle for the control of this vital work.

Unhampered by accurate defensive fire, the Imperialists began to climb the east face of San Martino, cutting steps as they went. By 5 June they were close enough to the top to use stones of their own against the defenders.[52] On 6 June a straw man, clothed and armored, was lifted over the parapet on a halberd to draw the defenders' fire. Having emptied their weapons, the defenders tried to grab the dummy with the hooks of their own halberds and the success of the trick drew great shouts of appreciation from the Imperial lines.[53] Bombs and fireworks were used in attempts to destroy the timber works that the defenders now employed to raise their own parapet. Pikes, halberds, and swords were all in play, as well as smoke bombs, *trombe di fuoco* (scatterguns),[54] swarms of bees, and other traditional devices. The flavor of this fighting is vividly conveyed by the *Giornale* account for 12 June: "Today an armed man appeared at the bastion, fired an arquebus, and shouted, 'Rabble, soon we'll have you in our hands!' Immediately he ducked down to a place where we were only able to reach them with boiling water and quicklime, which we were throwing over continuously, causing them much annoyance, so that they worked in great danger and often got a shave without a barber."[55]

Attackers and defenders were now close enough to touch each other and in some parts of San Martino the Imperialists were actually above the Sienese. The struggle for the bastion had become a race for height, both sides building up their works to gain the advantage of a foot or two of overlook. Even the cavalier behind the bastion was being pushed skyward so that, according to one account, by the end of the siege it had reached the prodigious dimensions of "more than one hundred feet high and sixty wide."[56] While the need to "overlook" was an obsession typical of the sixteenth century, the preoccupation with sheer height runs counter to the commonly accepted trends in Early Modern fortification. Indeed, one is struck by the similarity between the race of the *cavalieri* and the medieval use of siege towers.

The End of the Siege

Without relief Montalcino could not long have survived the loss of the San Martino bastion, which by mid-June was clearly imminent. Further resistance at the retrenchments could only have delayed the city's fall. The vast numerical superiority of the Imperialists would have proved decisive once fighting could take place all along a much wider front than the saddle. Although no attempt was made to raise the siege with local forces, the Franco-Turkish alliance provided the necessary relief. With French and Sienese ports open to them, a large Turkish fleet was expected in the western Mediterranean in summer 1553: when it appeared in Italian waters, Don Garcia would be obliged to abandon the campaign against Siena to defend the Neapolitan coastline. Franco-Sienese expectations in this matter were known from captured documents in early March.[57] By the middle of May, Genoese sources reported Turkish plans for seventy galleys, commanded by the admiral Dragut Bey, to sail from North Africa at the beginning of June.[58] News of the fleet's passage of the straits of Messina reached Tuscany by 7 June.[59] Two days later, Cosimo dispatched orders to his own officials with the Imperial army to ensure the security of the Florentine artillery in what he feared might be a disorderly retreat.[60]

By 14 June there were a number of indications at Montalcino that the siege was almost over. In the morning a mine had been discovered and destroyed under the cavalier being built behind San Martino; yet the serious fighting spirit seemed to evaporate from the Imperial troops during the day. A Spaniard with a guitar serenaded the women laboring in the new ditch, camp followers were seen to move off, and the artillery in front of the Rocca was withdrawn—but not without a final salvo in reply to the snipers in the keep. Evidence of a near complete breakdown of Imperial discipline came to light when Don Garcia discovered numbers of Montalcinesi in the camps, trading and fraternizing among the Italians of his command. Orders were given to round them up but, hearing of this, Orsini had the gates closed to confine "more than three hundred" Imperial soldiers inside the city! Evidently Giordano Orsini had given permission for this intercourse, which was likely to help the defenders by bringing provisions and messengers into the city.[61]

On the morning of 15 June, when vast palls of smoke were seen rising from the direction of Montalcino, the citizens of Siena were convinced that they signified the destruction of the camp shelters, which presaged a general withdrawal.[62] When the Imperial troops "formed battles," the inhabitants of Montalcino reached the same conclusion and gathered on the walls to heap final insults upon them. Amid bell ringing, victory salvos, and the rattle of a thousand pots and pans, the Imperialists moved off in the direction of San Quirico, shadowed by Sienese cavalry and the grim-faced relatives of unransomed prisoners hoping to capture stragglers to use in an exchange.[63] Inside the town, Mass was celebrated and a solemn procession made its way through the streets. "All injuries were forgiven, as people came together to exchange the kiss of peace."[64]

As always, the Sienese were more inclined to credit their deliverance to the miraculous intervention of the Holy Virgin than to the human agency of the Turks. For our purposes, it is important to consider how the defenders managed to hold out for as long as eighty days on a site which, when Montaigne visited the place in 1580, was still considered too badly overlooked to be defensible.[65]

No answer is to be found in the quality of the fortifications. Indeed, the incompleteness of the outer works eventually posed the most serious threat to successful defense: the blind spot on one face of the principal bastion was a fundamental failing and far more serious than the battle damage sustained by the fortifications. But considerable damage had been caused by the 2,500 cannonballs fired by the Imperialists.[66] Giovambattista Peloro's postwar sketch of the city clearly shows the fortifications of the southern front in a bare landscape, deeply scarred by the remains of batteries and trenchworks (fig. 62). Although the vulnerable and antique *merlatura* of the Rocca had been stripped before the siege and the keep lined with wool bales, the superstructure was now badly knocked about. Maggi and Castriotto's woodcut of the siege shows the keep to be seriously cracked (fig. 60). The bastion of San Martino was a ruin. Peloro's view shows the trenchwork leading to the salient of the blind face, which had been broken open to form a rough ramp up and into the bastion. In the weeks following the siege, successive Sienese commissioners complained of soldiers

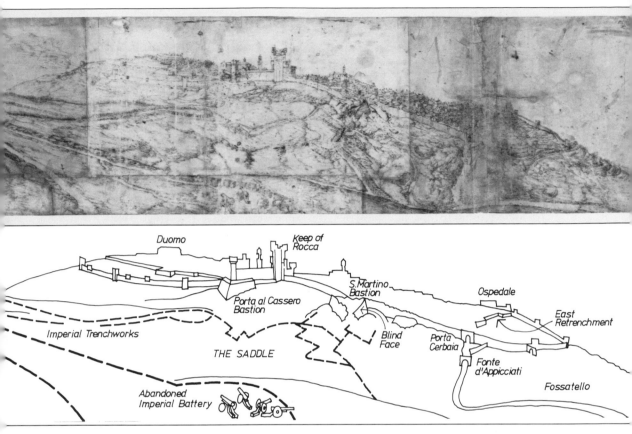

Fig. 62. Giovambattista Peloro, View of the Siegeworks at Montalcino. Executed after the siege, this is the most accurate view of the fortifications, showing the bastion of the Porta al Cassero (left), the Rocca and San Martino (center), and the east retrenchment (right back). The artist took his view from the Poggio Albergheria, looking across the saddle, with the gabions of an abandoned Imperial position in the foreground.

going in and out of the city at this point, as if through "an open gate."[67] Three months after the fighting, the bastion was still in such a derelict state that it was said to be no obstacle to thieves.[68]

What probably saved the city was the aggressive quality of the defense organized by Orsini against the rather ponderous initiatives of Don Garcia. Constant raids harassed the Imperialists in their trenches and camps and helped to keep the besiegers on the hills for the first weeks, while Sienese convoys kept Montalcino supplied with food, ammunition, and money for the troops. Morale was sustained by regular communications promising relief and telling the defenders of their growing fame. Don Garcia used all of the available siege techniques—bombardment, mining, sapping, and blockade—but failed to make full use of his much greater manpower to pursue several of these options simultaneously from the outset. By allowing all of the fighting to be concentrated on the narrow saddle, Don Garcia played into the hands of his weaker opponent. The sheer size of the Imperial army, with its attendant problems of supply and discipline, became a positive disadvantage.

The fighting on the saddle, however, cost the defenders dearly. Garrison and civil population together sustained 16 percent fatalities: 500 dead from the 3,000 inhabitants in the town, with probably much the same number wounded.[69] The Montalcinesi had been poverty-stricken before the siege: after it they were destitute and anxious above all things to be relieved of the burden of the soldiers. A grateful republic paid the soldiers off as soon as it could afford to do so, endowed scholarships and dowries for some orphans of the siege, and voted general tax exemptions to the citizens—a real privilege in the long term, but one that brought no immediate relief. Public honors, however, cost nothing. It was resolved that henceforth Montalcino would take precedence before all other towns of the Sienese dominio.[70]

Fig. 63. Porta Cerbaia, Montalcino, as Seen Today. Buildings now occupy the area of retrenchment behind the gate, which has been largely rebuilt since the siege. The modest scale of this gate and its flanking walls contrast markedly with the size of comparable medieval works in Siena (see above, fig. 18).

6

THE SIEGE OF SIENA

THE second and decisive phase in the war began at the end of January 1554, when a surprise night attack was launched against Siena from Florence. In truth, the only unpredictable aspect of the Florentine attack was its timing in midwinter. Cosimo's neutrality during the 1553 campaign had been a diplomatic fiction. Following the Spanish withdrawal from Montalcino, a number of events combined to persuade the duke of Florence to take the leading part in the next campaign as well as convincing him of the need for a preemptive strike.

When the Turkish fleet arrived off the Tuscan coast in August 1553, the Florentine island of Elba had been the first "enemy" target to be attacked. Later in the same month, Franco-Turkish forces based on the Sienese harbor of Port'Érated the Genoese island of Corsica, and by the end of September they had captured nearly all of this strategically vital Imperial position. Many of the French regular forces in Tuscany were transferred to Corsica under Thermes. In spite of Sienese efforts to represent these "troop reductions" as a conciliatory gesture towards Florence, Cosimo saw them only as a temporary weakening of his troublesome and dangerous neighbor and began in earnest to make his own preparations to resolve once and for all the problem of Siena.[1]

By the autumn of 1553, Florence was planning for war: troops were hired, galleys armed, and fortresses refurbished. As his field commander, Cosimo had engaged Giangiacomo de'Medici, marquis of Marignano, no relative but a successful Milanese soldier who had taken the Medici surname as a tribute to his first commander and patron, Giovanni dalle Bande Nere.[2] Cosimo's private secretary, Bartolommeo Concino, was dispatched in secret to the Imperial court, where he secured guarantees of military and political support for a campaign to reconquer Siena in the name of the emperor.[3] Concino was himself to serve with the army throughout the operations against Siena, as secretary to the Imperial Council of War and as Cosimo's most trusted informant in the camp.

At the end of November, King Henry II of France provided Cosimo with an even more pressing personal motive for war when he nominated Piero Strozzi to command the forces of the Sienese republic. The appointment of the leading Florentine exile to a military command in Tuscany was a flagrant breach of the treaties of 1542 and 1547 whereby Florence and Siena had undertaken not to harbor each other's rebels. To Cosimo, moreover, Piero Strozzi represented a special threat. Filippo Strozzi, his father, had died in Cosimo's prison in 1538, either from maltreatment or by suicide following torture—the truth would never be known. Piero, the eldest son, spent much of his life as an exile in the service of France, acquiring a formidable reputation as a soldier.[4] With Piero Strozzi commanding in Siena any delay in the planned attack would serve merely to strengthen the position of Cosimo's most bitter opponents. When news of the appointment reached Florence, the existing war plans were accelerated.[5]

Strozzi arrived in Siena on 2 January 1554 and immediately began preparing to meet the attack that was expected at the opening of the spring campaigning season. He was away from Siena, on a tour of inspection in the Maremma, when the Florentine assault was launched (fig. 64).

The Surprise Attack, 26 January 1554

Early on 26 January 1554 Marignano left Florence, accompanied by his staff and a small escort of Spanish horse. As this little force headed southward, the gates closed behind them, and all over Florentine territory road blocks were set up, bridges closed, and ferries guarded. At Pisa, 600 Italian soldiers commanded by Federigo di Montaguto embarked on galleys for a secondary seaborne attack on Grosseto. The militia companies from Arezzo and Cortona marched toward Montepulciano, the Florentine salient into the Sienese Val di Chiana, which served as the mustering point for the third prong of the attack: that directed at Pienza and Montalcino. Most of the troops, however, had orders to rendezvous at Poggibonsi with "powder, lead, match, and bread for three days" not later than Ave Maria in the evening of 26 January. The companies marched independently by different routes in order to minimize the impression of troop movements, but by the appointed hour 4,000 foot, 400 horse, 600 pioneers, and a number of light artillery pieces carried by mules were mustered twelve miles north of Siena. As the winter evening darkened, the soldiers pulled white shirts over their corselets to assist in night identification and marched south again along the Via Cassia.[5]

Three hours after sunset, a horseman from Monteriggioni brought the first definite news of border incursions to Siena. A small force of cavalry was sent north to reconnoiter the approaches, and a proclamation issued calling upon citizens to arm and to be ready to gather at the houses of the standard bearers of the terzi at the sound of the Mangia bell. At about nine in the evening, the cavalry patrol returned reporting contact with the enemy near Fontebecci—some eight miles from the city.[7] An attack was clearly imminent.

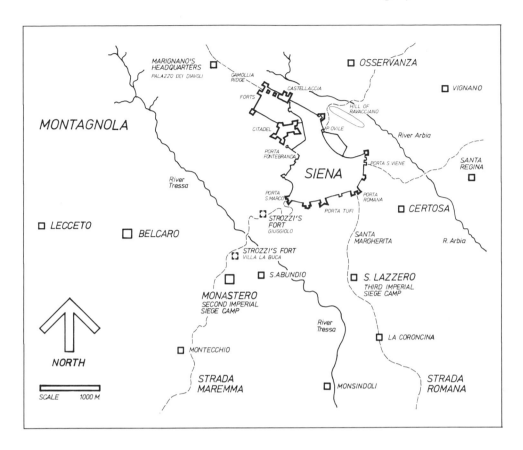

Fig. 64. Siena and Its Environs During the Siege. Squares mark the fortified positions on the approaches. Note also the Ravacciano area to the northeast of Siena.

In the absence of Strozzi, the Franco-Sienese command structure displayed near fatal weakness. Members of the Balìa were reluctant to risk panic by sounding the bell and only agreed an hour later to support the proposal of a French officer, Colonel Francesco Chiaramonti, to station three of the six companies of regulars in the Camollia forts while the other three companies marched north to the Palazzo dei Diavoli, from which point they could take the Imperial vanguard in the rear. In retrospect it can be seen that Chiaramonti's plan had a good chance of success. Cold weather and heavy rain had slowed the march of the Imperial column and caused particular difficulty to the inexperienced Florentine militia-men and the artillery. After the cavalry skirmish, Marignano could no longer hope to surprise the city and decided to risk splitting his force. With two hundred Spanish and Italian veterans and some of the cavalry, the general pressed on toward Camollia and would probably have proved no match for six fresh French companies fighting on familiar ground. But Chiaramonti's plan was rejected by the cardinal of Ferrara. Because the regular companies were ordered to remain within the main enceinte, when Marignano's little force approached Camollia the forts were held only by a few dozen men who fled at the first fusillade. "Skirmishing with the wind," as a Sienese chronicler put it, the Imperialists took the forts, pressed on past the Torrione Dipinto, the Prato, and the Torazzo di Mezzo, through the Castellaccia, and on to the Porta Camollia, where a Spanish sergeant stuck his sword through a crack and derisively demanded: "Open the gate! Don Diego Hurtado de Mendoza wishes to enter!"[8] This informal "summons" in the name of the deposed Spanish governor represented the formal beginning of the siege. By midnight all of Camollia north of the gate was in Imperial hands save for the Torrione Dipinto, which was held for Siena and France by a party of survivors from the forts (fig. 65).

Next day the French managed to recover some of the lost ground. Just before noon, regular infantry counterattacked from the Camollia gate; after three hours of house-to-house fighting in the confined space of the Castellaccia, the Imperialists had been pushed out of the *borgo*. The French advance, however, stopped at the Torazzo di Mezzo. No attempt was made to follow the Imperialists across the Prato, although the retreat from the Castellaccia had caused panic among

Fig. 65. Giorgio Vasari, Marignano Captures the Forts at Camollia. In the background can be seen the towers of Siena, and in the foreground the familiar architectural topography of the Castellaccia and the Camollia forts.

Note that the soldiers, in addition to swords, pikes, and muskets, are carrying ladders and, foreground right, a pair of *trombe di fuoco*. In the foreground left, a dwarf carries Marignano's helmet.

the mainly inexperienced troops establishing themselves in the recently captured forts, which were now once again temporarily abandoned and could have been retaken without a fight.[9] No proper explanation, besides the exhaustion of the soldiers and the confusion of battle, has been advanced for the Franco-Sienese failure to recapture the forts. The failure of the men in the Torrione Dipinto to tell their allies of the second abandonment of these important positions represented yet another highly damaging breakdown in Sienese communications.

Fixed Positions at Camollia

Both sides now began to dig in on opposite sides of the Prato (fig. 66). On 29 January the Torrione Dipinto was abandoned, only to be immediately reoccupied by the Imperialists.[10] For the next fifteen months a sniper duel developed between the Torrione Dipinto and the Torrazzo di Mezzo. The towers were about 500 feet apart, and the front lines somewhat closer, so that "one couldn't raise a head without getting wounded from those positions."[11] The French planned to install a culverin in the Torrazzo di Mezzo and during the first half of February managed to fill a large part of their tower with earth to give the gun a solid platform.[12] Hearing of this from a deserter, the Imperialists on 17 February concentrated all their artillery fire on the Torrazzo.[13] After the bombardment, the tower was unfit to mount artillery but continued to be used as an observation post and sniper base. The French general Monluc, who described the situation just before Christmas 1554, even infers that the holes made by the enemy artillery proved useful in these respects.

The Imperial gunners then shifted their aim to the two towers flanking the Camollia gate, which were protected, like the keep at Montalcino, with woolen mattresses. Their bombardment began on 20 February. At a range of about 1000 feet these were rather more difficult targets, and it was not until 14 April that the first collapsed. On 21 April, 235 shots were fired at the second tower, which collapsed the next day.[14]

With their towers knocked out, the French were compelled to concentrate on low-level fortifications for the Castellaccia. During 1554 the thin curtain became a low rampart about 6 feet high. Outside the rampart a ditch was excavated "as wide as a pike and equally deep."[15] A retrenchment was built in front of the Porta Camollia to make the Castellaccia into a self-contained fort.[16] In April a casemate (we would probably call it a *caponier* or a pillbox) was constructed in the ditch beside the Torrazzo di Mezzo, but this work had to be abandoned in November because of bad drainage.[17] During the spring the Imperialists were much concerned about the possibility of French mines, but the countermines

Fig. 66. Anonymous Master, View of Siena During the Siege. Dating from 1554–55, the painting shows the location of the forts and siegeworks with remarkable detail. In the foreground is the fifteenth-century Palazzo dei Diavoli (with the tower) used for some of the siege as Marignano's headquarters. The plan of the Spanish citadel is also confirmed from this painting. A large number of medieval towers still survived in the wartime city. Note that the city walls still have their *merli*.

excavated under the Imperial batteries suffered from the same drainage problems as the French casemate.[18] Somewhat surprisingly, no mines were sprung at Siena. It seems likely that the unusually high water table of the Camollia ridge prevented what otherwise would have been a most suitable tactic in the confined space between the forts and the Castellaccia.

During the summer of 1554, the French managed to construct two artillery positions on the north side of the Castellaccia. The Fortino di Santa Croce was built in May to give a field of fire into the Valle di Malizia and toward the Osservanza:[19] later in the siege a gun from Santa Croce performed useful work by putting shots into an Imperial battery some 2,000 feet away outside the Porta Ovile. Another battery described as the "new fort" or the "other fort beside that of Santa Croce" was constructed in June to engage the Imperial works north of the Torrione Dipinto.[20] These positions can be recognized in pictures of the siege as two blunt projections from the Castellaccia. Most of the artillery exchanges took place between the Imperial works on the southern edge of the Prato and the French positions on Poggio San Prospero. Here the guns were only silenced by shortage of ammunition or by bad weather. Rain, it must be said, was almost as destructive as enemy fire; despite frequent sorties to collect timber and brushwood for repairs, the Sienese regularly suffered from shortages of materials essential to reinforce the earthworks.[21] If they had not been well founded on the Spanish masonry, it is possible that a major breach would have been created. By the end of February, however, it was clear that San Prospero would hold.

The Campaign for the Approaches

Marignano's position to the north of the city was at first precarious. For a number of weeks early in 1554 he "besieged" a garrison that was repeatedly reinforced from Grosseto and Montalcino, while his own communications with his home bases within the Fiorentino were constantly threatened by raiders from the Sienese garrisons "behind" him at Casole, Monteriggioni, and Aiuola as well as from a large number of lesser strongholds—privately fortified country houses, hamlets, and medieval towers—in the wild and mountainous district to the west of Siena known as the Montagnola.[22] Marignano's first letter to Cosimo after the surprise attack requested cannon from Poggio Imperiale to employ against "certain little places where these peasants who raid the highways are based."[23] There can be little doubt that this raiding, coupled with the snows and heavy rains of February, was a major cause of food and ammunition shortages in the Imperial camp, and a steady trickle of deserters back to Florence and even into Siena.[24]

The "little places" of the Montagnola would have to be captured before Marignano could implement what had now become his strategy for the siege: the blockade of Siena by means of two further fortified camps dominating the supply roads to Grosseto (the *strada maremmana*) and Montalcino (the *strada romana*) and, when the western and southern approaches had been secured, the systematic destruction of the crops in the agricultural hinterland of the dominio. Marignano's developing strategic intentions are revealed in his regular correspondence with Cosimo and are summarized from time to time in major *discorsi* (position papers) prepared in the early months of 1554.[25] Franco-Sienese strategy, not so clearly expressed, was probably never so well formulated. Strozzi, however, seemed determined to maintain control of these approaches for as long as possible by means of the fortified outposts at Lecceto, Belcaro, and Monastero. As we shall see, further outposts were constructed during the course of the fighting to support the key position of Monastero. The defense of the rural strongholds in the Montagnola was less determined. The Imperialists quickly discovered that a single piece of medium-caliber artillery was often sufficient to force surrender or evacuation. But, the number of isolated positions and the difficulty of moving even small numbers of guns across the Montagnola in winter turned what should have been a rapid "mopping up" operation into a protracted series of actions.

Operations began on 21 March when an Imperial force of 1,000 infantry and 100 cavalry with one half-cannon and two sakers left camp and moved northwest along the Val di Staggia. By the evening of the next day, Chioccola, Fortezza di Santa Colomba, Villa Lionardo, Villa D'Arnana, Palazzo del Rosso, and Toiano were all in Imperial hands.[26] Pickets were put into these positions to secure the right flank for the second phase—the attack on Lecceto, Belcaro, and Monastero—which was meant to follow immediately. Although these places were reconnoitered on 23 March, the attacks had to be postponed when news arrived of disaster at Chiusi, where a large Imperial force had been ambushed and routed by the French. Piero Strozzi took advantage of the lull to order hundreds of men out of Siena to work on the fortifications at Monastero. As Monastero became daily more defensible, Marignano determined to move against the western outposts. On 4 April a force of 2,000 foot supported by 50 horse and two pieces of artillery took and sacked Belcaro after a bombardment.[27] Two days later, Lecceto surrendered without standing a battery.[28]

Strozzi now began last-minute efforts to protect the Maremma road. On 7 April a new fort was started between Monastero and the Porta San Marco, which was described in an Imperial report as 200 braccia (some 400 feet) in circumference and located "an arquebus shot" outside the gate on a site overlooking the valley and the road to the Badia. The Fortino di San Marco, as it was called by Sozzini, was on the north bank of the Tressa, probably near the modern suburb of Giuggolo, which would give the specified field of fire. Within three days it was defensible.[29] On 8 April, Marignano learnt of a second new fort "on the left hand side of Monastero (i.e., to the north) on top of a prominent hill."[30] It was certainly located between Monastero and the Tressa, probably on the high ground now occupied by the Villa la Buca. During the fighting that followed, the Imperialists encountered "various other forts built at the mouths of lanes": the context suggests small works—redoubts or blockhouses in modern terminology. However, it was the construction of the second new fort that precipitated Marignano's decision to attempt the incomplete defensive system of Monastero (fig. 67).

The assault force of 1,600 foot, three companies of horse, and two half-cannon left camp on 9 April in a thick mist. Two hours after dawn, the force

Fig. 67. Giorgio Vasari, The Capture of Monastero. Vasari's information about Monastero is good. The forts are shown as rectangular projections from the enceinte. The breastwork appears as a low curtain running out from the enceinte to the left.

halted to wait for the mist to clear; as Monastero came into view, it was seen to be defended by some 800 men and 50 lances behind a breastwork that was a little over three feet high.[31] Federigo di Montaguto with 500 arquebusiers moved along the Tressa valley to prevent any relief from Siena. Two further columns of 200 arquebusiers took up positions to fire into the defenders from the flanks while the rest of the infantry attacked the breastwork from the front. The main body of defenders was forced to fall back to Sant'Abundio, leaving 120 men under Captain Ventura in the convent of Monastero. The incomplete fort north of Monastero was then stormed and artillery brought up to batter the convent, which surrendered the next day.[32] The action was hailed in Florence as the first substantial victory of the war. The capture of the Camollia forts was still seen as a disappointment, although both events were later to be commemorated in Giorgio Vasari's decorative scheme for the Palazzo Vecchio in Florence. Fortification work continued almost unchecked at Monastero, which, as the second of Marignano's proposed siege camps, was now designed to accommodate one thousand men and to resist artillery. Imperial control of the Maremma road was consolidated when, a week later, two companies were put into the convent of Montecchio and a third stationed at Barontoli.[33]

Following the effective closure of the Maremma road, Marignano had planned to establish another fortified camp to block the road to Montalcino.[34] A suitable site for the third camp had been agreed for San Lazzero about a mile south of Siena; but now the general reported construction would not begin until the arrival of promised German reinforcements. Instead, Marignano proposed to patrol the strada romana with cavalry based some ten miles to the south.[35] To Cosimo and his advisers in Florence this looked like failure to grasp the nettle of a close blockade. The general seemed to be holding back from a commitment to establish the third siege camp, which, they had been encouraged to believe, held the key to success.[36] Yet from the often heated exchange of letters between Florence and the field headquarters outside Siena, it is clear that Marignano still faced considerable difficulties and real dangers as he attempted to consolidate his control of the approaches in April and May.

Many of the Imperial troops were detached from the main force on raids into the Sienese hinterland and on convoy protection duty. Around the city itself there were insufficient soldiers to create continuous lines of circumvallation: in any event, Marignano's pioneers were barely able to cope with the construction of siegeworks at Camollia and the fortification of Monastero. Hence the need to rely on patrols operating from a limited number of fortified camps. In the constant skirmishing near the walls of the city the Imperial patrols were always vulnerable to Franco-Sienese sorties in superior strength—particularly, as Marignano emphasized, because the broken ground made it difficult for one body of men to see and help another. To the man on the spot, unsolicited tactical advice from Florence was yet another burden of command. "I must speak my mind freely . . . ," protested Marignano when Cosimo had again urged aggressive action close to Siena's walls, "these are drawing room plans, which do not work in practice."[37] Shortly afterward the general was to complain: "If only you could see the ground, I know it would give you better understanding."[38]

Marignano, through Cosimo's extensive intelligence network, was becoming increasingly aware of the buildup of French forces in central Italy. As anticipated in his first *discorso*, it had taken the French some months to respond to the surprise attacks of 26 January. By May, however, troops were moving southward from Lombardy while others had landed at Port'Ércole and for weeks had been slipping into Siena in small bodies. With some kind of counteroffensive obviously in the air, the general was reluctant to divide his forces further by establishing a third siege camp.[39] For the time being, the route to the south remained open.

Strozzi's Raid to the Val di Nievole

A few weeks later, Marignano's caution was to be vindicated. On the night of 11 June, Piero Strozzi led a strong force of at least 5,000 foot and 1,000 horse out of the Porta Fontebranda and headed toward Casole. False letters had been allowed to fall into Medici hands implying that Casole was to be strongly rein-forced as a prelude to raids against San Gimignano and Colle di Val d'Elsa. Beyond sending more troops to the two Florentine border towns, Marignano took no action to forestall a movement apparently designed to draw the Imperial army away from the blockade. Late the next day it was realized that Strozzi had left Casole, bypassed both Colle and San Gimignano, and was making rapid progress northward with his outriders disguised in Imperial colors.[40] In response to Cosimo's frenzied and abusive demands for assistance,[41] a large Imperial force marched north in pursuit; but Strozzi passed through Pisa and crossed the Arno into the Val di Nievole. There he joined a contingent of French troops from Lombardy and moved with them to Viareggio, where between 10 and 15 June a Franco-Turkish fleet was to disembark artillery and more troops prior to the march on Florence. For reasons that have always remained unclear, the fleet arrived too late and Strozzi found himself on the "wrong" side of the river, with no artillery and fast becoming outnumbered by the forces gathering between his army and Siena.

Leaving Viareggio on 21 June, he managed to avoid a number of ambushes and brought his army to the banks of the Arno late on June 23. The river was swollen with unseasonable rain, so that Marignano was confident that, with the bridges and fords guarded, Strozzi was trapped. By mid-morning on 24 June, however, Strozzi had taken his army across the river on a makeshift pontoon bridge and headed south, closely followed by Marignano—who crossed at Pon-tedera—and a Spanish *tercio* (a brigade, in modern terms) which had been rushed from Corsica to Bocca d'Arno. By late afternoon, Strozzi's exhausted column had been overtaken near San Vivaldo, but took up a defensive position which the Imperialists were unwilling to attack without support from their artillery (which had fallen far behind in the chase). The armies skirmished indecisively throughout 25 and 26 June, and during the night of the second day Strozzi slipped away once more. By the morning of 27 June he was at Casole, by 28 June at Rencine; and by 30 June he had reached safety at Ponte a Bozzone, between Siena and Montalcino.[42] Strozzi's raid into the northern Fiorentino had been an attempt to bring the war home to its leading protagonist. His escape from the Val di Nievole, in particular the crossing of the Arno in the teeth of superior numbers, was the military high point of the conflict.

The presence near Siena of a sizable and well-led French field force posed special problems for the Imperialists, which were discussed at a council of war held at Basciano, just north of Siena, on the march back from the Val di Nievole. Chiappino Vitelli, marquis of Cetona, urged the continued pursuit of Strozzi in the hope of bringing him to battle with inferior numbers. Marignano, supported by Vincenzo Nobili and Mario Sforza, count of Santa Fiora, now argued that Strozzi would outrun them and that, by establishing themselves south of Siena, they would reinforce the blockade and eventually force Strozzi to fight in order to relieve the city. In the meantime the Sienese, who had not taken full advantage of the raid to reprovision the city, would suffer a severe drop in morale when they found the Imperialists camped to their south.[43] The position south of Siena was a bait to lure Strozzi into an offensive move.

On 3 July the third siege-camp was started in the plain of the Badia, about three-quarters of a mile from the Porta Romana. Concino's report placed the camp in San Lazzero and observed that a nearby church offered copious supplies of water.[44] Soon water was dwindling, however, and the site proved anything but secure from long-range artillery fire from Siena.[45] As few as four days after its foundation, the new camp was the main item on the agenda of another conference of senior officers. By this time further intelligence was available on enemy strength. An enemy officer—it is not clear whether he had been captured or had deserted—told them that Strozzi had now been joined by contingents from the Maremma and the Val di Chiana and, with the troops inside Siena, could field 12,000 infantry. Another report notified them that the French fleet had been seen off the Maremma coast—with a clear inference of yet further reinforcements. The meeting then pondered whether Strozzi planned to revictual Siena or to attempt a field engagement.

All those present, minuted Concino, were agreed that Strozzi was unable to carry sufficient provisions to satisfy his own army. Since Strozzi was evidently desperate to snatch victory from a battle, and since Imperial forces numbered no more than 8,000 foot, no one was prepared to recommend risking engagement until Camillo Colonna joined then with promised reinforcements. In the meantime, the army had to secure itself in a good camp. But where? The San Lazzero site could be invested from the south, forcing the troops to fight or starve. Monastero was no better, being exposed to attacks from Siena itself. Finally, the council resolved to pull the Imperial troops back to the Camollia ridge, where they would benefit from the natural strength of the site, its extensive fortifications, and the shorter and safer lines of communication and supply.[46]

Since news of the withdrawal was certain to infuriate Cosimo,[47] the council decided next day to send Concino to present the consensus view to the duke. Concino then managed to persuade them to send Chiappino Vitelli in his place; as a personal friend to Cosimo and a soldier well known for his boldness, he was a messenger who could scarcely be accused of timidity. Vitelli was also armed with a *discorso* that repeated the arguments of the conference and emphasized the other officers' enthusiasm for combat, but it concluded with the point that "we must be careful to fight when it suits us, not the enemy."[48]

The events of the next few days confirmed the accuracy of the field officers' analysis. On 14 July, heavy skirmishing at Sant'Abundio covered the approach of the French. On the next day, Strozzi's force entered Siena by the Porta Romana, passed through the city to the acclaim of the people, and occupied positions outside the Porta Ovile (northeast).[49] Instead of revictualing the city, the troops levied provisions from the citizens.[50] Since the French were now clearly looking for a fight, the Osservanza, Vignano, and Santa Regina—to the north and east—were abandoned by the Imperialists and promptly occupied by Strozzi. Marignano preferred to face Strozzi from behind his well-prepared defenses northwest of the city.[51] (Cosimo, as ever, was concerned lest these withdrawals should let supplies into the now open city. In fact, Strozzi's large force did little to help the food shortage inside Siena, consuming, as it did, rather more than the Sienese *vivandieri* could bring into the city.)[52] Strozzi was compelled to win a battle to save Siena. To bring the Imperialists to battle in anything like equal conditions, however, he had to drag them away from their Camollia entrenchments by threatening vital Florentine interests.

Marciano and Its Aftermath

On 17 July the French army left Siena and moved eastward into the Val di Chiana. Foiano, a Florentine border town, was captured and the Imperial garrison massacred. French forces then added insult to injury by demonstrating in front of Cortona and Arezzo. The loss of Foiano was a serious blow to the Imperial position in the northern Val di Chiana; even before the town fell, Marignano had left his entrenchments and marched in pursuit. By the end of the month, after a week of cautious maneuver, the two armies faced each other near Marciano.[53]

Here, for the first time, Strozzi had chosen unfavorable ground. Marignano was now between the French army and their base, interrupting the French supply route. Water was also a problem, for the Val di Chiana, unlike the Val d'Arno, had experienced a forty-day drought. The only water available to the French was from a small stream that was dangerously exposed to Imperial artillery fire. While Marignano played his usual waiting game and bombarded the French from long range, strong pressures mounted in Strozzi's councils for immediate attack or withdrawal. When casualties and hunger made withdrawal inevitable, opinion was divided as to whether Strozzi should attempt disengagement by day or try to slip away by night. The French general Blaise de Monluc, now commanding in Siena, heard of the debate and sent word urging a night withdrawal, arguing that Henry of France had earned great distinction and honor for a night retreat and that Strozzi himself owed his current high standing as a commander to a brilliantly executed withdrawal.[54] Contrary to the best-known accounts—those of Monluc and Montalvo—it seems that Strozzi did indeed attempt to get away on the night of 1–2 August. Marignano, however, managed to maintain contact, and on the morning of 2 August the two armies found themselves on opposite sides of another stream, the Fosso di Scannagallo. Again disengagement was urged. Cornelio Bentivoglio, commanding the French rearguard, even offered to sacrifice his force in the delaying action that would be essential to the success of the daylight maneuver.[55] Strozzi, however, now decided to fight. At first his infantry made a good advance to the *fosso* but, as soon as the Imperial cavalry moved, the Franco-Sienese horse bolted in panic, leaving the foot to fend for themselves. Most of the day the Gascons and Swiss held their positions along the *fosso,* but when the Imperial cavalry returned from the pursuit, the French infantry was broken and cut to pieces in flight. At the end of the day, 4,000 French soldiers were dead and an equal number wounded or prisoner.[56] The Imperialists, who had spent the day pouring artillery and arquebus fire into the defenseless mass of pikes, lost only a few hundred men. Strozzi's defeat marked a change in the war.

The destruction of Strozzi's field force left Marignano free to enlarge his regional siege to the scale envisaged in February. The capture of Lucignano immediately after the battle consolidated Imperial control of the upper Val di Chiana. Monteriggioni was taken at the end of August. With the removal of this threat to communications between Poggibonsi and the base camp at Camollia, Marignano was able for the first time to place the largest part of his army south of Siena. During September an Imperial fort was built on the Poggio di Monsindoli, overlooking the strada romana, and a siege camp was established at Poggiarella, near the Certosa.[57] During October, Imperialist expeditions captured a large number of places in the district between Siena and Piombino, among them the important positions of Casole, Radicondoli, Monterotondo, Chiusdino, and Massa Marittima.[58] Finally, in mid-November the Imperialists took Crevole, a small but important fortress in the rugged mountains between Siena and Montalcino which was used by the French as a base for blockade-running operations.[59]

The autumn of 1554 marked the beginning of real hardship for the besieged population. Strozzi himself commanded the last major food convoy, which had fought its way into Siena from Crevole on the night of 18 September.[60] Since then there had been only promises of further relief, a trickle of food smuggled through the lines to be sold at enormous prices on the black market, and French demands that the civilian population be reduced from 25,000 to 15,000 souls. On 22 September 1,000 men, women, and children left the city under escort, but this was to be the last convoy of civilian evacuees successfully to penetrate the Imperial blockade.[61] Two days later the terrified, humiliated, and nearly naked survivors of another party of evacuees were begging on their knees for readmission at the Porta San Marco.[62] This grisly event set the pattern for the future. The Imperialists continued to allow empty-handed civilians to enter the city but not to leave; on 3 October, Marignano announced that all males taken leaving Siena or bearing food in its vicinity were to be summarily executed. A bounty was offered for each man hanged, and the few trees remaining on the approaches to Siena were soon festooned with bodies.[63] Yet the French insisted on the expulsion of "useless mouths"—men and women too old or infirm and children too young to serve in the militia or labor on the fortifications. The expulsions that followed caused deep resentment as well as anguish, for a disproportionate number of those driven out to starve in no-man's-land came from the disadvantaged groups of the besieged city: orphans, foreigners, refugees from the dominio, and poor Sienese citizens with no family influence.

The autumn also brought difficulties to the Imperialists facing the dismal prospect of a second winter siege. Marignano complained persistently of serious manpower shortages and warned Cosimo of the unreliability of statistics based on under-strength units. Just before Marciano, Concino had given the Imperial infantry strength as 7,000.[64] Early in October, Marignano estimated his effective strength as low as 3,500 "combat-worthy infantry . . . the rest are all unfit."[65] Even these troops could not always be freely used. In August the Tercio di Corsica, a veteran Spanish unit, mutinied for its pay. After this event, the commander was unwilling to order the movement of unpaid troops lest it should provoke another mutiny or provide an opportunity for large-scale desertions.[66] The general manpower scarcity was compounded by specific shortages of gunners, pioneers, and ox handlers experienced in the transport of artillery.[67] Artillery and ammunition were scarce and often in bad condition.[68] On top of these problems, the weather frequently caused expeditions to be postponed, or slowed them to a near standstill. Many of these factors played a part in the operation that followed the decision temporarily to shelve the blockade policy and to attempt to bombard the city into submission before Christmas 1554.

The Bombardment of Siena

At the beginning of October 1554, Bartolommeo Concino wrote to Cosimo observing that the people of Siena were already murmuring against the famine and becoming fearful of the sack that would certainly follow a successful assault. A show of force, he suggested, might well produce a surrender. Concino also pointed out that a bombardment would demand a further eight to ten cannon and a large supply of ammunition. Some guns, he said, could be transported to the siege from Montepulciano and Lucignano, and it might prove necessary to transport further artillery from the fortresses of the Fiorentino.[69] Cosimo responded favorably to the proposal.[70] However, in October it seemed to Marignano more important to push ahead with the expeditions against the western Sienese strongholds before the worst of the winter weather. It was not until the very end of November that the artillery operation was set in motion. The count of Santa Fiora was ordered to lead a force of 800 Spaniards and 10 ensigns of Germans with two half-cannon to Montepulciano, where they were to collect ten of the twelve cannon that had been stored there after the siege of Montalcino. Santa Fiora was to capture Pienza on the way to Montepulciano and to return by way of Lucignano, where three more artillery pieces were to be collected.[71]

At the time of these actions the transport of artillery was not considered a major problem. Indeed, the early progress of Santa Fiora's expedition confirmed Concino's estimate that it would take at least twelve days, possibly more.[72] The bombardment was scheduled for Christmas, and it was the provision of qualified gunners that most exercised the Imperial commander.

Since very few gunners had been required during the maneuvers of the summer months, there had been no objection from the general when a number of them had been posted to the northern Fiorentino after the Val di Nievole scare. Others had left the army when their contracts expired. A few had been killed or captured. But the planned bombardment demanded at least eighteen guns with two gunners per piece; so the general urged Cosimo to obtain all available men, if necessary "by dragging them out of the Papal fortresses and Ancona . . . and the galleys of the Prince [Andrea Doria]."[73] Throughout the month of December, Marignano emphasized this problem with growing urgency. "I am counting on our artillery being here by Christmas," he wrote on 20 December; ". . . above all send as many gunners as you can."[74] By this time it was practically certain that the Christmas bombardment would have to be postponed. Postponement was made absolutely certain when a postscript to Marignano's dispatch of 23 December brought the astonishing news that Santa Fiora was still "bogged down" in Chianciano.

That Santa Fiora was experiencing some difficulty with the weather in the Val di Chiana was known to Marignano. Extra oxen and pioneers had been collected at considerable expense, and on 20 December Marignano had instructed Santa Fiora to bring only three or four pieces, "or however many pieces you can handle."[75] On 24 December, Marignano ordered him to concentrate on the transport of the guns from Lucignano.[76] It is not clear whether the orders went astray or were ignored by the count. In any event, Santa Fiora continued to haul all of the guns from Montepulciano, so it was not until 7 January that they reached Ponte a Bozzone, about one mile southeast of Siena.

Early in December, Monluc told the Sienese of the purpose of Santa Fiora's expedition, information which provoked a marked increase in building activity on the fortifications. The most urgent work was concentrated near the Porta Tufi and the Porta San Marco (on the south), where the Imperialists were pushing their positions dangerously close to the walls.[77] Not knowing which section of the wall was to be attacked, the defenders were compelled to build retrenchments behind all threatened sectors, making enormous demands on manpower and materials.[78]

The location of the bombardment site was, of course, a closely guarded secret. Even the Imperial dispatches which record disputes about the choice of site speak mysteriously—and possibly ambiguously—of "the place we discussed" or "the place Your Excellency knows." Secrecy was essential because, with a large civilian population still inside the city, it would not take long to construct obstacles behind any part of the wall clearly identified as the target.[79] For the same reason, a successful bombardment would have to be fast. Hence the need for a large number of guns served by experienced gunners and a well-synchronized plan to bring them quickly into action.

The orders issued after Marignano's Council of War on 8 January 1555 set aside 9 January for the preparation of arquebuses, powder, match, and lead. During the night of 9–10 January, Santa Fiora was to move his guns into position from Ponte a Bozzone, while Chiappino Vitelli was to bring his artillery from Monastero "to the place of the battery." To avoid confusion in the darkness, Vitelli and Santa Fiora were personally to reconnoiter their respective routes to the mustering point. The movement of artillery had to be finished before daylight, 10 January.

Early in the evening of 10 January, Captains Gabrio and Julio, the chief Imperial gunner-engineers, were to survey and mark out the battery, level the site, plant gabions, supervise the siting of the guns and bring up barrels of water to sponge out the hot gun barrels. One hour after dark the *tavole* (wooden shields) in Camollia and the Osservanza were to be brought to the battery and a guard posted to ensure they were not removed. At the same time, the Spanish infantry were to move into position near Camollia, leaving one ensign from each company to guard the camps. Two hours after dark, the Germans were to move to "the place of the battery"—again, no mention of the specific site. Possibly the staggered moves were designed to avoid confusion; but the Spanish infantry and the pioneers were responsible for filling the gabions with earth and for this reason needed to be in position before the Germans. Veteran Spanish and German troops were to deliver the assault, while recently arrived units of the Florentine militia were to assemble towards the Porta Romana, where a diversionary attack was to be staged.[80]

In spite of the security precautions, the defenders managed to piece together a number of clues to Imperial intentions. On 7 January the diarist Sozzini noted the construction of a cavalier "within the wall from the Torre del Giudeo to Camollia, above the orchard of the Casa Umidi, to overlook the hill of Ravacciano because [Monluc] had some intelligence of artillery being taken there."[81] On 8 January, before the detailed plans had been agreed at the Imperial Council of War, someone seems to have been careless or overzealous, for Sozzini recorded that it was possible to see the Imperialists leveling the ground behind the hill of Ravacciano. Immediately the Otto della Guerra issued orders that all shops were to be closed and that everyone was to work on the retrenchment of San Lorenzo (fig. 68).

A heavy mist soon obscured the Imperial works, and it was still not possible to be certain of the battery site. Indeed, on 9 January work had recommenced on all sides of the city when, according to Sozzini, Monluc received word from a spy that the Imperial Council of War had decided upon three simultaneous attacks from different directions. On 10 January, however, a prisoner captured by one of Monluc's patrols told his interrogators that fifteen large pieces of artillery were concealed behind the Ravacciano ridge. Sienese efforts were now once again concentrated on the trench and rampart enclosing the area of land behind the stretch of wall from the Porta Ovile to a point some distance northwest of the Barriera San Lorenzo. To the north of this area the approaches were too steep for an attack, while east of the Porta Ovile they were overlooked by the heights of San Francesco. The ground behind the San Lorenzo-Porta Ovile stretch of wall was free of buildings, suitable both for an assault and for the type of defense planned by Monluc, who wanted to lure the Imperialists through their breach into a killing ground, bounded by the retrenchment and swept by cannon loaded with chains, nails, and pieces of iron.[82]

However, Monluc's hopes of inflicting heavy casualties on the enemy were dashed when, three hours after sunset on 10 January, the moonlight revealed two batteries pointing not at San Lorenzo but at the new wall that had been built in the late fifteenth century to bring San Francesco and the Piccolomini tombs within the enceinte. This wall, being the strongest part of the medieval circuit, at first seems a curious choice of target: but the space behind was then crowded with houses that would greatly hinder the construction of retrenchments. Monluc's account continues with the description of the demolition of more than a hundred houses by "not less than four thousand souls" led by the patriotic

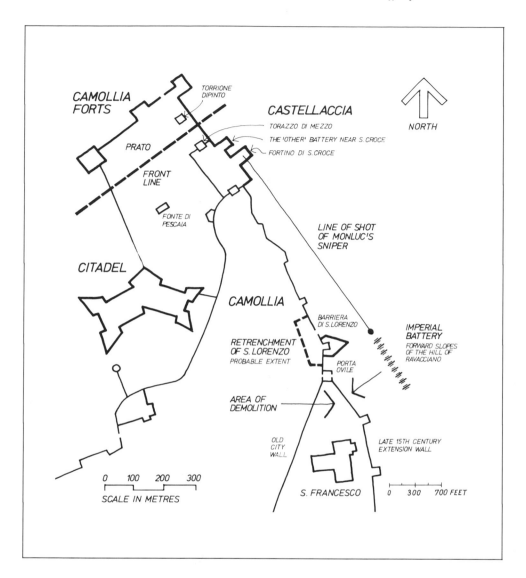

Fig. 68. Siena under Attack from Ravacciano

householders and assisted by the famous three companies of Sienese women. During the night and the following day a space of about eighty paces was cleared, and a trench and bank "not much above the height of a man" was built facing the target area. Behind this retrenchment the houses were loopholed and knocked through to give covered access to the rampart. The anteportal of the gate was reinforced with earth; embrasures pierced the side flanking the rear of any breach.[83]

The bombardment began at dawn and continued until an hour before sunset. During the course of the day some 260 rounds were fired, but most sources are agreed upon the relatively small amount of damage to the wall. The official Sienese version reports a target of "fifteen or sixteen braccia [about twenty-five feet] of wall, of which they did no damage of importance, destroying only two-thirds of a braccia [about fourteen inches] on the outside of a wall that was three braccia [five feet] thick."[84] Monluc tells us that at first a cutting technique was used "one foot or two above the ground, to cut the wall from the bottom." Later in the day the aiming point was raised: "Toward midday they ceased this low battery and began to shoot into the middle of the wall."[85] Near the end of the day, fire was shifted onto targets inside the city, which, of course, put an end to Marignano's hopes for a breach.[86]

The failure to concentrate on one target could be attributed to lack of discipline or experience among the Imperial gunners, although Sozzini suggests that even before the aiming point was raised, many of the shots went harmlessly into the ground in front of the wall because of the difficult angle of fire.[87] Another factor which possibly explains the increasingly wild shooting toward the end of the bombardment was Monluc's decision to attempt some long-range artillery sniping into the enemy battery.

Shortly after noon, Monluc noticed that from the Castellaccia it was possible to see "all the recoil of their artillery," which presumably meant that he was looking directly into the flank of the Imperial battery. On his orders a demicannon was hauled into the fortino di Santa Croce, served by a Sienese bombardier who was so well practiced with the gun that he could hit a small target with it "as if it had been an arquebus." Monluc continues:

> I gave ten crowns to our Sienese that he might make some good shots with that piece here, as he had done several at the citadel before. The enemy had placed gabions on the flank of their battery toward us. Bassompierre [a senior French officer] and I went a little on the right hand and observed the bullet in the air like a hat on fire, flying very wide on the right hand, and the second as much on my left, which made me ready to eat my own flesh with rage. Monsieur de Bassompierre always assured me that he would presently take his right level. . . . The third shot landed on the bottom of the gabions, and the fourth played directly into their artillery and there killed a great many of their men; whereupon all those that assisted fled behind a little house which was in the rear of their cannon. At which I ran and took him [the gunner] in my arms, and seeing him with his linstock ready to fire again, said to him, "My brother, let them have it; I'm giving you another ten scudi and a beaker of Greek wine." I then left him the French captain, who had the guard of the fort, to furnish him continually with such things as he stood in need of, and Monsieur de Bassompierre and I returned to our post.

And this Sienese made so many brave shots that he dismounted six pieces of their cannon, and their artillery remained totally abandoned till the beginning of the night without playing any more than two pieces of cannon that were covered with gabions and flanked towards the fort Camollia.[88]

Concino confirmed the essentials of Monluc's somewhat colorful account when, in the dispatch explaining the failure of the battery, he mentioned that "the enemy emplaced a piece of artillery in their fort at the orchard of Santa Croce, which harassed our battery from the flank so much that seven or eight of our Spaniards were killed."[89] These relatively trifling casualties merely confirmed the Imperial officers in their decision to abandon a project that had failed before the first shot had been fired. The plan required at least eighteen guns for a rapid bombardment; but, after the long delay of Santa Fiora's expedition, probably rather more than this number had been collected.[90] The plan had foundered, as Concino explained in the dispatch dated midnight of 11 January, on the inability of the Imperialists to haul all of their guns up the hill where the battery was to be sited. Only nine pieces were in action on 11 January, and two of these were not full-sized siege cannon.[91]

After this further striking demonstration of the practical limitations on the use of siege artillery, the Imperial guns were dispersed northward among the Florentine fortresses. The decision clearly indicated the abandonment of all plans for a quick solution to the siege.[92]

The End of the Siege

The Imperial blockade was now intensified. Marignano had been greatly reinforced in the weeks before the planned assault; thus, following the failure of the bombardment, most of the Imperial troops in Tuscany were concentrated around Siena. Spanish, German, and Italian veterans constituted about half of the 30,000 men available for the siege in the early months of 1555; the remainder came from the Florentine militia. An army of this size was able to man a continuous line of pickets between the forts and to do so on a proper day-and-night shift system.[93] Determined troops could still fight their way through the lines. On 29 January a force of 800 German soldiers sustained heavy losses but reached Montalcino, to the relief of those remaining in Siena, where (in Bardi's words) they had eaten as much food as 3,000 Italians.[94] On 5 April, on the very eve of surrender, another force of Imperial and Florentine rebels—who could expect no quarter from Cosimo—fought their way out with surprisingly few losses.[95] Peasant guides, such as the heroic Tirantallo, Carlotto, and Callocci still managed to penetrate the line with messages, relying on their expert local knowledge as well as disguise to postpone their almost inevitable capture, torture, and death.[96] For the 10,000 civilians still in Siena there was little chance to escape. At the end of March, a final expulsion of "useless mouths" brought yet new horrors as the survivors showed themselves at the gates with noses and ears hacked off as a grim warning that escapees would now be mutilated first and hanged only on a second escape attempt. Sozzini paints a dismal picture of the starving inhabitants, "men and women, all ravaged, thin, and pale from the continuous suffering and hardship of life," dying with surprising speed once sickness took hold because of their weakness and the total lack of restoratives.[97]

Outside the walls was a scene of desolation. When he arrived in Siena in mid-1554, Monluc had been much impressed with the prospect of palaces and convents around the city.[98] In February 1555 one of Bentivoglio's soldiers wrote that for ten miles around Siena there was not a wall standing, while the country was infested with dogs devouring the corpses.[99] Before the siege, affectionate patriotic descriptions never failed to mention the mature forests surrounding the city.[100] By 1555 the hills around Siena were bare—stripped for fuel, shelter, and material for fortifications as well as to deny cover to the blockade runners.

The Sienese made their first overtures for surrender early in February 1555. Strozzi from Montalcino and Monluc inside the besieged city attempted to stiffen the Sienese with promises of certain relief in the spring.[101] By March, however, the Senate of the republic had resolved upon direct surrender negotiations with Cosimo, who held plenipotentiary powers from the emperor. The Sienese had little to bargain save further desperate resistance. Their French allies declined to recognize the negotiations, still less to offer concessions such as the surrender of fortresses in the large areas of the dominio as yet unconquered by the Imperialists. Almost certainly it was Cosimo's anxiety to occupy Siena and to begin operations as quickly as possible against French-occupied southern Tuscany that finally persuaded him to offer acceptable formal terms—to the immediate outrage of the emperor, who considered himself humiliated by them and, later, to the disappointment of those Sienese who had not expected to be deceived.[102] The city, of course, would return to its former state of obedience to the emperor. A general pardon would be offered to all save non-Sienese rebels. The citadel would not be reconstructed without the agreement of the republic, and the siegeworks would be demolished as soon as circumstances permitted. Even the traditional institutions of republican government would be retained; this, despite the revocation in 1554 of all Siena's Imperial privileges.[103] Finally, the French contingent with their belongings would be permitted to leave the city with full honors of war—colors flying, bearing arms—free to choose their own route of march.[104]

The leaders of the republic signed the surrender document on 17 April. Shortly before the surrender, Monluc consigned the citadel and the Castellaccia to the Sienese republic: the crown of France would surrender no fortress to the enemy, but was prepared to return them to their ally.[105] On 21 April 1555, Monluc left the city for Montalcino accompanied by his own soldiers and a miserable convoy of Sienese patriots who, with their families, preferred exile to submission.[106] The republic-in-exile, supported by France, was to fight on from Montalcino for another four years.

7

THE CAPTURE OF
PORT'ÉRCOLE, 1555

AFTER the fall of Siena, four defended localities remained in French hands. Montalcino, visible from much of the Val d'Arbia, was probably the most galling symbol of resistance. Grosseto in the Maremma and the group of strongholds around Chiusi were also capable of prolonged resistance, provided that reinforcements, supplies, and money continued to arrive from France. The fourth site, Port'Ércole, was the key to Sienese Tuscany, for it was through this small harbor on Monte Argentario—a volcanic island joined to the mainland by a single, sandy causeway—that most of the French munitions of war entered Italy. [1]

The importance of Port'Ércole was clear to both sides (fig. 69). The Sienese and their French allies began its fortification in October 1552, only weeks after the expulsion of the Spaniards. [2] As the Imperial blockade tightened around Siena in the autumn of 1554, Marignano planned to seize the seaport, which he then described as "the most important objective after Siena." [3] Indeed, at that time the general hoped that the capture of Port'Ércole would force the surrender of Siena itself. A plan of attack had been formulated following reconnaissance missions and the interrogation of a captured officer who had worked on the fortifications. As events turned out, however, no Imperial troops could be spared from the operations around Siena, and it was nearly a month after the occupation of the capital before a decision was finally taken to force matters at Port'Ércole.

The siege that followed is of interest for a number of reasons. It was a combined operation; both land and naval forces being opposed to each other on each side. The defensive system was based entirely on a system of seven detached forts, a novel concept in fortification which we will see here tested in battle. Further, the events of the siege are depicted in considerable detail in one of Giorgio Vasari's major frescoes in the Palazzo Vecchio, Florence. An account of the fighting and the battlefield topography will show that Vasari recorded these details with much attention to "documentary" accuracy; his painting has provided interest for its courtly iconography, and its political—even propagandistic—overtones. [4] Yet on many occasions in his writings, Vasari claimed that he strove to achieve historical and natural accuracy; and it may be that this claim should be taken seriously.

140

The Forced March to Port'Ércole

On 16 May 1555, Marignano reported to Cosimo his departure from Siena to Pienza prior to the move southward. His letter bears a rough note at the bottom—presumably added in Florence on the following day—reminding the secretary to

Fig. 69. Map of the Monte Argentario Peninsula

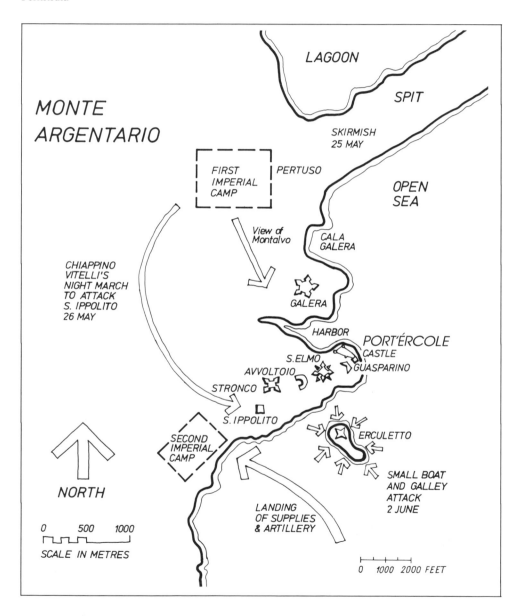

"write to the marquis and advise him of the new fort they are building at Port'Ércole, sending him the copy of the prince's letter."[5] This note almost certainly refers to a report just received from Prince Andrea Doria, whose Imperial galleys were patrolling the Tuscan coastline in anticipation of the arrival of another Turkish fleet from North Africa. Doria must have received word of the tree felling and brushwood clearance that would signal the construction of a new fort on the heavily wooded slopes of Monte Argentario.

From this moment the campaign against Port'Ércole was prosecuted with a great sense of urgency. On 18 May, Marignano reported his decision to leave two guns in Montepulciano and to force-march the infantry toward Port'Ércole with no other artillery support and, for speed, with provisions for only three days. The mules that normally carried ammunition for the guns were loaded with food for the march. Artillery, ammunition, and further provisions for the siege were to be brought down the coast from Livorno and Piombino by the galleys of Andrea Doria.

This accelerated plan meant that Marignano's land force would be almost

Fig. 70. Port'Ércole as Seen Today. The old Cassero above the town is now incorporated into the postwar Spanish Fortress of Sant'Elmo at the top of the hill.

entirely reliant upon Doria's fleet for a supply system that had often proved unsatisfactory when operating overland between Poggibonsi and the Camollia camp outside Siena. Bad weather at sea—galleys were fair-weather vessels—or the premature arrival of the Turkish fleet could leave him with no more attractive option than to join the besieged Spanish garrison of Orbetello. That Marignano decided to go through with the combined operation says a great deal for his strategic insight, and much for his nerve.[6]

Although fast, the march to the sea took longer than the three days for which supplies were carried. On Monday, 20 May, the army left Pienza, captured Castiglioncello, and camped at Castel di Piano. On Tuesday, as soon as the march started, it began to rain heavily "with a cold wind and much mist," and the discomfort of the soldiers was increased by their inability to reply to shots from Arcidosso. They spent a miserable night at Triana. On Wednesday they left camp in fine weather and reached Saturnia. On Thursday they camped at Marsiliana and on Friday they reached the coast at Ansedonia, where they received provisions from galleys in the Stagno di Orbetello. Some 65 miles had been covered in five days, over hilly terrain and in some bad weather. On Saturday, 25 May, the army moved along the sandy spit of land (known as the Tombolo di Feniglia) that linked Monte Argentario to the mainland and, after a sharp skirmish, established their camp at Pertuso, just beyond range of the guns of Port'Ércole.[7]

The Fortifications of Port'Ércole

Now a bustling resort town some two hours' drive from Rome (fig. 70), Port'Ércole in the mid-sixteenth century was a village of only about three hundred inhabitants, clinging to the steep, north-facing slope overlooking the harbor that gave the place its name.[8] The top of the hill was dominated by a small medieval castle with a square keep. Vestiges of the keep can still be seen in the lower levels of the great fortress built by Giovan Battista Camerini in the 1560s, when the place had become part of the Stato dei Presidii, the Spanish enclave in central Italy.[9] From the keep, two curtains, some 24 feet high, descended to the harbor wall. A number of the round mural towers shown on contemporary plans and in Vasari's fresco have survived and can be seen to offer little accommodation for defensive artillery (fig. 71). Indeed, the only recognizably modern fortification to appear on the early plans was the polygonal battery at the seaward end of the harbor wall. Guns placed here could flank the lower wall of the town and sweep the harbor entrance. A polygonal work containing two tiers of gun galleries can still be seen in this position and may well be the "casemate" surveyed in 1531 by

Fig. 71. Giorgio Vasari, The Capture of Port'Ércole. The line drawing simplifies the fresco so that we may pick out the major elements of the defense system. **A:** The sandy spit joining Mont'Argentario to the mainland. **B:** First Imperial camp at Pertuso. **C:** Piero Strozzi's escape by sea. **D:** The Rocca of Port'Ércole. **E:** Harbor of Port'Ércole, showing westward extension of waterline. **F:** Fort Galera (now site of Fort Filippo). **G:** Fort Guasparino. **H:** Fort Erculetto, surrounded by small boats from night attack. **J:** Fort Sant'Elmo. **K:** Fort Avvoltoio. **L:** Fort Stronco. **M:** Imperial batteries engaging the Stronco. **N:** Second Imperial Camp.

Baldassarre Peruzzi, who found it in serious disrepair and warned that "in a very short time [it] will fall completely into the sea."[10] Altogether, the fortifications were not impressive. The vulnerability of Port'Ércole was made plain in 1544 when it was captured, sacked, and burned by the Turks after an attack that could scarcely be called a siege.

During the War of Siena the defense of Port'Ércole became very much a French responsibility. Contemporary sources credit the key planning decisions to Thermes, Piero Strozzi, and his brother Leone—none of whom have left records of their own day-to-day activities.[11] Fragments of information, however, can be pieced together to give some idea of the construction program. Work seems to

have started on the forts (the plural form is used) in October 1552, when one hundred laborers were drafted from Siena to Port'Ércole.[12] At least one fort was finished and garrisoned by May 1553, when a Florentine officer visited the place in search of escaped galley slaves.[13] Marignano's scouts first reconnoitered the position in October 1554, by which time six forts had been built.[14] As we shall see, a seventh fort, which did not form part of the original scheme, was under construction in May 1555 when Port'Ércole was attacked. It was an impressive achievement for a normally underpopulated part of the dominio, which had suddenly become congested by an influx of foreign soldiers, sailors, and vivandieri. One letter from Siena acknowledges the real hardships of the local people, promising urgent measures to get them back into their own houses.[15]

No contemporary plans of the wartime fortification system are to be found. However, we do have a coherent eyewitness description of the works from the pen of Don Antonio da Montalvo, in his *Relazione della Guerra di Siena*. Montalvo was a Spanish officer who fought throughout the second phase of the War of Siena, after which he joined Cosimo's household, rising eventually to the office of chamberlain. Since he was resident in the Palazzo Vecchio while Vasari painted his *salone* frescoes, it is likely that he would have been consulted by the artist. From Montalvo we have the names and the general disposition of the seven forts, information which can be correlated with a modern topographical map as well as with other accounts of the fighting to give a plan of the defensive system.[16]

To the south, the offshore island of Erculetto had been fortified and armed with a gun that could fire onto the *cala sbarcadello,* the landing cove, indeed the only landing beach between the harbor and the Punta Avoltore. To the north of the harbor another fort, partly built of masonry, was sited on the mountainous promontory. The Forte della Galera, as it was known, overlooked the Cala Galera, swept the harbor, and covered the northern approaches to the village. However, Port'Èrcole was still exposed to attack from the hills that overlooked it from the southwest, and it was along this series of peaks that the other forts were located. Fort Guasparino protected the level approach to the medieval castle, and the remains of this fort (i.e. Guasparino) are probably beneath the site of the horn-work of the extant Spanish Rocca di Santa Barbara. Fort Sant'Elmo was below the hornwork on the saddle, occupying ground which offered a possible starting point for an attack on the curtain of old Port'Èrcole. Fort Avvoltoio occupied the high ground to the southwest of this saddle, and Fort Stronco a neighboring hill of the same height.

The Stronco was the key to Piero Strozzi's defensive system. It was, Montalvo tells us, bigger and stronger than the other forts and blocked the approaches to Port'Èrcole from the north and the west. Any attack from these directions would have to be delivered across a small but steeply banked stream followed by a steep uphill slope. To the south, however, a hill now known as the Poggio della Stella (from the Spanish fort of the same name) rises nearly 200 feet above the Stronco at a range of about 1,000 feet. Another saddle joined the Stronco to the Stella and this approach, which could be covered by long-range fire from the Stella, represented the only viable direction of attack on Strozzi's strongpoint. By October 1554, Marignano's scouts had identified the Poggio della Stella as the weak spot. "Maestro Giulio, the gunner," he wrote, "reckons the taking of Port'Èrcole is feasible and says that the hill they [the French] have fortified has another one above it."[17] Since then, Imperial plans for the siege of Port'Èrcole had been based on the capture of this neglected hill and it was the news of its fortification that had precipitated Marignano's decision to accelerate the expedition.

When Marignano reached Monte Argentario, he discovered the reason for the last-minute work on the Poggio della Stella. It seems that the site had been reconnoitered again early in May by Maestro Giulio and Captain Giovanni Pazzaglia, who found nothing to upset the long-standing plans. Shortly afterward, however, the French had been alerted to the danger by a bungled patrol from Orbetello. A Spanish officer had been captured by the French and, threatened with torture, revealed the Imperial plans. The French immediately began to fortify the hill "con ogni diligentia"; by the arrival of the Imperial army they had made considerable progress.[18] This last fort was known as Sant'Ippolito.

The Siege of Port'Ércole

When Marignano and his army arrived at Pertuso, they found that nine days' work had been completed on Sant'Ippolito "so that it is already in being and defensible, and the ground around it is so diabolical with trees and rocks that in fifteen days one could not level it for artillery, not even in twenty."[19] Of course, the difficulties of emplacing artillery were really irrelevant because the army had no guns on site at this time. The commander's choice lay between an immediate infantry assault of some danger against defensible but incomplete fortifications and delay, which would give Strozzi time to improve Sant'Ippolito and increase the risks to the exposed and unsupported army.

On the night of 26 May, Chiappino Vitelli left the camp at Pertuso with 1,500 German and Spanish foot and moved into position to storm Sant'Ippolito. Their route is described by Marignano only as "lungo e fastidioso"[20] but almost certainly took them through the heavily forested lower slopes of Monte Argentario to a position due west of Sant'Ippolito. Surprise was impossible, for as Montalvo explained, the Spaniards had to hack a path through the undergrowth with their swords, creating so much noise that when the fort was reached two hours before dawn, its garrison was thoroughly alert and standing to its defense.[21] The scaling ladders, however, were placed against the rampart in a number of places, and after an hour of fighting, the 150 defenders were overwhelmed. Simultaneous demonstrations in front of the other forts prevented relief.[22]

The pace of the attack then slackened. A large part of the army was moved around the island to camp behind Sant'Ippolito, almost certainly on the sloping ground above the landing beach, now the location of an estate of vacation chalets.[23] This move put the army into a good position from which to attack the remaining forts, but made them almost totally dependent on the galleys for supplies, and rendered them vulnerable to bombardment from the gun in Erculetto and even from the French galleys.[24] At this stage of the operation, the French galleys were not only able to bombard the Imperial army but made frequent trips to the Papal port of Civitavecchia to bring supplies into Port'Ércole. These breaches of neutrality were the subject of protests to Rome and a somewhat contradictory demand for similar facilities. Marignano, however, reserved his most bitter criticism for Andrea Doria, who with sixty-four galleys seemed unable to keep him either supplied or protected.[25] The final days of May saw further bad weather,[26] and it is not difficult to imagine the sodden spirits of the Imperial soldiers as they camped on the rain-swept slope above the beach, subjected to intermittent bombardments from Erculetto and the French galleys.

The problem of Erculetto was complicated by the fact that the Imperial galleys were separately commanded (and many of them owned) by Andrea Doria, who was reluctant to risk them against a shore battery. Following Marignano's complaints to Florence, it seems that some ducal pressure was used against Doria, because in the early hours of 2 June, Erculetto was attacked. Two galleys and a number of skiffs landed three hundred men on the island, and after an hour the fort was in Imperial hands. Nearly all of the one hundred defenders were killed in the fight or immediately afterward thrown into the sea to drown.[27] The landing beach was now open to the Imperialists.

At daylight the first artillery was brought ashore but was found to be in bad condition, "having broken carriages and other defects."[28] Attempts were then made to drag the piece that had been captured in Erculetto up to Sant'Ippolito, but these efforts proved unsuccessful "because of a shortage of pioneers as well as the roughness of the terrain."[29] In his letter dated 3 June, Marignano tried to shock Cosimo into recognition of his difficulties. Two defensible positions had been captured, he reported, and with forty days and proper supplies they would be confident of taking Port'Ércole. But, he notes, there is not much time; supplies are quite insufficient; only four pieces of useless artillery have been received; pioneers are few, in bad physical condition, and short of tools. In short, writes Marignano, the situation could become critical if the Turkish fleet should arrive before proper supplies have been lain in. Even so, he ends on a determined note, we are now preparing to attack the Stronco despite the difficulties of "these absolutely diabolical locations."[30]

Marignano's battery of the Stronco did not, however, begin until 7 June. By then more artillery must have been landed because shortages of gun carriages and wheels were identified as the main reasons why only six pieces could be brought into action. The artillery was not now the only problem. After many days of continuous skirmishing, the arquebusiers were running short of powder, lead, and match. These shortages combined to force the Imperial Council of War to decide on another bold stroke—an infantry assault on the Stronco.

Three hours after sunset on 8 June, the fort was assaulted on all sides by German and Spanish infantry. Marignano mentions "two assaults, each lasting more than an hour," which gives the impression that two consecutive assaults had been planned. Montalvo's account, however, makes it clear that the Germans and Spaniards were to have attacked simultaneously, but that because of the usual confusion in getting into position the two assaults were delivered separately and consecutively. The disorganization resulted in heavy casualties as well as failure to capture the fort. The general's account was probably not deliberately misleading. His letter was evidently written early on 9 June, for the first casualty figures ("not more than 100 killed and wounded") are corrected in two further dispatches bearing the same date, which revised the cost of the night attack upward to 100 killed and 400 wounded and, finally, to 125 killed and more than 500 wounded. Later a German deserter brought word that the enemy fatalities had been even higher; he delighted the Imperialists with the news that Piero Strozzi had left Port'Ércole with his two galleys; "he's pushed off, but God knows where."[31]

There can be little doubt that Strozzi's departure damaged the morale of the garrison. Contrary to the impression created by Montalvo and other Medici historians, however, resistance did not collapse immediately. Because the Imperialist attacks on the night of 8–9 June had been repulsed with heavy losses, Marignano decided to order no further assaults before establishing a new battery to the north of the Stronco and constructing a major trenchwork, which by 11 June was within 120 feet of the fort.[32] Two hours before sunset on 12 June the defenders of the Stronco attempted to break out through a sally port, but as luck would have it their attempt coincided with the changing of the guard in the siege works. The escaping defenders ran straight into both the old and the new guard and lost 150 men in the retreat.[33] The Stronco, of course, was captured.

Yet even this important loss did not precipitate a collapse. The Avoltoio now commanded the approaches to the port, and it was not until the night of 14–15 June that Marignano "planted" his battery against this position. Rain held up the bombardment on 14 June.[34] After a fine day's battery on 16 June, the Imperial troops were drawn up for an attack early on the following morning. A herald was sent forward to deliver a final summons, which to the surprise of the Imperialists was accepted by the Austrian commanding the fort. As an Imperial rebel, this officer had an obvious motive for wishing to surrender on terms. While terms were being discussed, however, Spanish soldiers broke into the fort: the garrison panicked and fled down the hill towards Port'Ércole, vigorously pursued by the Spaniards.[35] Those who reached the town were cut down as they begged for quarter on their knees in front of the locked gates. In the confusion, a number of Spanish soldiers managed to scale the wall and, true to form, immediately abandoned the chase and started to loot. At this point the defenders, "to gain goodwill," opened the gates, and a general sack followed.[36] With the main objective already in Imperial hands it was not difficult to persuade the garrisons of the Galera, Sant'Elmo, and Guasparino forts to surrender, so that by the end of the day the castle was the only position held by the French. At dawn on 18 June, Monsieur De la Chapelle des Ursins and 400 men surrendered at discretion.[37]

The Vasari Fresco

Two days after the surrender, Marignano's men began to demolish the forts, "except those above Port'Ércole and the Galera."[38] By the time Giorgio Vasari began to work on the frescoes for the Palazzo Vecchio,[39] both Guasparino and the Galera had almost certainly been obliterated by the postwar Spanish works. For this reason we are compelled to treat all our pictorial records of the siege and its fortifications with caution.[40] In Vasari's fresco we may have the most accurate record of the architectural forms of the six forts. None of the documentary sources for the siege mentions the shape of individual forts. However, the pentagon of the Galera and the square plan of the Stronco are standard traces. The half-moon trace of the Avoltoio is unusual; but Belluzzi's treatise illustrates a similarly shaped work in Normandy, which must have been constructed during the middle of the century.[41] It would be surprising if Sant'Elmo had been equipped with mid-curtain ravelins, although these features—which did not become common until the seventeenth century—are illustrated in Francesco de'Marchi's treatise, written not long after this time.[42]

Vasari's fresco (fig. 71) thus provides useful confirmation of the layout of the forts as well as all the principal events of the siege. His viewpoint is taken from the site of Sant'Ippolito, which gives foreshortened views of the Tombolo di Fenigalia (left background) and Erculetto (right middle distance), both of which are recorded with sufficient topographical accuracy to suggest that sketches were drawn in situ, although not necessarily by Giorgio himself. This is not to say that the view is reproduced "photographically." The natural topography has been artistically distorted in order to show the ground that in reality is hidden from Sant'Ippolito by the Poggio delle Bicche (the site of the Avoltoio). The Avoltoio should have been shown at the same elevation as the Stronco, but has been depressed to reveal Sant'Elmo, the harbor, and the curtain wall of the village of Port'Ércole. On the other hand, the plan relationship of these works is well recorded; with the solitary exception of Erculetto, which seems to have been placed a little too high on the fresco—no doubt for compositional reasons.

Vasari provides a self-justification for similar topographical distortion in his panorama of the Siege of Florence of twenty-five years earlier in the Fourth *Ragionamento* (fig. 72). On the second day of their tour of the Palazzo Vecchio, Vasari and the prince have arrived in the Room of Clement VII. "Now look, Your Excellency, at this picture in which Florence is shown 'al naturale' from the hilly side [i.e., from the south] and measured in a way that varies little from the truth." The prince then asks the artist how he gets the view "that to my eyes is different from others that I have seen portrayed." Vasari agrees, "but one has to appreciate how difficult it is to tell this 'history' by means of a natural

Fig. 72. Giorgio Vasari, View of the City of Florence during the Siege of 1529–30. Among the architects active during the siege were Antonio da Sangallo the Younger and Peruzzi, on the Imperialist side, and Michelangelo, for republican Florence. The scene is rich in topographical, military, and anecdotal detail.

view." From the hills, he argues, one cannot see what goes on at the bottom of the valleys, and besides, Monte del Gallo and Giramonte block one's view of the Porta San Miniato and Porta San Niccolò and a number of other important places. To ensure that his picture of a large battlefield was "exact" and "fully comprehensive," the artist used what he clearly considered to be a novel means of site sketching, which produced a necessarily distorted perspective. Vasari then relates how he mounted rooftops with a compass and made sketches along a northerly bearing. Each linear sketch included "hills, houses, and closer places" (i.e., background, middle distance, and foreground). By adding together a series of such sketches, each one correct along its own bearing, he was able to produce a composite view that compressed an enormous panorama into about ten feet of measured wall space. The view included all of the army and put each senior officer at his post or the house where he lodged. After all this, says the artist, it was easy to sketch in the far background; the hills of Fiesole, the Uccelatoio, the beach of Settignano, the plain of San Salvi, and, finally, all the plain of Prato with the edge of the hills up to Pistoia.[43]

Here Vasari advances the proposition that pictorial distortion can help one to get to the essential truth of the situation, an interesting paradigm of the artist's concept of *natura* and typical of the late sixteenth-century *maniera*. At Florence the "truth" for Vasari comprised documentary facts—location of batteries, the quarters of senior officers, and so on—as well as a somewhat idealized view of the city, an entire city, surrounded by its enemies. The idealized depiction of "Florence as Florence versus the rest" was perhaps a deliberately neutral statement for Medici clients, who must have entertained somewhat ambiguous attitudes to that episode in the history of the dynasty. Moreover, it is significant that a large part of the discussion that follows takes the form of tea-time chatter about friends and allies of the family who served in the Imperial camp—conversation clearly designed to demonstrate the artist's familiarity with the events depicted as well as to ingratiate himself with his patron.

At Port'Ércole, Vasari's idealizing tendency must be seen to be motivated by artistic ("getting to the essence of things") and documentary requirements. The historian's concern for a complete record of the fortifications and the fighting has led him to compress all the main events of the siege into one picture. The first Imperial camp is shown at Pertuso: while tents in the right middle distance represent the second camp above the landing beach with its beached ships. Erculetto can be seen surrounded by a cluster of boats (the night attack of 2 June), while in the background Strozzi's galley is pursued toward Civitavecchia (his flight on 8 June). The figure on horseback is probably Chiappino Vitelli (not Marignano as is normally supposed), who, with characteristic Vasarian tact, is depicted from behind to avoid representing his enormous protruding belly, famous in the camps of Europe.[44] The mounted officer is at the head of a column of soldiers which follows the route of Vitelli's night march to the assault on Sant'Ippolito. From this latter position attacks are being launched against the Stronco, supported by the six pieces of artillery mentioned in Marignano's dispatches. The artist has done his homework. It is in fact an extremely detailed and well-informed depiction of a complex series of events, all of which are supported by alternative documentary evidence.[45]

The Defensive System—an Evaluation

It is necessary to draw a distinction between the functions of the superficially similar systems of forts at Port'Ércole and Siena. At Siena the French defended Osservanza, Lecceto, Belcaro, Monastero, and other outposts in an effort to prevent the interruption of their lines of communication with Montalcino and the Maremma. When these positions were captured by the Imperialists, they were used in the blockading role advocated by Maggi and Castriotto. At Port'Ércole the availability of a good harbor and the restricted land access to Monte Argentario meant that any blockade would have to be carried out by the fleet. The seven forts must be regarded, therefore, not as a means of controlling lines of communication into the port but, simply, as an obstacle. In these terms, far from accepting Montalvo's verdict of "enormous expense but little consideration,"[46] Port'Ércole's fortifications must be seen as highly innovative.

By the middle of the sixteenth century, the bastion-rampart system was well understood in Italy, even if sometimes imperfectly applied. The essential characterisics of its evolution had been the improvement of the obstacle components (the rampart and the ditch) and the development of the bastion itself as an offensive component capable of matching the firepower of the besieging batteries. In a properly designed system the flank batteries covered every part of the trace, while the face batteries sent fire far out into the surrounding country. It was not until the second half of the eighteenth century that the theorists Montalembert[47] and Carnot[48] took this concept toward its logical conclusion with the proposition that, given sufficient firepower, it would be possible greatly to reduce the physical obstacles of ditch and rampart. Carnot's theory of vertical fire—by which the approaches to a fortification could be saturated with plunging fire from mortars— appealed to some intellectuals in the Prussian army but was furiously attacked by British and French traditionalists, who would no doubt have been astounded to discover that some 250 years earlier Francesco de' Marchi had suggested that a well-planned pattern of fire could allow one to dispense altogether with continuous physical obstacles.

Francesco was led to this proposal when he considered the defense of an anchorage by a number of isolated forts built in the sea. In the figure illustrating the concept (fig. 73) he shows that all internal and external faces of the forts could be "cleaned" by gunfire; and he argues that no ship, however large or well armed, would dare to penetrate an area of certain destruction. Francesco then expands on the wider implications of his idea. Towers (for which we can read, detached works) can be used on terrain broken by rivers, lakes, marshes, or steep valleys. "In many places," he concludes, "they make shelters where one defends the other, and no wall or other work is built from one to the other."[49]

In the absence of any specific statement of intentions it is impossible to know for certain whether in fact Port'Ércole's forts were conceived as a system of mutually supporting works. Yet the treatise writer Girolamo Cataneo evidently assumed this to be the case for his criticism of the Port'Ércole system is based on a kind of domino theory—if one fort falls, the others will follow. The Sienese mistake, suggests Girolamo Cataneo, stemmed from initial economies in the defense of Port'Ércole, which they should have realized would leave them unable to check a breakthrough. "Because of some ill-considered scheme of fortification," he wrote, "it happened that as soon as one of their [forts] was lost . . . in a short while they lost all the others."[50]

Girolamo Cataneo's comments were published a number of years after the fall of Port'Ércole. To a readership who probably remembered that the siege had been a fast one, his criticism might well have suggested that the entire defensive system had collapsed after the initial loss of Sant'Ippolito. As we have seen, this was not so. Sant'Ippolito was captured on the night of 26–27 May; the Stronco

Fig. 73. Francesco de' Marchi, Sea Forts from *Della architettura militare.* The placement of "floating bastions" is a seaborne equivalent of the land-based forts of the Port'Ércole defense.

held until 12 June; and it was only after the fall of the Avoltoio on 17 June that the defenses of Port'Ércole could have been said to have collapsed. Both the Stronco and the Avoltoio were surrendered, not taken by storm. Even making allowances for the difficulties of the Imperial army, the performance of individual forts can be compared favorably with the resistance of positions such as Monastero, Crevole, or Casole.

There can be little doubt that the French failure to fortify Sant'Ippolito until nine days before the arrival of the Imperial army was a serious error of judgment. Although Marignano reckoned the position to be defensible, the fortification was not yet complete and, because of the speed of construction, was probably not as big as it should have been. On the night of 26–27 May the garrison of 150 men was outnumbered 10 to 1 by Chiappino Vitelli's force and received no support from the other forts. Marignano reported diversionary demonstrations in front of the other forts, which seem to have been quite sufficient to keep the defenders inside their walls. A few days later, however, the Imperial commander reported shortages of small arms ammunition (powder, lead, and match) "because we are continuously in action a large quantity of it is expended."[51] This suggests that after the fall of Sant'Ippolito the French had started to counterattack more energetically.

One is also struck by the apparent inability of the forts to support each other by artillery fire. Only three guns replied to the battery of the Stronco.[52] Yet the Imperial pieces were located between Sant'Ippolito and the Stronco and should have been vulnerable to counterbattery fire from the French guns in the Avoltoio. After the fall of the Stronco, Marignano reported that only three small pieces and some *moschettoni* had been found in this the biggest and strongest of the forts.[53] Erculetto had been armed with a single medium-caliber gun and a number of *archibusoni*.[54] Yet when Port'Ércole itself was captured, the Imperialists found a vast store of munitions as well as "four full cannon and many other pieces and *moschetti*."[55] Had these guns been brought into action against the inadequate Imperial artillery, events at the Stronco and the Avoltoio might well have taken a different turn. Strozzi can justly be blamed for failing to make proper use of available artillery to provide the mutual fire support that was the sine qua non of a system of forts.

Other criticisms of the system seem to be less merited. Indeed, when one visits what Montalvo called "this strange site,"[56] it is difficult to see how the Spaniard could justify his strictures on the cost and the lack of consideration of Strozzi's system. Seven forts no doubt cost a lot of money; but it is unlikely that their combined cost would exceed that of a single rampart across the peninsula to the south of the harbor. In both practical and military terms the use of individual forts can be defended. Each outwork could be defensible relatively quickly—witness the construction time of Sant'Ippolito—and improved later. One or two well-placed works, the Stronco and the Avoltoio for instance, would provide a good deal of protection for the port; while the strength of the system would be increased with each subsequent addition. By contrast, a continuous rampart would remain indefensible until completion and, once breached or escaladed, would present no further obstacles to the enemy.

8

CHANGING PATTERNS OF MILITARY ARCHITECTURE AND SIEGE WARFARE

The End of the War

FORTUNE favored the bold at Port'Ércole. Marignano's forced march to the sea, followed by nearly three weeks of fierce fighting, saw the Imperialists in possession of the principal Franco-Sienese port by the middle of June 1555. When ninety galleys of the Turkish fleet arrived off Elba on 11 July, Imperial forces had already taken the villages of Capalbio, Castiglione della Pescaia, Scarlino, and Gavoranno and were preparing to assault Grosseto, the major town in the Maremma. Despite these gains, the Turks presented a potent threat. Raiding parties went ashore at a dozen places, and a force of some 3,000 Janissaries seized Campiglia and was poised to fall upon Piombino. Since many of Marignano's troops were dispersed in the recently captured positions, it seemed for a few desperate hours that Piombino itself might replace Port'Ércole as an enemy base. The situation was retrieved by Chiappino Vitelli, who managed to catch the lightly armed Janissaries between a body of German foot and his own cavalry and drive them with heavy losses back to their ships.[1] The Turks withdrew to raid Elba and Corsica before returning to North Africa with their captives and loot.

With the Maremma coast secured, Marignano's exhausted and depleted forces marched back to the Val d'Orcia, where, in their absence, the French had reoccupied Pienza and Crevole. By any measure, French and Sienese resistance should have been crushed during the winter of 1555–56. Events in Northern Europe, however, contrived to prolong the struggle of Siena's republic-in-exile. By Christmas, negotiations were in progress at Vaucelles for the truce which was to confirm war-weary France and Spain in their territorial holdings for five years.[2] The truce went into effect in April 1556—too late to save Cetona, which was captured and sacked on 3 February, or Sarteano, which was defended for nearly six weeks until 2 February in the final contested siege of the war.[3] Outbreaks of fighting disturbed the truce for another three years as each side took reprisals for breaches of the peace. Montalcino, Grosseto, Chiusi, and Radicofani finally surrendered to Cosimo in 1559. Then, under the Treaty of Cateau-Cambrésis, France renounced all of her Italian claims. Italy enjoyed the first peace since the French invasion of 1494, and Siena retreated from the central stage of action to become a part of Florentine Tuscany.

The Postwar Building Campaigns

Peace was marked by a final and sustained fortress-building program as the victors consolidated their gains. Philip II, to whom Siena had been ceded on the abdication of the emperor Charles V, retained Orbetello and Monte Argentario for the Spanish crown when he granted Cosimo the rest of his conquests to repay the Imperial war debt. Orbetello was defended with a new land front, Monte Argentario with a chain of coastal watchtowers, and Port'Ércole with a complex of new forts designed by Giovan Battista Camerini, Cosimo's military architect.[4] Over the ruins of Strozzi's last structure, Sant'Ippolito, the Spaniards built a small outwork, Forte Stella. Around the Franco-Sienese works above the town rose the Rocca di Santa Barbara, with its gigantic hornwork. To the north of the harbor, on the site of the Galera, the hill was crowned with a new work, Forte Filippo. Peruzzi's casemate, much repaired, covered the southern entrance to the harbor: the northern shoreline was swept by a new battery, the Forte Santa Caterina. The fortresses of the Stato dei Presidii were the only formerly Sienese positions to see further active service when they were attacked by the French in the War of Spanish Succession in the early eighteenth century.

Cosimo's building program was even more ambitious. Grosseto was given an entirely new enceinte during the 1560s, comprising six massive bastions approximately along the foundations of the wartime Sienese fortifications. Sorano, close to the unfriendly duchy of Castro, was strengthened to resist subversion in the remote and mountainous south. A new citadel was built at Radicofani, dominating the Papal frontier and the pilgrim route along the via Cassia. The work of fortification continued at Montepulciano, which had been part of the Fiorentino for many years and controlled the Sienese settlements in the lower Val di Chiana most effectively. A major new fortress was begun on a hill just outside Lucignano. Montalcino's wartime works were dismantled, the rocca was repaired, and a single gigantic bastion was constructed on the side of the castle that had once been overlooked by the Spanish positions in 1553.[5]

At Siena the Camollia outworks were slighted to provide materials for a new massive citadel, which was begun in almost indecent haste in 1561 (fig. 74). Two years later Baldassarre Lanci had completed an enormous rectangular en-

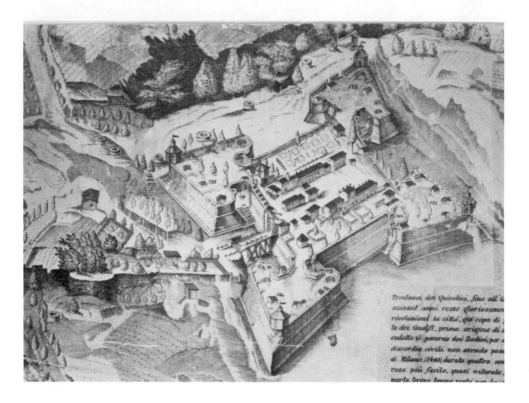

Fig. 74. Baldassarre Lanci, Fortress of Santa Barbara, Siena. This detail from Francesco Vanni's map of Siena shows the ruined remains of Peruzzi's bastion at the Sportello di San Prospero in the foreground to the left. Also visible are the mysterious circular works in the area just beyond the bastions facing San Domenico.

ceinte with four bastions, sited above those parts of the Spanish and Franco-Sienese works that crowned the hill of San Prospero.[6] It was a severe and simple fortress, enlivened only by the Medici arms (fig. 75). The hornwork that lay beneath the Lizza gardens and made the earlier citadel an integral part of Siena's northern walls was demolished. Cosimo's new citadel was isolated from the city it overlooked. When Michel de Montaigne approached the citadel too closely in 1581, he was driven off by the sentries with insults and stones.[7]

There was much skill but little variety to be seen in the regular polygonal layouts of the fortresses in occupied South Tuscany. They represented the new orthodoxy of bastioned fortification and a massive investment of money which must have strained even Florentine and Spanish treasuries. The earlier generation of Sienese fortifications, however, exemplified an experimental phase of modern fortification design. And in the middle years of the century one could still speak, as did Giancarlo Severini in his study of the fortification work of Giuliano da Sangallo, of military architectures—in the plural.[8]

Fig. 75. The Stemma of Cosimo de' Medici, Fortress of Santa Barbara, Siena. These elegant figures are located on three of the salients of the bastions.

Baldassarre Peruzzi's Designs

The best-known parts of Siena's fortification system were the bastions designed by Peruzzi. When built, they excited considerable interest outside the republic. Letters came from as far away as Milan asking for information and drawings of works that were evidently considered to have added greatly to the strength of the city. Since the sixteenth century, however, they have generally been treated disparagingly and regarded more as throwbacks to the towers of Francesco di Giorgio than as part of the developing tradition of the Italian bastion.[9] Of course, it is true that by the mid-sixteenth century the development of the bastion had led to the general use of much lower and wider bastions of the gun-platform type; indeed, by the beginning of our period many such works had already been built in Italy. By the mid-sixteenth century, too, covered casemates had been generally abandoned in favor of works open to the sky, and casemates remained little used until their revival in the late seventeenth century as a defense against explosive shells.[10] In the 1520s and 1530s, however, many leading military architects made use of tiered casemated designs. Leoni's bastions at Verona and Antonio da Sangallo's double bastion at Rome were certainly not backward-looking. In northern Europe, casemated bastions with a number of floors of guns were the rule rather than the exception at this time.[11] In this context, Peruzzi's designs were not really out of step with current practice. They also served well in a limited and rather special role, namely, the defense of Siena's gates and the weak area of Camollia. Here the sites were restricted because of the steep slope of the ground away from the walls, and it was entirely sensible to obtain a concentration of defensive firepower by stacking the guns at more than one level. At San Viene, three tiers of casemates were provided, including a vaulted upper gun platform. A lower work would have been denied a level field of fire onto the ridge which overlooked the bastion and the gate from the north. An uncovered gun platform would have been dangerously exposed to fire from the same northern ridge. In short, all of the characteristics of the San Viene bastion which identify it as old-fashioned are explicable on strictly functional grounds.

The same is true of the much more unusual fortino at Camollia. Shaped like a bastion in plan, it seems to have served as a pillbox, accommodating a large number of relatively small guns capable of bringing considerable firepower to bear on the ground below the Camollia wall. It is difficult to identify precise contemporary parallels with Peruzzi's fortino, although the circular advanced work at Colle di Val d'Elsa and many of the ditchworks illustrated in the treatise of Francesco di Giorgio Martini contain similarities. So far as we know, the arrangement of a double tier of galleries housing as many as twenty-seven gun positions (possibly more in the original) is unique for a work of this small size. It was also tactically effective, bringing much of the low ground that approached the northern walls into the defensive fire plan and doing so at relatively small expense.

Fully to understand Peruzzi's entire system of fortification, we have to see it as a modification to the medieval wall. This point applies to Peruzzi's bastions, but there is physical evidence that the wall itself was modified in a number of places to incorporate gun embrasures, the best example being the double tier of embrasures in the curtain between Porta Laterina and Porta San Marco. Traces of embrasures—now blocked—are also to be seen between Porta San Viene and the adjacent Peruzzi bastion, in the curtain between Porta Camollia and the Peruzzi fortino, in the barbicans to Porta Ovile, Porta San Viene, and Porta Romana, and in the square medieval tower beside the Barriera San Lorenzo. When these works were carried out is difficult to say, but the size of the openings suggests the late fifteenth century or early sixteenth century, and some of the brickwork detailing is very similar to that in Peruzzi's own buildings. Yet even with these improvements, Peruzzi's remained a limited scheme, amounting to no more than the reinforcement of an enceinte that remained substantially medieval. When we recall the length of time demanded for the construction of the four-teenth- and fifteenth-century walls and the economic burden of Peruzzi's five bastions, it is hardly surprising that the Sienese went no further at this time toward complete urban refortification. Complete refortification was probably considered unnecessary from a military point of view as well as prohibitively costly. All of the early sixteenth-century schemes of comprehensive urban refortification—involving new rampart curtains as well as bastions—were for flat sites: the extension of Ferrara (ca. 1492), Treviso (1509), Padua (1509), and the first angle-bastioned enceinte of Civitavecchia (1515).[12] These places could be attacked from many directions, while Siena's irregular topography of sharp ridges and long, deep valleys offered only a limited number of vulnerable approaches. A handful of well-placed works provided, if not complete security, at least significant improvements without altering the traditional political character of the city's defenses.

The scheme of urban fortification that offers the closest architectural parallel to Peruzzi's Sienese project is probably that for Urbino (fig. 76), where small, tall, but not nearly so elegant bastions were added in the early 1520s by Giovanni Battista Comandino at a few key points on an otherwise impregnable hilltop enceinte.[13] This selective approach was shared with Michelangelo's scheme—

Fig. 76. G. B. Comandino, Bastion below the Convent of Santa Chiara, Urbino. Comandino's bastions at Urbino have been more heavily restored than those of Peruzzi; in a number of instances stone cornices have been replaced with concrete. This bastion appears to be in relatively good condition.

carried out simultaneously with that of Peruzzi—for the defense of the last Florentine republic, which in 1529 was preparing to meet an assault from the combined Imperial and Papal armies.[14] Michelangelo placed his elaborate earthworks at threatened gates and embarked upon a new rampart-and-bastion fortification only for the San Miniato sector, an area of high ground overlooking the southern defenses and offering the new artillery a field of fire into the reinforced medieval walls and the city itself. This kind of selective extension, rather than comprehensive reconstruction, was to be the hallmark of Siena's later-sixteenth-century schemes of fortification.

The Spanish Citadel

Although the Spanish citadel was not conceived primarily as an improvement to the city defenses, its outer works eventually formed an important element in the northern fortifications. With their curious banana-shaped trace, the Spanish works were much better adapted to the defense of the city than was Cosimo's later fortress, with its rectangular plan and acutely angled bastions.[15] The Spanish works presented two stretches of curtain and the faces of three bastions to the Prato and the Camollia ridge—the main sources of danger to the city. During the siege of 1554–55, the French were able to mount a large weight of cannon on San Prospero with which to engage the Imperial batteries on the Prato. To mount a heavy weight of artillery was, after all, one of the principal functions of the new military architecture. As Machiavelli put it, "More guns beat less."[16]

Could modified medieval works have served equally well? Evidently the medieval wall was modified yet again to provide further gun positions during the siege. The rear of the wall along Via Malta (from Porta Camollia to Peruzzi's fortino) shows clear signs of rough openings probably dating from this period; and the defenders certainly demolished parts of this wall to accommodate heavy guns during the siege.[17] This kind of gun position, however, was in many ways much less desirable than an open and wide bastion or rampart; guns pointed through small holes in a thick wall would have had very limited traverse. Large unsupported openings at a low level would have risked weakening the whole structure. Gunners working near such openings would have been vulnerable to falling masonry shot away from the wall above them. Although all of these shortcomings could be tolerated in an emergency, purpose-built bastions and ramparts provided a much more flexible base for artillery operations. The earthwork parapet could quickly be adapted to provide embrasures for extra guns and could be built up or repaired by sandbags and gabions. Earthworks, whether turfed or lined with a brick or stone revetment, tended to absorb incoming shot.

If the forward positions suffered particularly bad damage, earthwork and timber platforms could be built behind them to provide alternative gun emplacements. Should a bastion or rampart curtain be breached, the opening could be swept with gunfire from the adjacent bastion. In short, there were substantial functional advantages to a properly built rampart-and-bastion system—even one that employed nonpermanent materials.

Earthwork Construction

Here we should draw attention to a factor that is often overlooked in the balance of advantage between medieval and Early Modern fortification systems. The bastion and rampart system in its most basic forms used simple building materials: earth, turf, loose rubble infill, bundles of brushwood and twigs, rough green timber for reinforcement, and the wicker gabions which formed the sandbag of Early Modern warfare. Many Sienese documents from the siege speak of the difficulties faced by the civic authorities attempting to provide sufficient quantities of these raw materials. Numerous sorties had to be made to collect timber and brushwood, and the use of wood for cooking and heating was strictly controlled. [18] However, simple building materials were available locally: certainly much more readily available than the bricks, stone, and iron needed in permanent fortifications. All that was required to take full advantage of earthwork materials was picks, shovels, axes, wheelbarrows, and large numbers of laborers. Indeed, the value of a well-motivated, able-bodied civilian population for this kind of work is another much underrated aspect of the siege. Conventionally, the civil population is regarded merely as so many useless mouths to feed, or to be driven from the city when food supplies became critical. Yet the existence of a large civilian labor force—which included all able-bodied men, women, and children—permitted the defenders of Siena not merely to construct new earthworks but to repair damage during the siege, to build retrenchments behind threatened sectors, and to throw up a large number of outworks commanding the approaches to the city. [19] These outworks became the third important element in Siena's fortification system.

In the months immediately before the siege the civilian population was mobilized to construct three outworks on the Camollia ridge, a curtain connecting them to the front, and a trenchwork which was to have joined these forts to San Prospero. In the event, the Camollia forts were captured practically without resistance on the night of 26 January 1554, the penalty for inexcusable lack of judgment and decision on the part of the Franco-Sienese command. Some of the opprobrium for this setback seems to have attached to the forts themselves, which after so much effort from the civilians gave so little service. In their disappointment the Sienese chroniclers hint at almost treasonable misguidedness on the part of those who built the works where they could be taken and used against the city.[20] The system of seven detached forts surrounding Port'Ércole came in for similar criticism. Girolamo Cataneo saw them as an intrinsically insecure defensive concept; to Montalvo they were both expensive and ill-considered.

Yet fortification by means of outworks represented a policy that was both economical and well adapted to the topography of towns like Siena and Port'Ércole. Forts were also militarily effective when properly defended. At Port'Ércole some of the detached forts resisted assault for many days and, considered as a whole, the system took three weeks to fall. Clearly the forts at Camollia could have been expected to hold out for very much longer than they did.

Elsewhere on the approaches to Siena the tactical value of relatively simple

Fig. 77. Albrecht Dürer, The Cannon. Dürer shows a cannon on the road, with its trail hoisted up and mounted on a second bogey and the wheels chocked to prevent it slipping back down the slope. As many as twelve yoke of oxen and a much larger number of horses were needed to move heavy pieces over rough terrain. The operation illustrated by Dürer seems to have run into difficulties, and there appears to be roadside conference between drover (left), gunner (in soldier's uniform, leaning on the barrel), and various officials.

outworks was demonstrably much greater. Small Franco-Sienese garrisons in Lecceto, Belcaro, and Monastero helped to keep open the western and southern routes into the city from January to the beginning of April 1554. Yet none of these was strongly fortified. Lecceto was a hamlet with rudimentary medieval walls. Belcaro was a villa ingeniously remodeled by Peruzzi inside oval medieval walls on what in northern Europe would be described as a motte.[21] Monastero was a religious house, partly fortified by low earthworks at the time of its capture. Although a number of new earthworks were constructed between these places and Siena, the entire western defensive system evidently fell far short of the standards expected of modern fortifications, for when attacked or even seriously threatened, they quickly capitulated. The same was true of the other outlying Sienese fortifications: Sant'Abundio to the south; the Certosa di Montecelso, Santa Regina, and Torre di Vignano to the east; and the monastery of the Osservanza to the north. The military value of the outworks was not determined solely by their ability to resist attack—an ability that clearly had its limitations—but by their very existence, a fact which compelled Marignano to divide his forces in attempts to suppress them. Unless constantly and closely patrolled, the outworks threatened persistent trouble, for they served as staging posts for block-ade runners on their way into the city and as secure bases for raiders striking at Imperial communications. To reduce them by bombardment meant diverting men and guns from the principal siege. To be sure, modern artillery when properly handled would quickly bring down old-fashioned or hastily constructed works, but to bring the guns into position was frequently no easy task, as we have shown.

The Artillery

The count of Santa Fiora's expedition to bring the guns from Montepulciano for the bombardment of Siena is well documented, allowing us to be precise about the speed of artillery transport under different weather and road conditions.[22] The expedition took three days to move two half-cannon from Monastero to Pienza by way of Asciano and San Giovanni d'Asso, a distance of about 26 miles. Thus Santa Fiora was able to achieve a daily average of approximately 9 miles with two medium-caliber guns, over hilly but not steep country, in good winter weather (fig. 77). The occasional sharp frost would help to keep the roads firm. On the way back from Montepulciano the expedition hauled nine cannon and one half-cannon to Lucignano, where they collected another three cannon. For the most part the Val di Chiana–Piano di Sentino road runs over level ground, but after some weeks of rain the artillery train was able to achieve a daily average of just over three miles for the 43-mile journey. When we consider individual stages of the journey, it seems likely that some extraneous factors, such as the desirability of camping at or in an Imperial-held town, influenced the distance traveled in a day. Thus, the fastest stage recorded was the 5 miles traveled on 3 January between Rapolano and Grillo. This was followed, however, by the slowest phase of the journey when the artillery train took three days to move a little over 7 miles across the broken country between Grillo and Montaperti.[23]

The slow movement of Cosimo's artillery train in support of Don Garcia's 1553 campaign against Monticchiello and Montalcino so extended the first operation that the second was unfinished when the approach of the Turkish fleet forced the Imperialists to raise the siege. Transport problems compelled Marignano to rely on Andrea Doria's fleet for his artillery at Port'Ércole and forced the general to use only two medium-caliber pieces for the mobile actions around Siena in the early months of 1554.

Ammunition posed further difficulties. In response to a specific request from Marignano, a pair of half-culverins had been supplied for operations against the "small places."[24] Early in March 1554, the provveditore of the arsenal at Poggio Imperiale informed Cosimo that all of the stockpiled ammunition had already been issued to the army outside Siena, but that Marignano and Albizzi were now demanding powder and ball from the fortress magazine.[25] By the end of the month the general was protesting directly to the duke that his demands for iron balls for the precious half-culverins had been met with an offer of quite unsuitable stone shot.[26] The incident seriously delayed operations in the field. It also provided a classic illustration of the difficulties that bedeviled the use of nonstandard calibers. The exhaustion of balls for a particularly heavily-used pair of guns, employing custom-made projectiles, put those weapons out of action just as surely as enemy fire. Shortages of guns, ammunition, gunners, drovers, and oxen—together with defects in the equipment—meant that the effective artillery of an army in the field was a small fraction of its paper strength.

The quality of the gunnery also left much to be desired. This is not to deny that individual sixteenth-century gunners were sometimes capable of surprising feats of marksmanship. Monluc's sniper managed to put shots accurately into the Spanish battery on the Ravacciano ridge from the Castellaccia, a range of at least 2,000 feet. Another Sienese marksman gave Concino a scare when he put a shot into the senior Imperial officers' quarters at the Palazzo dei Diavoli, about one mile north of the Franco-Sienese batteries at Camollia or San Prospero.[27] The skill of "Il Lupo," who served a saker on the campanile of San Miniato al Monte, was one of the legends of the siege of Florence.[28] These men were artists: the élite of the "brotherhood" of gunners who jealously guarded the secrets of their private powder formulas and continued for much of the sixteenth century to regard themselves more as craftsmen privateers than as rank-and-file soldiers.[29] But such feats should not blind us to the generally low performance of the artillery in this war. The set-piece bombardments of Montalcino and Siena achieved only trifling damage to relatively insubstantial targets. Only in their rates of fire did the performance of Don Garcia's and Marignano's gunners achieve the standards set out in the technical treatises.[30]

These facts of the artillerists' life may take us some way toward an explanation of the defense of positions which, in the conventional military-architectural terms of the mid-sixteenth century, can only be described as obsolete.

In February 1554, two weeks after the surprise attack on the Camollia forts, Marignano advised Cosimo of the need to capture Monteriggioni (fig. 78). At that time the Imperial general was of the opinion that more artillery would be needed than the two pieces then available for mobile operations.[31] It was not until the end of August, after the victory at Marciano, that Marignano was able to collect sufficient troops and artillery to launch a full-scale attack on the fortress that had threatened Imperial communications for seven months. On 28 August, a battery of four cannon and two half-cannon created "a good breach"; the next day the fortress was surrendered.[32]

That the walls immortalized by Dante[33] were breached in a single day will surprise no one who has visited Monteriggioni (fig. 79). Yet on the evidence of contemporary reports these quintessentially medieval structures were considered a significant obstacle. Marignano found "the wall very strong" and advised that "with very little expense Your Excellency will make the place very strong."[34] Montalvo described the place as "fortified *alla moderna.*"[35] Concino quoted Jacopo Tabusso, the newly appointed governor of the fortress, "The place is very important . . . and truly he says that he gives to Your Excellency the most beautiful fortress in Italy."[36] Concino also provided details of these highly regarded fortifications. The walls themselves, he said, were 16 braccia (33 feet) high and just over 8 palmi (5 feet) thick, with a circumference of some 650 paces. The outer works took the form of a "steep almost precipitous" scarp, 32 braccia (66 feet) high and with a perimeter of 1,000 paces "of good measure." Between the wall and the scarp was a small ditch providing cover for arquebusiers and others, and a wide space overlooked by the walls.[37] Evidently the modernization of Monteriggioni's medieval fortifications involved the construction of a wide earthwork platform; perhaps as much as 30 or 40 paces broad but certainly wide enough— as Concino reports—for the lower 6 braccia (13 feet) of curtain to be shielded from the Imperial artillery fire. Probably the scarp would have been staked or palisaded. Certainly it would have been swept with fire from the upper ditch and, very likely, from the curtain and the towers.

Monteriggioni is a striking but by no means exceptional example of a modified

Fig. 78. Monteriggioni as Seen Today. The *glacis* is now barely visible and is slowly being eroded by the vineyards that climb up almost to the walls. The walls, too, have been much changed. As a result of an overzealous modern restoration, the towers were raised in reinforced concrete to make the walls better conform to Dante's poetic image.

medieval structure which was evidently considered not merely defensible but formidable by the soldiers of the mid-sixteenth century. Such a verdict is surprising to those who have been brought up to accept the vulnerability—some would say, indefensibility—of medieval works when confronted by modern artillery. Our study of actual siege operations in the War of Siena suggests that this view needs to be qualified in a number of ways. First, even major set-piece bombardments such as those of Montalcino or Siena could be much less effective in practice than the somewhat hysterical descriptions of 1494 might lead one to expect. Second, the very real limitations on the availability and movement of guns meant that fortified positions of only moderate strength would rarely have to face heavy artillery. Third, the tactics of siege warfare current in the middle years of the century often made somewhat different demands on fortifications than resistance to the *attaque à outrance* implied in Guicciardini's statement that after the 1494 invasion the speed of siege operations changed radically.[38]

Positional Tactics at Siena

The War of Siena provides numerous examples of small towns and villages battered and stormed in circumstances that support Guicciardini's blitzkrieg thesis. Attack on a major position, however, was conducted along altogether different lines. At Siena, bombardment was attempted only as a final resort. After an initial attempt to storm the city by surprise, the Imperialists committed themselves to a siege by blockade, and the operations around Siena became one component, albeit the most important, of a diffuse campaign waged on a regional scale.

The French response to these tactics suggests a developing understanding of what later was to become known as positional warfare. Marignano's communi-

Fig. 79. Giovanni Stradano, The Capture of Monteriggioni. Stradano's engraving (by Gallé) is based on a fresco by Giorgio Vasari in the Palazzo Vecchio, Florence. It shows at least two substantial fortifications projecting from the glacis and gun platforms described in the documents. Note the five yoke of oxen used to pull the cannon and their drovers: these must have been fairly light guns. In among the tents, to the right, and just behind the small battery, can be seen another team of oxen pulling a cannon.

Mons Regonis, oppidum, situ et manu munitum, magna tormentorum ui quaßatum, praesidio metu perculso, 'a Caesariams et Aethruscis superatur.

cations with Poggibonsi and his intended movements toward the Maremma road
were threatened by the defensive outposts at Lecceto, Belcaro, and Monastero.
When the Imperialist movements towards Monastero became serious, further
defensive forts were constructed outside the Porta San Marco and to the north
of Sant'Abundio. Finally, when Marignano began to close the strada romana
with the third siege camp, the French responded with threatening troop movements from the south and, later, a deep raid into the Val di Nievole, which
forced Marignano to consolidate his forces at Camollia. Evidence of French
tactical intentions must remain largely circumstantial; but in one letter from
Monluc we have a revealing example of pure positional thinking dating from the
post-Marciano period, when Marignano was finally closing the ring around Siena.

> I have heard that the enemy have abandoned the fort of Montecchio, which
> is about one mile beyond Monastero and overlooks it so that no one can go
> in or out without being discovered; and I have been informed by people I
> have sent there—among others Captains Combasso and Sciarry—that it is
> a fortified place and could be held if there were two companies of foot and
> one of horse. With these men, and with twenty-five more in Barontoli and
> fifteen on the Poggio a'Frati, places close by, I will block the road that comes
> from the Camollia fort in such a fashion that in a few days those in Monastero
> will be reduced to extreme necessity . . . Thus, if Your Excellency would
> send me up to five hundred infantry in all, I would reduce them in a short
> time to such a condition that the marquis [of Marignano] would be compelled
> either to detach a large force from this front to reinforce that front, or to
> lose Monastero: either one or the other would be of great importance . . .
> We have learned also that the Palazzo dei Diavoli is abandoned by them,
> and perhaps from that side one might be able to seize some little place to
> make a large obstacle. If Your Excellency will send me those troops, I will
> make shift to seize some *castelletto* on their flank by the road to Florence and
> cut their supplies into the forts [at Camollia]. And if they wish to come out
> from the forts with artillery to recapture it [the *castelletto*], there will remain
> in the fort so few people that I will be able to attack the fort and take it
> from them. So if they do not wish to lose it, the marquis will be forced to
> draw back on himself on this [the southwest] side.[39]

Relatively feeble forts could play a useful role in this kind of warfare. They
could be constructed or improvised cheaply and quickly; indeed, the logic of
positional tactics as practiced by Marignano, Strozzi, and Monluc discouraged
excessive investment in any single work. Here we part company with most of
our military-architectural theorists, who, while accepting a role for the free-
standing outwork, nevertheless caution against the construction of forts that
might be too small to defend.[40] The idea of an expendable position which could

be abandoned when threatened by superior forces had no place as yet in the theories of the military-architectural treatise writers.

Earth Fortifications as Architecture

It is easy to understand the neglect of temporary earth structures by many modern scholars. Most of these works, after all, were razed soon after the fighting or abandoned to the weather. Crop marks on air photographs, or an overgrown mound, are often all that can be seen of surviving Early Modern siegeworks. While some were encased in stone or brick, the great majority of the outworks have simply disappeared without trace. Yet their importance in sixteenth-century siege warfare is clear from the primary documents as well as the published treatises, even if the more architecturally sophisticated of the treatise authors make it plain enough that, in their view, earth fortifications rank far below permanent military architecture in brick or stone.[41] But there can be no doubt that even temporary fortifications were invested with the formal significance of permanent works.

Soldiers observed the strict medieval conventions of siege warfare in the attack and defense of temporary works, as they would a feudal castle. A herald would "summon" an isolated earth fort or reinforced civil building, calling in the name of his prince on the defenders to give up the place or risk death as the penalty for contumacious disregard of a sovereign's summons to surrender.[42] Although the generals might be willing enough to concede an outwork in the chess game of positional tactics, the officer commanding an outpost often felt obliged to defy such a summons at the risk of condign punishment should he be taken alive.[43] The harsh code of honor that separated the siege from other forms of warfare recognized no distinction between fortified places—certainly none based on their size or permanence or on the durability of their materials.

There are also fragments of information which suggest that efforts were occasionally made to impart an architectural character of some distinction to temporary works. The superstructure of the Sienese citadel on San Prospero was finished, at least in places, in stone, and plans were made to face the Camollia forts with a masonry skin.[44] Leone Strozzi, we are told, did the same for the Galera fort at Port'Ércole.[45] At Siena, moreover, the cardinal of Ferrara proposed to reward the citizens for their efforts at Camollia by donating funds with which to build a proper gateway and drawbridge, decorated with the arms of the republic and the French crown. The gate was to be known as the Porta di Francia.[46] In both of Vasari's views of the siege this gate appears, rising somewhat above the level of the frontal curtain, with prominent dressed-stone quoins and voussoirs.

Beside Siena's medieval gate towers it probably seemed a modest structure, but the intention of the cardinal can hardly be in doubt. These works were meant to be architecture.[47]

The military architecture of mid-sixteenth-century Siena can now be seen to cover a very broad field. The decorated, three-dimensional shapes of Peruzzi's brick and terra-cotta "bastions" bear comparison with the military art of Bramante, Michelangelo, and the Sangalli. They present original and in some respects unique solutions to Siena's defensive problems, influenced but by no means bound by the increasing orthodoxy of the Italian bastioned system. Indeed, bastioned fronts play a relatively small part in Sienese military architecture. By the end of the war, Grosseto was the only fully bastioned town in Sienese Tuscany, although smaller and less complete examples were to be found at Siena, at Orbetello, and on the saddle at Montalcino. The last-named system, however, was seriously flawed. At Montalcino the defenders put much of their effort into a system of retrenchments, an enormously expensive and essentially passive manifestation of "defense in depth" (and one that was not favored by most contemporary authors). Siena's defenders adopted a different approach when they advanced substantial new works beyond the main enceinte. Outside each gate on a level approach to the city, the Sienese built works which not only swept the curtains with gunfire but would have to be taken before the main walls could be engaged. These advanced works were not conceived of as a true bastioned system, however; for although each of them flanked long stretches of the medieval curtain, they were too far apart to sweep each other's faces—the basis of fortification on the Italian method. Instead, the front of each complex of advanced works outside the Porta San Viene, the Porta Romana and the Porta San Marco was defended by a self-contained, small-scale bastion system which, in some case, very closely resembled the hornwork, an innovation of the previous twenty years (first seen in Siena on the lower wing of the Spanish citadel). Detached outworks on the more distant approaches provide yet another relatively new development which must have evolved directly from positional tactics. The adoption of a similar pattern of dispersed fortification for the defense of Port'Ércole gives a glimpse into the distant future of military architecture, when effective long-range, rapid-firing artillery made real the sixteenth-century vision of fortification based on firepower rather than on continuous physical obstacles.

9

NEW PATTERNS
OF MILITARY
ARCHITECTURAL PRACTICE

THUS far we have dealt but little with matters of authorship and attribution or matters of personal architectural style. By and large, fortifications are the product not of a single designer or an individual shaping force but of collective decisions. Baldassarre Peruzzi, of course, has been credited with the design of Siena's early sixteenth-century bastions and seems to have been accepted by contemporaries as the prime mover of the committee appointed to modernize the city's fortifications. Yet, even there, the architect was flanked by an expert on ordnance and reported to the civilian government. Later in the sixteenth century, when Siena was threatened or under siege, decisions were delivered through a military officer and responsibility for design became diluted. In the case of the Camollia forts, at least one part of the attribution ought to go to Thermes, the soldier, in addition to Peloro, the architect. The location and general disposition of the Spanish citadel is known to have been a somewhat wider collective decision, achieved only after much discussion and some disagreement among military and architectural experts advising the governor. The final proposals for the citadel, it appears, had to be approved by the emperor himself. The role of the model-maker, Giovambattista Romano, is not completely clear. Montalcino's wartime fortifications offered yet another paradigm of what might be called creative disagreement. The double lines of defenses that so dangerously diluted the efforts of the builders resulted from the different priorities urged by the military commander, the architect, and the civilian population. When one is dealing with building programs of these kinds, it can become positively misleading to attribute designs.

All of this may well appear unsatisfactory to historians who regard fortifications—along with other works of architecture—as products of individual creative genius. Even if such a situation obtained in military architecture in the days of Brunelleschi or even Francesco di Giorgio Martini (which seems unlikely), it no longer seems to have been true of the mid-sixteenth century. Predictably, the picture that emerges from our study of warfare in the mid-sixteenth century is confusing. Not only do medieval fortifications remain effective and in use alongside "modern" ones; even architects whose training and experience might be judged irrelevant to the modern needs of military affairs remain active and productive. In this chapter we will attempt to explain how and why such a confused picture of change must be presented so long after the supposedly decisive revolution in artillery and military architecture of around 1500.

Generalists and Specialists

Renaissance art historiography, following the Florentine biases of Vasari and others, has always placed a high value on the universal abilities of those blessed with *disegno,* a general sense of design and skill in drawing which could be very widely applied. Versatility in the many branches of the arts, crafts, and technical sciences was an important factor in the reputation of Leonardo da Vinci and Michelangelo as well as numerous other lesser figures. So far as most architects were concerned, this was a virtue born of necessity. Since architecture had no recognized professional structure, not even an apprenticeship within the established craft guilds, it was almost inevitable that building design should form part of a much wider artistic workload and that many of its earliest practitioners should be compelled to tackle all kinds of civil and military commissions. Specialization, in the dual modern sense of specific training and a defined professional role, came late to architecture.[1]

Military architecture, however, demanded many areas of special expertise. Not only did the principles of fortification and gunnery have to be mastered, but solid competence was needed in surveying, estimating, and plan making as well as in the practicalities of site management and building construction in both temporary and permanent materials. Then as now, such skills came only from years of experience. It seems realistic, therefore, to draw a distinction between occasional fortification designers—whatever their talents and originality—and those who became specialists by virtue of long experience. Leonardo da Vinci, Bramante, and Michelangelo should all probably be classified among the former, while Michele Sanmicheli and the Florentine Sangallo family—Giuliano, Antonio the Elder and Younger, and their relatives—carried out so much fortress building that it must have consumed the greater parts of their professional lives.[2] As Horst de la Croix pointed out in connection with Sanmicheli and Antonio da Sangallo the Younger, "while not yet specialists to the exclusion of their other interests, they were the first representatives of a trend that was to accelerate throughout the sixteenth century and finally lead to the complete exclusion of civil architects from military construction."[3]

During the first half of the sixteenth century, yet another type of fortification designer was becoming established in Italy. Frequently these men are known as "military engineers" by modern authors anxious to distinguish their skills from those of the "civilian" architects. In fact, contemporaries drew no such titular distinction between *ingegneri* and *architetti.*[4] The newcomers, however, were primarily soldiers—holding military ranks rather than civil titles—skilled in the design of permanent and field fortifications, camps, trenchworks, bridges, and mines. Some of them would undertake general building tasks, and a few achieved architectural competence. More often they combined their engineering with expertise in artillery, although here it should be added that not even gunnery was held in the first half of the sixteenth century to be an exclusively military accomplishment. Niccolò Tartaglia (1506–59) and Vannoccio Biringucci (1480–1539), both civilians, were acknowledged artillery experts,[5] and gun founding continued for much of the century to be practiced by *tragittatori,* artist-technicians also employed in the casting of bronze sculpture. What firmly identifed the new specialists was their practical military experience. Gabriele Tadino da Martinengo (1480–1543), Jacopo Fusto Castriotto (1510–63), and Francesco de' Marchi (1504–77) were veterans of numerous sieges and traveled widely on campaign service, often changing their engagements among the best military employers in ways that would have seemed scandalous if not treasonable to later generations. Peripatetic devotion to fortification and siege warfare separated them from civilians, much as the mercenary *condottiero* had been differentiated from the medieval militiaman or feudal levy.[6]

Martinengo served the republic of Venice against France and the empire at the sieges of Padua (1509), Brescia (1512), and Bergamo (1516), after which he was posted to Crete as engineer general with the rank of captain of infantry. He left this post in clandestine circumstances almost immediately to join the Order of the Knights of St. John in their defense of Rhodes, 1522–23, where he distinguished himself in the countermining operations. In 1525 he was created a knight of the order and appointed prior of Barletta, by which name he appears in later treatises. He then served the emperor in Spain, North Africa, Sicily, and Vienna, and as general of artillery at Pavia (1525) and Genoa (1527). At the siege of Genoa he called for his brother and cousin, then fighting under the Venetian flag, to join him. This episode, which has appealed greatly to historians seeking to find the origins of the strong family bonds of Italian society, suggests the kind of freedom allowed the fighting man in the sixteenth century. Indeed, after his release from Imperial service in 1533, Martinengo returned to Venice, where despite his previous "desertion" he ended his days peacefully and honorably.[7]

Martinengo was one of the first technically qualified soldiers to achieve high rank by the exercise of these accomplishments. His ancient family connections were doubtless no hindrance in a military career, but for others technical skills increasingly opened the door to active service, and the social advancement that attached to the profession of arms. Francesco de' Marchi, author of one of the most important mid-sixteenth-century treatises on fortification (not published until 1599) and no mean civil architect, worked at different times for the Medici, the Papacy, and the Habsburg empire—serving in the Low Countries and, briefly, in England. Francesco retired with the rank of captain, as Imperial pension, and landed estates in Italy.[8] Castriotto, who also styled himself captain, began his military career with the duke of Urbino, but later served the viceroy of Naples and the Papacy, for whom in the years 1548–52 he built fortifications at Anagni, Sermoneta, Pesaro, and Urbino. He fought with the forces of Julius III at Mirandola in 1552. In 1553 he was with the Imperial army at the sieges of Monticchiello and Montalcino, as we have seen. During the late summer truce of 1553, however, he joined the French and served with Thermes in Corsica (1553) and at the sieges of Marienbourg (1554), St. Quentin (1556), and Thionville (1558). After the recovery of Calais from the English in 1558, Castriotto went there to rebuild the fortifications. He died in Calais five years later, by which time he held the post of chief superintendent of the fortresses of the kingdom.[9] Girolamo Marini was another Italian technical expert to serve the French crown. He fortifed the northeast frontiers during the years 1544 to 1546, was knighted and later awarded the exclusive military order of St. Michael.[10] If civilian architects in the sixteenth century moved gradually from craftsman to professional standing, military architecture offered a much quicker route to the status of officer and gentleman.

The relatively brief service career of Giovanni Battista Belluzzi (1506–54), Cosimo's chief military architect during the early phases of the War of Siena, provides our final illustration of the special standing that could be achieved by the architect on active service. Belluzzi, of course, was born a gentleman. A native of San Marino, he spent some years in the wool trade of Bologna and at the Roman court of the Colonna before marrying into the family of the Urbino architect Girolamo Genga (1476–1551) in 1536. Genga obtained posts for his son-in-law in the administration of his many building projects and gave him a training in architecture. Belluzzi's first contact with his future patron came from an embassy to Florence in 1543 as representative of the republic of San Marino. When his diplomatic mission was complete, Cosimo engaged him as military architect. Commissions quickly followed. In 1544 he worked at Pistoia, Castrocaro, Borgo San Sepolcro, and Florence, where he completed the permanent fortifications of San Miniato. The next two years saw Belluzzi engaged on general surveys of the Fiorentino, and in 1548 he initiated the fortifications for the new city of Cosmopolis (present-day Portoferraio) on the island of Elba.[11] In 1551 Belluzzi had his first experience of active service at Mirandola. In 1553 he accompanied the Imperial army on some of the early sieges of the Siena campaign at Monticchiello and Montalcino, where in June he was wounded in the thigh. He recovered in time to enter Siena in disguise at the end of July to reconnoiter the earthworks near the Porta Camollia and to make suggestions to Marignano about their attack. By the end of the year he was in action again at San Firenze in Corsica. On 12 Feburary 1554 he was granted the rank of captain of infantry and given command of 300 foot at the siege of Siena. Almost certainly Cosimo intended the captaincy as a reward for his conduct in the field rather than as an active command. In February he entered Siena through the underground water courses to reconnoiter a possible route of attack. Belluzzi's patent as *ingegnere del campo* was delivered on 2 March, and it was in this capacity that he directed the Imperial trenchworks on the Camollia ridge and demolished parts of the Sienese aqueduct system. Cosimo was furious with Marignano when he received word that Belluzzi had been gravely wounded on 6 March 1554 while leading his company in the assault on Aiuola, a small and relatively unimportant Sienese fortress, and he was deeply saddened by news of Belluzzi's death at the end of March. A promising career had been cut short by a Sienese arquebus ball.[12]

Bernardo Puccini (d. 1575), Belluzzi's successor as chief engineer to the Imperial army at Siena, apparently did not share his predecessor's enthusiasm for action. Although paid the same high salary of 200 scudi per annum, Puccini was never awarded a captaincy, a rank which then seems to have enjoyed much greater status than its modern equivalent. Giovan Battista Camerini (1500–1569) and Bernardo Buontalenti (1531–1608), Cosimo's other principal fortress builders, remained on the civilian side of their profession.[13]

While the distinction between sixteenth-century military and civilian architects probably had as much to do with the personal qualities of individuals and their opportunities for active service, the published treatises stressed the increasing militarization of military architecture. Francesco de' Marchi considered knowledge of artillery of crucial importance, while Antonio Lupicini (1530–71) accepted the architect provided only that he worked under military supervision.[14] The hands that prepared Belluzzi's treatise for posthumous publication took a more uncompromising position. Architects, together with other civilian *dottori*, were to keep out of a subject of which they knew nothing and could learn nothing from their classical libraries, "because . . . books don't fight." Belluzzi's editors not only rejected the notion of the *uomo universale* beloved of the earlier treatise authors, but argued that no single individual—soldier or civilian—could master all of the skills needed for modern fortification construction. Instead, a partnership was proposed between soldier and builder. Only an experienced soldier would be capable of appreciating the defensive and offensive potential of a site, and of anticipating the tactical situations likely to arise during a siege. The soldier would be supported by *un buon Capitano maestro di muratori*, that is to say, a builder combining the functions of master mason and foreman, or clerk of works. The builder was explicitly not required to have all of the architect's skills. It would be sufficient to have a knowledge of mathematics and the qualities of materials, as well as the ability to draw plans and to estimate costs.[15] Implicitly, the education and authority of an architect were represented as impediments in a strictly subordinate role.[16]

It is not our intention here to dispute the general validity of de la Croix's contention that, by the middle of the sixteenth century, the split between civil and military architecture had become decisive.[17] De la Croix based his conclusions on the published treatises, and it would not be surprising to find them running somewhat ahead of day-to-day practice as well as adopting a harder polemical line. Our own research into the military architecture of Siena is partial too but suggests a much longer lease of life for the kind of designer who, in a small and restricted professional market, had probably always had to tackle a variety of commissions. Indeed, if we consider the major figures of military architecture in Siena during the second quarter of the sixteenth century, we see that the change from civilian all-rounder to military specialist did not take place overnight.

Prewar Sienese Military Architecture

Baldassarre Peruzzi was a classic example of the early sixteenth-century generalist. When he arrived in Siena in 1527, he had, so far as we know, no specific experience in military architecture,[18] although it seems unlikely that someone so closely associated with Bramante and the Sangallo family would have been completely ignorant of this subject. From 1527, when he left the sacked city of Rome, until at least 1533, fortifications were becoming an important part of a highly varied workload.[19] The new bastions designed and built for Siena were his largest military project, but he was also called upon to make numerous journeys into the dominio to inspect town fortifications. While we can identify no surviving work on these provincial sites, the documentary evidence and drawings prove that various new projects were considered. At Sarteano and Cetona, to which Peruzzi was called late in 1528, his plans show bastions similar in size, shape, and strategic intention to those in Siena. The drawings that have survived seem to have been rough drafts composed on site and would have served Peruzzi while formulating his explanations and proposals for the government (fig. 80). No attempt was made to hide the purpose of Peruzzi's visit. On the contrary, it was hoped that the local spies would see his presence as proof of the importance of Chiusi to the republic.[20]

Peruzzi was often on such journeys (fig. 81). One is documented to Montorio

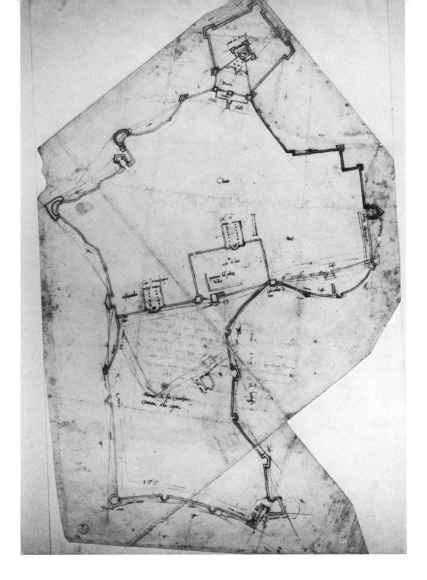

Fig. 80. Baldassarre Peruzzi, Fortifications at Chiusi. One of the largest and most complex of Peruzzi's refortification proposals for the Sienese republic. Peruzzi had to account for the difficult topography of the town as well as sort out troubles with a major local landowner whose property flanked the walls. Peruzzi's proposals seem not to have been built.

and Castel Ottieri in February 1529 and another to Asciano in May of the same year. At Asciano the *commissario* makes an effort to describe the visit and Peruzzi's proposals in one letter but admits, in a second, that on his return Peruzzi will fill them in on the details orally.[21] Peruzzi visited Orbetello and Port'Ércole in the Maremma in early 1530. His visit drew a confused response from a semiliterate commissioner: "A master Baldassarre who makes works of architecture has turned up."[22] Peruzzi advised this incredulous servant of the people to repair a half-ruined seaside casemate. From all these visits we may deduce a similar pattern: a request from the field for aid and advice; the government instructs Peruzzi to investigate;

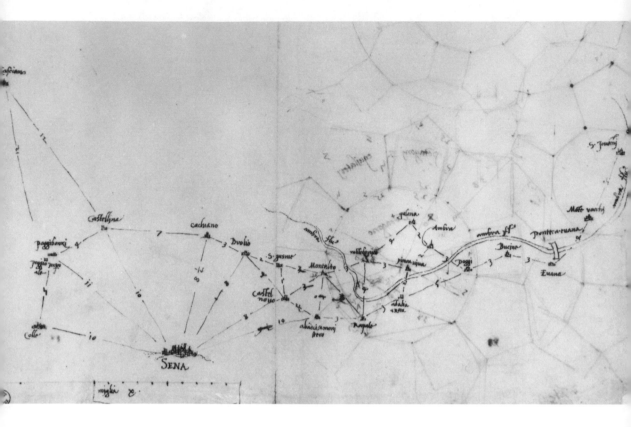

Fig. 81. Baldassarre Peruzzi, Villages along
part of Siena's Northern Border. Distances
and bearings are marked between the villages.
Rough maps of this sort may have been common among traveling military architects.

Peruzzi travels to the site to consult with the local representatives; Peruzzi advises
the government; governmental action or, more usually, inaction. As a public
servant, Peruzzi seems generally to have acted at one remove from actual decision
making; his role is basically that of a consultant.

Peruzzi also went to war on the specific request of the Imperial commanders
at the siege of Florence.[23] The architect arrived there early in 1530 and stayed
for three days in conference with Antonio da Sangallo and the generals. It was
a trip that he undertook reluctantly—Peruzzi protested that he had business back
in Siena that prevented him from remaining longer—but it shows the value given
to his opinion and the way in which, in times of emergency, even an unambig-
uously civilian architect could be seconded to the military.

Quite apart from work on fortifications, the office of Architect to the Republic
carried many other responsibilities. Repairs to the bridge at Buonconvento oc-

cupied Peruzzi in 1527, 1531, and 1532. In 1532 he built dikes against the sea of Castiglione della Pescaia and, probably at this time, he attempted to reconstruct the fifteenth-century dam on the River Bruna.[24] Francesco di Giorgio Martini had collaborated in the construction of the original structure, designed to provide a lake for fish for the Siena market, but it had collapsed in late 1492. It is fitting that Peruzzi should have been able to work on the project of the older man, seemingly his intellectual model. Work on the minting of devalued coinage occupied him in 1530.[25] The design of a house for the Florentine ambassador was an official commission in 1532, when he was also involved in the design of a new altar for the Duomo.

Peruzzi was also able to undertake private commissions; although it was this outside work that led to disagreements with the Sienese civic authorities and eventually to his dismissal. In the period 1527–35 he worked on the tomb of Pope Adrian VI and as *capomaestro* for St. Peter's, Rome; investigated on behalf of the pope the possibility of a canal linking the valleys of the Chiana and Tiber; reconstructed sections of the Villa at Belcaro; and built the Palazzo Neri-Pollini, Siena. Peruzzi was already working in Rome when his appointment as Architect to the Republic was terminated, and it was there that he died in 1536.

Antonio Maria Lari (act. 1521–49), Peruzzi's student and successor as Architect to the Republic of Siena between 1537 and 1543, also mixed civil and military work. Fortification was not being undertaken in Siena itself during this period, but between his various civil and ecclesiastical projects Lari toured the dominio, much like Peruzzi, carrying out inspections and improvements to the defenses of Cetona and Chiusi in 1537, Chiusi again and the towns of the Maremma in 1539, Grosseto in 1540, Talamone and Sovana in 1541, Port'Ércole, Pitigliano, and again Sovana in 1542.[26]

The impetus for Lari's program of refurbishment of fortifications on or near to the coast was almost certainly the resurgence of Turkish naval power following their victory at Prevesa in 1538. During the 1540s the raiding increased in its frequency and ferocity, stimulating a large number of repair and improvement projects along the threatened seaboard. These works provided commissions for the two leading Sienese official architects, Pietro Cataneo and Giovambattista Peloro.

Cataneo was of course the quintessential Renaissance polymath: author, architect, mathematician, and administrator in the tradition of Francesco di Giorgio Martini. He has been credited with the design of the Palazzo Francesconi in Siena and with numerous engineering projects in the Maremma, where at different times he served as civil commissioner and castellan.[27] His book on measurement and surveying dealt with the most practical applications of mathematics and geometry.[28] Cataneo's treatise on architecture embraced all branches of the subject from city planning to perspective, including a substantial section on fortification. The treatise has been described as one of the last of the generalist books on architecture,[29] and it is certainly true that the broad scope of the work and the academic approach of its author sets even the fortification chapters apart from most of the soldiers' writings. But it is not the work of an amateur. Cataneo's technical abilities and experience of civil and military administration in the Maremma during the 1540s compel us to take him seriously as a military architect.

Peloro's career also included diplomatic and administrative duties for the republic during the 1520s and 1530s, as well as service as a military architect in Piedmont between 1536 and 1540 with the marquis of Vasto, and with Pope Paul III at Ancona and Fano (1541–45).[30] He designed the severely classical interior of the church of San Martino in Siena (fig. 82) and is credited with the invention of a papier mâché technique for the copying of ancient sculpture.[31] Despite his skill and experience of fortification on active service, not even Peloro seems to have been regarded in Siena as a military man. Like Peruzzi, Cataneo, and Lari, he remained an architect: a citizen and public servant rather than a soldier.

French Soldiers and Engineers

With the arrival of the French in the 1550s in Siena many of the important decisions on fortification were taken by soldiers. Blaise de Monluc organized the building of the retrenchments and the extra gate defenses during the winter of 1554–55. Piero Strozzi (1510–58) authorized the construction of the outworks toward Belcaro and Monastero by means of which it was hoped to secure the southwestern approaches during the spring of 1554. Thermes ordered the construction of the forts on Siena's Camollia ridge, probably initiated the system of seven forts at Port'Ércole, and certainly took key decisions at a number of other places. Cornelio Bentivoglio (d. 1585) and Carlo Caraffa, both in the rank of *maestro di campo,* are credited with planning decisions: in one case Caraffa is said to have left a drawing of works at Monteriggioni, although whether by his own hand or another's is unclear.[32]

It is often difficult to establish whether officers of this seniority are weighing the evidence and taking their own decisions about fortification, or merely lending their authority to the advice of others. In the case of Thermes, however, there is much in the chronicles and the primary documents to suggest that this distinguished light cavalry commander took his own decisions. Agnolo Bardi describes how Thermes conducted his tours of the dominio in the autumn and winter of 1552. He would enter a place after first having cantered around the

Fig. 82. Giovambattista Peloro, Church of
San Martino, Siena. Its highly Romanized interior, recalling the work of Antonio da Sangallo the Younger, is extremely unusual in
Siena. The later marble frames of the altars
make it difficult to see the somber doric of the
nave frieze.

walls and, before being received, would lead his party on an internal circuit. Then he would address all the men in a public square—something no architect would do—giving them his opinion of the defensibility of the position. If it was to be held, he would promise aid and seek to rouse the community in their own defense.[33]

Giulio Buonsignori, commissioner of Chiusi, described very similar events when his city was surveyed by Cornelio Bentivoglio and Peloro in October 1553. "Signor Cornelio arrived here yesterday evening when it was almost dark and, before dismounting, rode completely around the outside of town and saw the fort. Then this morning at break of dawn they went round inside and again on the outside at the weakest place where he planned to fortify. And he considered everything together with Peloro and put it into two drawings. . . Signor Cornelio says that he wishes to confer with his Most Reverence of Ferrara and ordered that Peloro return to raise the plan."[34]

Here soldier and architect appear to be working as an effective team. Joint decisions were reached swiftly and recorded in duplicate by Peloro, who was evidently expected to return to supervise construction after the scheme had been approved by Ippolito d'Este, the cardinal of Ferrara. The need to confer with the cardinal possibly reflects the difference in rank between Bentivoglio and Thermes or, more simply, may reflect the return to "normal" official processes in the period between the two Sienese campaigns. It seems clear, however, that in this case Peloro was acting as an architectural consultant to the soldier—trusted and valued for his expertise, perhaps, but subordinate in the eyes of the commissioner.[35]

A number of French engineers—or, at least, French-employed engineers—served with the army of Siena. Someone with the curious name of Malagrida worked at Chiusi, Rocca d'Orcia, Casole, Montalcino, and Lucignano di Val di Chiana in 1552 and 1553, and built the batteries on the north side of the Sienese Castellaccia at Camollia in the spring of 1554. Another, described as Maestro Guglielmo Francese, worked at Caparbia in 1553; while as late as December 1554, an unnamed official inside Siena was described as Engineer to the King.[36] Because these men were French employees, we have little chance of identifying them save by a chance mention in a document—often in connection with some friction with civilians. It may be that other French engineers worked on Sienese fortifications. However, the normal response to calls for technical assistance from the commissioner of a provincial town was to send one of the civilian architects then serving the republic. A survey of the activity of these architects in this period not only overwhelms one—for they were very busy—but goes a long way to support the view that the civilian architect still had a firm place in the wartime military architectural practice of the mid-sixteenth century.

Siena's Wartime Architects

Giovambattista Peloro, for example, was engaged as architect to the republic in the autumn of 1552. Although by then sixty-nine years of age, he had evidently gone to the Maremma immediately following the expulsion of the Spaniards and had made drawings of the works at Port'Èrcole, which had been captured from the Spanish early in August, and Orbetello, where the Spanish garrison was still being besieged by the French. Early in October the Otto della Guerra wrote to him offering employment and asking him to bring his drawings of Port'Èrcole and Orbetello for discussion with Thermes.[37] By this time he had moved to the duke of Florence's court at Poggio a Caiano and at first seemed in no hurry to respond to the Sienese ambassador's urgings that he return immediately to take up what he must have realized was to be a demanding post. However, on 10 October he was appointed architect at the generous salary of 150 gold scudi per annum.[38] Probably he started his duties on or about the 16 October, because on this date he was given a first payment of ten scudi "per cortesia del collegio."[39]

Peloro's main responsibilities in Siena were on the works at San Prospero and, early in 1553, the design of the three forts at Camollia. He also worked in the dominio at Lucignano (December 1552), Monticchiello (early 1553), Montalcino (September 1553), Chiusi (October 1553), Casole (November 1553), and again at Lucignano (December 1553 and January 1554), where a new fort was being built on a hill overlooking the important Sienese border town in the Val di Chiana. During the war of maneuver around Siena in the spring and summer of 1554, Peloro continued to travel in the dominio: Monticchiello, Chiusi and Montalcino (March), Casole (April) and Lucignano (May). He remained inside Siena when the blockade tightened in the winter of 1554–55, being rewarded for his work, in the last days of the siege, by a special ration of grain. Following the surrender, Peloro briefly joined the exiles in Montalcino before moving to Rome, where he died in 1558.[40] The last years of Giovambattista Peloro's long life were packed with action.

Pietro Cataneo, another of the architects, was employed in October 1552 to fortify Caparbia.[41] He may also have worked briefly at Montalcino early in November. At the end of the month, he wrote from Campagnatico reporting that this place was now "secura dalla artiglieria" and that on his return from Pienza he would, as instructed, survey Sinalunga.[42] Early in 1553 he worked on the reservoirs of Acquasena.[43] No further archival references to his wartime activities have been found; the Sienese antiquarian Ettore Romagnoli supposes that he may have gone to Venice to supervise the production of his treatise *I quattro primi libri di architettura*, which was published in 1554. It would have been possible for him to leave Siena quite honorably during the hiatus between the two campaigns.

Bartolommeo Neroni ("Il Riccio") was best known as a painter, but he too served as a military architect and was able to draw upon some prewar experience in building design.[44] In November 1552 he produced a drawing of the fortifications of Sinalunga. December 1552 saw him in Chiusi, where he received instructions to survey the "torri della Montagnola," the mountainous district to the west of Siena which gave so much trouble to the Imperial troops in 1554. In the spring of 1553, Il Riccio was active on the northwest borders of the dominio: at Massa in January, Monterotondo and Monteriggioni in February, Chiusdino in March, and back to Monterotondo in April, when he became involved in argument with a certain Captain Leonbruno di Urbino, the garrison commander, over the extent of the fortifications to be carried out. The architect, it seems, wished to restrict the works to a scheme which could be completed in the foreseeable future. During the second phase of the war, Il Riccio remained in Siena, where he painted a deposition scene in the Chiesa delle Derelitte, Siena (1554) and supervised the construction of a guard house in January 1555.[45]

The fourth of the Sienese civilian architects was Dionigio Gori (1510–86?), a mathematician and the author of a treatise on measurement. As a *maestro d'abaco* at the University of Siena, he followed in a line of Sienese mathematicians active in all phases of architectural practice. Before the war he had practiced civil engineering: surveys for river flood control dykes, mapping, bridgeworks, and timber roofing.[46] In January 1553 he was appointed site architect to the three forts at Camollia, with letters patent giving him wide ranging powers to draft and organize labor on what was then the most urgent Sienese project.[47] The forts were practically finished by April 1553 when Gori was posted to Monterotondo, one of the republic's sixteen fortified towns.[48] Here affairs were already in disorder, with the local commander in dispute with the architect (Il Riccio) and the civil commissioner appealing to Siena for a decision. Whether Gori managed to bring the situation under control is unknown; but at about this time the stream of disputatious letters ceased. In June 1553 he visited the Val di Chiana on a survey tour. In August he was in Cetona and in October once more in the Val di Chiana. Following the surrender of Siena he retained his academic post but, so far as is known, did no further building work of any kind.

Giorgio di Giovanni was a painter by trade. He had been trained in the studio of Domenico Beccafumi and assisted Giovanni da Udine in the decoration of the Vatican *logge*. In his native city he decorated the portico of the Palazzo dei Saracini and, with Il Riccio, made the triumphal arch that the Sienese planned to raise in honor of Pope Paul III as he passed through the city on his way to the Congress of Nice.[49] It is as the painter of the *tavolette* commemorating the major scenes of the Sienese rebellion (figs. 41, 42, 58) and war against the empire that he is probably best known today. During the war, however, he was second only to Peloro as the most heavily employed military architect in the republic. Indeed, before the war he must have obtained considerable experience of building, for immediately after the expulsion of the Spaniards he was appointed architect to the citadel site. Maestro Giorgio's appointment to this important project on 7 August 1552 predates by just over two months Peloro's patent as Architect to the Republic.[50] Later in the year Maestro Giorgio, like the other architects, was despatched to numerous towns in the dominio: Montalcino, Chiusi, Radicofani, Monteoliveto di Chiusure, San Giovanni d'Asso, and San Gusmé. One of his letters, reporting the death of his horse, records that he was fired upon by a Spanish patrol near Orbetello in the far south.[51]

Maestro Giorgio's activity at Montalcino both before and during the siege of 1553 provides our best information on the nature of wartime architectural practice. Like Il Riccio at Monterotondo, Giorgio clashed with the senior military officer, Colonel Giovanni da Torino, who commanded the garrison throughout most of the building program and had evidently begun to set out some new fortifications before the architect arrived at Montalcino in November 1552. Giorgio immediately took issue with the colonel on the design of the bastions beside the Rocca, which, in his view, failed to flank each other properly.[52] After an acrimonious correspondence with Siena, the civil commissioner managed to convene a meeting, and the matter was resolved in the architect's favor.[53] Maestro Giorgio also urged the construction of a third bastion outside the Porta Cerbaia to eliminate the blind spot on the bastion of San Martino. Works outside the walls, he maintained, should enjoy greater priority than the retrenchments favored by the leaders of the civil population, none of whom seemed confident of their ability to hold the outer defensive line.[54] As we have seen, the third bastion was started late and never completed, with nearly disastrous consequences for the defenders.

Soldiers and civilians might not always accept Maestro Giorgio's views on the strategy of fortification design, but they relied implicitly on the architect's technical judgment.[55] On one occasion Giorgio was recalled from a nearby site to rule on the depth of foundations. In this case the colonel had been enraged by the time wasted, as he saw it, on excavations far deeper than those indicated on the architect's drawing, an incident which also sheds an interesting light on the authority vested in the plan.[56] At other times the architect was dispatched to Siena as the most convincing supplicant for men, money, and materials. Once Giorgio was away from the site, however, the commissioner would desperately urge his return.[57] Although many of the details of Maestro Giorgio's duties remain obscure, a picture emerges from the letter books of a key figure controlling site operations, entrusted with enormous sums of money, valued and supported by the local civil authorities, and on some occasions able to persuade senior officers to reverse their decisions on military matters.

Neither architect nor colonel, however, could persuade or coerce the civilian residents of Montalcino to exert themselves in their own defense. Driven to distraction by their reluctance, the colonel was moved to declare that he was not about to dishonor himself by attempting to defend an indefensible position, "not if ordered to do so by the Most Christian King or even by Christ himself!"[58] Maestro Giorgio sadly observed that he had never before seen such unwillingness: "It seems they are expecting friends, not enemies."[59] Only money could persuade the Montalcinesi to work. Maestro Giorgio himself, it seems, worked for long periods without reward. In his most miserable letter from Montalcino the architect requests permission to resign and for someone else to be appointed to implement his proposals, as had been done with his drawings from Chiusi. Since the capture of the Spanish citadel (in August 1552) he had worked as engineer, foreman, and laborer, wearing his clothes bare and aging prematurely. For these efforts he had received a mere ten scudi. When he hears himself addressed "Signiore Engeniere," he looks in his purse and there isn't a cent! "Questo fumo senza arrosto no fa per me" ("The aroma without the roast won't do"). He now sees his error and wishes to return to his trade as a painter.[60]

This letter—undated but probably written in February 1553—marked the nadir of Maestro Giorgio's fortunes. In March he received some pay[61] and in April was given a further ten scudi by Giulio Vieri, the newly appointed commissioner general of Montalcino, "because he was so unhappy about his lack of funds."[62] Montalcino by now being under siege, Maestro Giorgio was working continuously on the repair of the fortifications, the construction of further retrenchments, and the underground countermining operations. At the end of May, Giulio Vieri reported that the architect was "utterly exhausted by danger and fatigue."[63] Giorgio, however, survived to paint *tavolette* of the sieges of both Montalcino and Siena. He remained inside the capital throughout the operations of 1554–55 and, in its closing days, was given authority to go up the Mangia, the bell tower of the Palazzo Pubblico, to make a plan of the city and its fortifications.[64] This plan was probably to serve as a definitive, up-to-date record of Siena's defenses, for use by the leaders of the republic-in-exile at Montalcino.

These brief records of public service show how difficult it is to determine the point at which the civilian architect is squeezed out of military architecture. Of the five men employed by Siena in the mid–1550s, all were primarily civilians. Peloro and Cataneo, to be sure, had a great deal of experience in fortifications from the 1540s; and Peloro was so old that he could be regarded as a survivor of early sixteenth-century practice. Gori, however, was a mathematician and civil engineer. Riccio and Maestro Giorgio were both painter-architects. Gori, Il Riccio, and Maestro Giorgio are not known to have had previous experience of fortification although all of them were clearly experienced builders. Even so, Maestro Giorgio seems to have impressed the civil and military leaders of the republic with his efficiency and skill as a fortification designer, as well as with that quality which marked out the soldier-engineer: the ability to work under fire.

Working Methods

The documents recording the payment and movement of Siena's "wartime emergency military architects" also yield a number of clues to their working methods. One is struck at once by their mobility. Peloro, despite his age, probably covered the greatest distance on his duties, though the other architects on the team traveled extensively in all seasons. No doubt they often took roundabout routes to minimize the risk of an encounter with enemy patrols. A good horse must have been a great asset to a Sienese architect: indeed, money to meet the increasingly high charges for horse feed was paid as a supplement to their professional fee.[65]

On a few major projects—the works at San Prospero and Camollia at the northern entrance to Siena, at Lucignano, and at Montalcino—architects were kept on site for many weeks. On most projects, however, the architect did not remain long enough for the works to be both planned and implemented under his continuous supervision. For the brief visits, therefore, it seems reasonable to suppose that the architect's task was to evaluate the works, perhaps to draw plans, and to prepare an estimate of the men, money, and materials needed. Many of the soldiers, as we have seen, could make a strategic decision on the defensibility of a place. But the architect would still have been required as a plan maker and estimator—in modern building terminology a quantity surveyor, building surveyor, sometimes even a general contractor. In these terms it is not difficult to appreciate how civilian architects, painters, and surveyors could so quickly become useful fortification builders. Basic geometry would be sufficient for making an accurate survey, setting out the pegs and strings for the foundations of new works, and calculating the volume of earth to be shifted. Knowledge of local tradesmen, materials, and prices was probably as important as military experience.[66]

The other essential skill was drawing. Today the architect is sometimes seen as little more than the author of finely drawn plans, sections, and elevations which, at their best, are works of art in their own right. The military architecture of the sixteenth century itself is often conceived in much the same way as a somewhat academic paper exercise in applied geometry.[67] It is a misconception that probably has its origins in the publication of treatises on fortification, many of them beautifully illustrated with woodcuts or engravings (fig. 83) of regular polygonal plans.[68] Often the pattern quality of the layout is enhanced by the addition of a thin tracery indicating the crossfire from cannon at every embrasure. It must be said at once that very few original drawings of this quality have survived for fortifications designed in the first half of the sixteenth century. The Setta Sangallesca—much the largest early sixteenth-century architectural practice—produced splendidly rendered presentation plans for the Florentine Fortezza da Basso and the Fortezza Paolina in Perugia (fig. 84). However, Antonio da Sangallo's numerous freehand studies for the walls of Castro or the refortification of Rome (figs. 85 and 86) are altogether more typical of surviving plans in that they include—often on the same sheet—preliminary survey and rough work-up sketches, construction details, and rough projections showing three-dimensional arrangements.[69] These were the working drawings. As Ackerman has shown, most sixteenth-century architects used large-scale and very accurately made models to present their proposals to clients.[70] Presentation models, of course, cost considerable sums of money, and it was to reduce this expense that Pietro Cataneo urged architects to develop their drafting skills and to use drawings not merely as the basis for models but as the principal means of presentation.[71] By the middle of the century, however, the elevation and the perspective offered no real challenge. It was a model of the Spanish citadel at Siena that was taken to Charles V for his approval. When Vasari painted the ceiling panel of Cosimo planning the conquest of Siena (fig. 87), he represented the duke, dividers in hand, studying a model of the city.[72] Then as now, few nonarchitects could read technical drawings with any facility. The unusual forms of modern fortifications and the broken topography of so many defended sites no doubt ensured that in this branch of design the wooden, wax, or clay model continued as the principal medium of presentation.

It comes as no real surprise, therefore, that so few architectural drawings have survived the Sienese wars and that we have been compelled to rely heavily upon other forms of illustration and the testimony of the archives. No doubt many working drawings were made. In the case of Peruzzi's visit to Chiusi in 1528–29 to inspect the defenses, not only did government documents call upon him to supply drawings, but an official body known as the committee "sopra el vedere li disegni di maestro Baldassare per Chiusci"[73] was formed to consider them. These drawings and others surviving from his hand are all for the towns of the dominio; there are none of Siena. They take the form of survey records, showing the basic dimensions of the walls and some proposals for defensive additions. Peruzzi's drawing for Chiusi (fig. 80) almost certainly indicates the kind of work submitted by Peloro, Il Riccio, and Maestro Giorgio.

To some extent, of course, Peruzzi was a special case. His architectural working methods seem to have been predicated on drawing as a means of un-

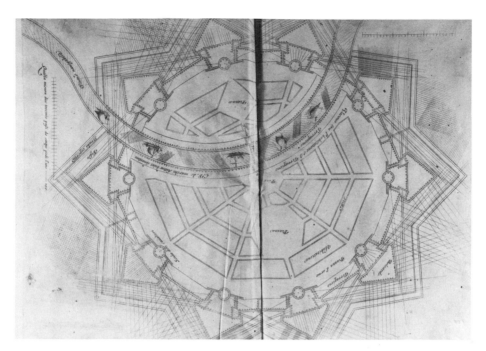

Fig. 83. Francesco de' Marchi, Radial Town Plan on a River. In light of the supply of weaponry in the sixteenth century, de' Marchi's proposed lines of fire seem rather denser than could be mustered by most towns.

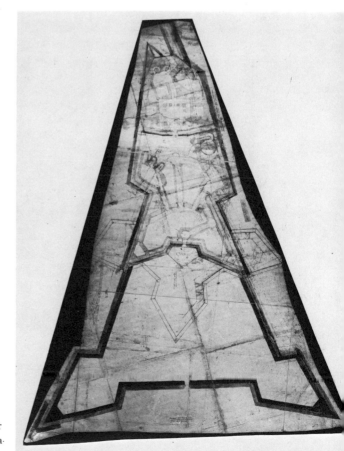

Fig. 84. Antonio da Sangallo the Younger, The Fortezza Paolina, Perugia. Drawings of this size were inherently troublesome due to the relatively small size of individual sheets. Given the complexity of the strata in a work like this, built into a hillside, it is no wonder that models were generally preferred for explanations to princes and political leaders.

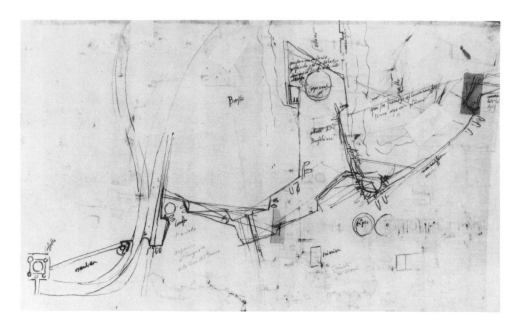

Fig. 85. Antonio da Sangallo the Younger, Study for Fortifications on the Northern Front, Rome. In this sheet, Sangallo explores the nature of the crossing fire created by the new bastion system in relation to the old walls.

Fig. 86. Antonio da Sangallo the Younger, Double Bastion near Porta Ardeatina, Rome. This sheet shows a plan of the countermine gallery and a series of rampart sections. These are all dimensioned and scaled and come close to modern working drawings. Even here, however, Sangallo mixes ruled and freehand lines.

Fig. 87. Giorgio Vasari, *Cosimo Studies the Plan and Model of Siena*. Vasari's painting depicts Cosimo before a model and plan. There are other Sienese images which lead one to believe that models were not uncom-

mon. Among the Biccherna panels, see Neroccio de' Landi's image (1480) of the *Virgin Recommends Siena to Christ* (Archivio di Stato, Siena).

derstanding form, and there can be little question that he was one of the most accomplished draftsmen of the period.[74] Other architects, however, used their artistic skills to record completed Sienese fortifications. Maestro Giorgio's painted *tavolette*—despite their primitive quality—may be regarded as official records of the most important republican projects. No doubt they were also accurate records. No one would have known the works better than he, and many of the details correspond closely with documentary evidence as well as with Vasari's history paintings. In the case of the Montalcino *tavoletta* (fig. 58), moreover, it is possible to confirm Maestro Giorgio's details from the very closely observed panoramic study by Peloro—the only contemporary drawing (fig. 62) to show how the wartime military architecture actually appeared from the ground.[75] The drawing extends over a number of sheets, pasted together to form a picture some six feet wide. Its size and the degree of topographical and urban detail suggest that the panorama was no idle sketch by the overworked Peloro but another form of offical record; possibly intended as the basis for a larger painting or fresco depicting the scene of the single important Sienese victory. One can only speculate about the possible roles of Peloro, Il Riccio, and Maestro Giorgio in the artistic program that would certainly have celebrated the survival of Siena's last republic. This kind of political history painting, however, was only to be executed in Florence.

NOTE ON SOURCES

Much of the material in this book has come from two archives, the Archivio di Stato, Florence (hereafter ASF), and the Archivio di Stato, Siena (hereafter ASS). Archival references are generally followed by a *fondo* reference. The Florentine *fondo* references are generally to the *Mediceo del Principato* (hereafter *Med. Princ.*), which contains a vast collection of documents relating to the period prior to the formation of the *Granducato*. Most of the documents we cite from this source are letters, which have been bound into numbered volumes, with a page or folio number, and of course a date. In one instance, *Med. Princ.* 1853, there is no folio number, and so we have cited only the date. Letters received from the field are kept as bound originals. Letters sent from Florence are recorded in volumes of copyletters (with volume number, folio and date, as above) containing either the entire text verbatim, or a comprehensive summary of its contents.

The other important Florentine *fondo* is the *Carte Strozziane*, or Strozzi papers, which are seventeenth-century transcriptions of documents bearing on the activities of the Strozzi family (and thus comprehensively embracing the War of Siena). Often the originals are no longer to be found in the principal archive of the Medici principate.

In the case of Siena, the *fondo* refers to the government agency—the *Consiglio Generale, Concistoro, Biccherna* or the *Balìa*, the central committee of the republic. *Balìa* references are much the most numerous and embrace not only correspondence but the *deliberazioni* (or minutes) of the committee and its many ad hoc subcommittees, as well as the copies of notarial records of building works, draft letters patent, proclamations, and so on. Correspondence was handled in much the same way as that of Florence, although each surviving letter has been given a number.

Where folio numbers are cited in our own references, *v* indicates the *verso*, but *recto* is normally assumed (and only cited when both sides of the folio need to be consulted).

NOTES

(Works listed in the Bibliography are cited in shortened form in the Notes)

Introduction

1. See, for example, Forster, "From 'Rocca' to 'Civitas'; Marconi, *La città come forma simbolica.*

2. Ludwig H. Heydenreich, *Leonardo da Vinci* (New York, 1954), 1:83.

3. See David Mackenzie, "Marx and the Machine," *Technology and Culture* 25 (1984): 473–502.

4. John Keegan, *The Face of Battle: A Study of Agincourt, Waterloo, and the Somme* (New York, 1976), p. 29.

1

1. Hale, "The Early Development of the Bastion," p. 466.

2. De la Croix, "Military Architecture and the Radial City Plan in Sixteenth Century Italy."

3. De la Croix, The Literature on Fortification in Renaissance Italy."

4. This section is developed from Simon Pepper, "Firepower and the Design of Renaissance Fortifications," *Fort* 10 (1982): 93–104.

The key English-language sources on the general development of early artillery are Ffoulkes, *The Gunfounders of England;* Hall, *Ballistics in the Seventeenth Century;* O'Neil, *Castles and Cannon;* Lewis, *Armada Guns;* Cipolla, *Guns and Sails in the Early Phase of European Expansion;* and Guilmartin, *Gunpowder and Galleys.* This subject, which has particularly interested historians of naval warfare, has also been dealt with in the context of military strategy by Contamine, *War in the Middle Ages.*

5. Hall, *Ballistics,* pp. 9–14, gives a good account of the casting techniques. See also Schubert, "The First Cast-Iron Cannon Made in England," p. 131. Biringuccio's *Pirotechnia* (1540) describes similar techniques for brass casting.

6. O'Neil, *Castles,* pp. 32–33; Contamine, *War in the Middle Ages,* p. 145.

7. Leseur, *Histoire de Gaston IV, Compte de Foix,* 2:157–58, quoted in C. T. Allmand, ed., *Society at War: The Experience of England and France during the Hundred Years War* (Edinburgh, 1973), p. 122.

8. Fuller, *The Decisive Battles of the Western World and Their Influence upon History,* 1:393. General Fuller notes that wheeled gun carriages for the lighter pieces began to appear about 1470, but that the heavy weapons for the siege of Cambil (1492) were built-up "Lombards" (i.e., bombards) some 12 feet long and with 14-inch bores, bedded on wooden trucks without wheels. In this last respect the Spanish siege artillery seems to have lagged some way behind contemporary French guns. On the conquest of Granada see Quesada, *Castilla y la conquista del reino de Granada.*

9. Guilmartin, *Gunpowder and Galleys,* pp. 158, 170. In "The Guns of the Santissimo Sacramento," p. 591, Guilmartin suggests that the change from stone to iron may have had to do with the cost of labor. He notes the casting of stone-throwing cannon in the Ottoman empire in the eighteenth century. The last Portuguese stone-throwing cannon was cast in 1578.

10. For the continued use of stone projectiles during the War of Seina, see chapter 8 below. It has been suggested that standardization of calibers was a *late* sixteenth-century development, brought about by the special difficulties posed by mixtures of guns and shot calibers on board ships. Hale, "Men and Weapons." Guilmartin, "The Guns," notes the continued use of guns of different vintages on board ships as late as the seventeenth century.

11. "Innanzi al 1494 erano le guerre lunghe, le giornate non sanguinose, e modi dello espugnare terre lenti e difficili e se bene erano già in uso le artiglierie, si maneggiavano con sì poca attitudine che non offendevano molto; in modo che chi aveva uno Stato era quasi impossibile lo perdessi. Vennono i Franzesi in Italia, e introdussono nelle guerre tanta vivezza, in modo che insino al [15]21, perduta la campagna, era perduto lo Stato." Francesco Guicciardini, *Ricordi politici e civili,* no. 64, in *Opere inedite,* ed. Giuseppe Canestrini (Florence, 1857), p. 102.

12. Francesco Guicciardini, *The History of Italy,* trans. Chevalier Austin Parke Goddard (London, 1754), 1:148–49.

13. Leseur, *Histoire de Gaston IV,* 1:123 for Barcelona; Jules de la Pilorgerie, *Campagne et bulletins de la Grande Armée d'Italie commandée par Charles VIII, 1494–95* (Nantes and Paris, 1866), pp. 63ff., and Lot, *Les effectifs des armées françaises des guerres d'Italie,* for Naples; Pieri, *La crisi militare italiana nel Rinascimento,* says that the defenders of Padua themselves mustered 120 cannon. Similar figures are cited by Contamine, *War in the Middle Ages,* pp. 148–49. An excellent overview is provided by Taylor, *The Art of War in Italy 1495–1529,* in his chapter "Artillery."

14. Ffoulkes, *The Gunfounders,* pp. 71–81, and Cipolla, *Guns and Sails,* pp. 36–41. Laughton, in "Early Tudor Ship Guns," shows that some cast-iron guns were made in England as early as the period 1485–1515. Ffoulkes and Cipolla describe the beginnings of large-scale manufacture around the year 1543, when Henry VIII's straitened circumstances prevented foreign arms purchases for the impending war of 1543 (the "Enterprise of Boulogne").

15. Guilmartin, *Gunpowder and Galleys,* p. 175, and Cipolla, *Guns and Sails,* p. 42, note that bronze guns could cost four times as much as iron guns.

16. D'Addario, "Burocrazia, economia e finanze dello Stato Fiorentino alla metà del Cinquecento." The very small number of guns in some of the fortresses is confirmed in the *visite* of Bernadino Pagni and Giovanni Orlandi, "Libro delle visite delle fortezze del dominio di S. Ex.ᵃ tenuto per me Bernadino Pagni da Pescia" (1539), in A.S.F. *Med. Princ.* 624, and "Visite e inventari delle artiglierie, munizioni, vettovaglie, e soldati che si trovano nelle fortezze, fatte per Giovanni Orlandi da Pescia, 1543–1569," in A.S.F. *Med. Princ.* 625.

17. Seventeenth- or eighteenth-century perriers, of course, fired iron shot. The name of the gun then indicated only that it shared the physical characteristics of the original stone-shotted guns, i.e., short-barreled, thin-walled weapons which were relatively lighter and more manageable than the cannon class. The older perriers were also capable of firing a large load of stones, pieces of scrap iron, and chain shot and, according to Collado, served very well in flanking batteries (being held in "low esteem only by ignorant men"). Luigi Collado, *Pratica manuale di artiglieria* (Venice, 1586), fol. 62ff.

18. Lewis, *Armada Guns,* pp. 220–22, where the musket shot is given as "about 1 lb weight." De' Marchi, *Architettura militare,* book 4, chapter 12, p. 6, regards the *moschetti* as a whole class of light, long guns firing balls of from one to twelve pounds' weight. Elsewhere (book 4, chapter 19) he provides dimensions of a typical *moschetto* firing a two pound ball. By the end of the century, however, Lewis shows that the musket had its modern meaning of a handgun. This is confirmed in Collado, *Practica Manuale,* book 3, chapter 7, p. 89, who still lists it among the artillery but gives it a point-blank range of 200 paces and a two-ounce lead ball.

19. The best figures for Siena's arsenal are secondhand but still confirm the point that most artillery was of the light wall-mounted *moschettone* type. Bardi, *Storie Senesi,* fol. 203 *v.* notes that when the Spanish disarmed Siena in 1548 they found 30 pieces of "artigliaria grossa" with 200 iron cannonballs, 200 "moschetti altretanti archibusi da mura," 1,500 arquebuses and 9,000 pikes. These weapons were stored in a guarded magazine at the convent of San Domenico. Clearly "artigliaria grossa" is a phrase used by Bardi as a term embracing all guns bigger than the wall-mounted *moschetti.* Note the small number of iron cannonballs available for the bigger guns. Sozzini, "Diario," pp. 89–90, describing the expulsion of the Spaniards in August 1552, mentions that "30 pieces of various types" were removed from the citadel and lodged in the Campo and the Camera del Pubblico in the Palazzo Pubblico. These 30 assorted guns must constitute the nucleus of Siena's artillery on the eve of war.

20. De' Marchi, in *Architettura militare,* book 4, chapter 12, p. 6, is the only treatise author seriously to tackle the question of rates of fire. Under "ordinary conditions" and employing "ordinary powder" the following performances are given for a twelve-hour shooting day. Cannon types range from 90 rounds per day from a 20 pounder to 25 rounds for a 100 pounder. "Long guns" have a generally slower performance, no doubt because of the extra barrel length and the correspondingly greater difficulty of charging with a ladle and ramming the shot along a fouled bore. Culverins, according to de' Marchi, deliver from 75 rounds per day (20 pounders) to 20 rounds (100 pounders). Muskets, classified by the author amongst the *artigliera longa,* have the highest rate of fire; 120 rounds per day being delivered by a one-pounder musket.

It is important, of course, to distinguish between normal expectations and exceptional feats. Girolamo Cataneo, *Dell'arte militare* (Brescia, 1571), book 2, fol. 39*v.*, reports the astonishing achievement of Giordano Orsini (defender of Montalcino) who, on 29 August 1564 in Brescia, fired 108 rounds in five hours from a 50 pounder cannon. However, this was a set-piece demonstration, designed to settle a dispute between certain captains about Italian and French supremacy in rapid fire. The cannon weighed 6,634 pounds, and was mounted on an inclined bed, so that gravity returned it to the loading and firing point after each recoil. Cataneo tells us that the 25 pounds of powder used for each shot was loaded in a single motion, presumably in a bagged charge (see note 21 below). He also mentions that the only cooling was from the sponges which were dipped in pails of water. An average fire rate of 2.7 minutes per round for five hours must have made Orsini's gun very hot indeed.

21. Laughton, "Early Tudor Gun Ships," says that "cartouches" were listed among the ammunition supplied to Henry VIII's ship the *Mary Rose.* Patterns for cutting out fabric cartridge cases are given in a number of mid-sixteenth century treatises, and de' Marchi, *Architettura militare,* book 4, chapter 14, pp. 7–8, declares that they not only assist rapid fire but achieve more accurate (i.e., more consistent) charging of the guns. Biringuccio, *Pirotechnia,* p. 418, describes this method using paper rather than linen: "using this method," he writes, "is a very quick way."

22. Guilmartin, *Gunpowder and Galleys,* p. 163.

23. Laughton, "Early Tudor Gun Ships," 245–46, suggests that each such gun had between three and four chambers. In 1485 the *Grace Dieu* contained 22 guns with 89 chambers, the *Mary of the Tower* 54 to 140, and the *Governor* 70 to 265. Similar figures for land service artillery are suggested by an inventory of weapons in the then Florentine castle of Sarzana in 1496; for example: "Spingardam unam ferri cum tribus cannonis," Buselli, *Documenti sulla edificazione della Fortezza di Sarzana 1487–1492,* pp. 102–7.

24. Good illustrated descriptions of these "wooden guns" are to be found in Della Valle, *Vallo,* book 1, chapter 2, and Biringuccio, *Pirotechnia,* pp. 409–16; pp. 425–28. Biringuccio says that with a stone ball one can expect half the ordinary effect of artillery, but the noise sounds as if the gun was of iron or

bronze. Other later authors assume a "canister" type or "incendiary" load.

25. Held, *The Age of Firearms;* and Lavin, *A History of Spanish Firearms,* pp. 39–50.

26. Lavin, *Spanish Firearms,* p. 44, has recorded early sixteenth-century Spanish weapons of this type weighing 27 to 35 pounds, with barrels more than 5 feet long.

27. Sir Roger Williams, "A Brief Discourse of Warre" (1590), in *The Works of Sir Roger Williams,* ed. John X. Evans (Oxford, 1972), pp. 35–38:

"To prooue Musketiers the best small shot that euer were inuented.

"My reasons are thus; the Musket spoyles horse or man more thirtie score (paces) off, if the powder bee any thing good, and the bearer of any judgement. If armed (i.e., armored) men give the charge, few or any carrie Armes of the proofe of the Musket, being delivered within ten or twelve score (paces). If any great troupes of horse or foote, offers to force them with multitude of smaller shot, they may discharge foure, five or sixe smal bullets being delivered in a volley . . . By that reckoning 100 Muskets are to bee valued unto 200 Calivers shot, farre or nere & better cheape: although the Musket spend a pound of powder in 8 or 12 shot, and the other smaller shootes twentie and thirtie of a pound. Considering the wages and expences of two to one, the Musket is better cheape and farre more serviceable."

28. Parker, *The Army of Flanders and the Spanish Road 1567–1659,* p. 277, provides a useful breakdown of the officers, musketeers, arquebusiers, corselets (armored pikemen), and other pikemen of the Spanish Army of Flanders in 1571 and 1601. The proportions varied somewhat between the Spanish, Italian, German, Burgundian, and Walloon units; but the overall percentages were as follows:

| | Muster Date | |
	1571	1601
Total troops (excluding camp followers and pioneers)	7,509	22,453
Officers	6.0%	8.5%
Muskets	8.0%	19.4%
Arquebus	20.0%	22.8%
Corselets	35.0%	37.6%
Pikes	32.5%	11.6%

29. Bury, "The Early History of the Explosive Mine."

30. Paolo Giovio, *Historie del suo tempo* (Florence, 1551), fol. 126*v*, quoted in Bury, "The Explosive Mine," 25. Other contemporary accounts of the Castel Nuovo fighting are to be found in Taylor, *The Art of War*, p. 134.

31. For discussion of later sixteenth-century mining and countermining techniques, see Pepper, "The Underground Siege."

32. Hale, "The Bastion," p. 478, quotes an early document specifying these modifications to the walls of Foligno in 1441.

33. For the morphology of gunports, see O'Neil, *Castles*, pp. 7–21, and Kenyon, "Early Artillery Fortification in England and Wales," and "Early Gunports." Relatively little has been published on Italian gunports, but see Mallet and Whitehouse, "Castel Porciano."

34. Machiavelli, "Relazione di una visita fatta per fortificare Firenze," in *L'Arte della guerra e scritti politici minori* ed. Sergio Bertelli (Milan, 1961) pp. 295–302.

35. Francesco di Giorgio Martini, *Trattati di architettura, ingegneria e arte militare*, 2:474. For illustrated accounts of the military architecture of Francesco, see Bardeschi, "Le Rocche di Francesco di Giorgio nel ducato di Urbino"; Pepper and Hughes, "Fortification in late 15th Century Italy"; Scaglia, "Francesco di Giorgio's Chapters on Fortresses and on War Machines"; Volpe, *Rocche e fortificazioni del Ducato di Urbino*.

36. Truttman, *La Forteresse de Salses*.

37. Francesco di Giorgio, *Trattati*, 2:433–44, where he claims that *capannati* are "newly invented." Casemates and other ditchworks have been strangely neglected by archeologists and architectural historians. Mid-sixteenth-century authors, such as Zanchi, *Del modo di fortificar le città*, or Maggi and Castriotto, *Della fortificazione delle città*, Book 1, Chapter 10, fol. 20, took them seriously. By the end of the century Busca remarked of them: "Io non sò se cosi le chiamano, perche pazzi sieno quegli che li hanno a star dentro, quasi case dei pazzi . . ." But he then goes on to give a good account of the different types that had been "much used by the French and Germans in the early stages of modern fortification" and were still considered useful in some circumstances. Busca, *L'Architettura militare*, p. 187.

38. Hughes, *Military Architecture*, pp. 23–66, provides numerous illustrations of the concentric principle in medieval fortification. De' Marchi, *Architettura militare*, book 3, chapter 102, p. 166, illustrates and describes a classic concentric scheme which, he maintains, was one of the standard Italian solutions in the late fifteenth century. This author, together with most other late Renaissance authorities, disapproves of duplicated fortifications, which were believed to sap the fighting spirit of those manning the outer walls.

39. Eugène Viollet-le-Duc, *Dictionnaire raisonnée de l'architecture française du XIe au XVIe siècle*, under "boulevard."

40. The gallery was built after the earthquake of 1456. Filangieri, *Castel Nuovo Reggia Angoina ed Aragonese di Napoli*, pp. 51–72. Hale, "The Bastion," p. 480, is uncertain that the gallery was a mounting for heavy guns, but points to similar low-level advanced works at the Neapolitan castle of Gaeta as well as the Orsini fortress of Bracciano.

41. Rusconi, *Le mura di Padova*, p. 34; de la Croix, *Military Considerations in City Planning*, p. 43; Brenzoni, *Fra Giovanni Giocondo Veronese*.

42. Guicciardini, *History*, 4:338 (Book 8).

43. Albrecht Dürer, *Etliche Underricht, zur Befestigung der Stett, Schloss, and Flecken* (Nuremberg, 1527). See also Malachowicz, "Fortification in Poland," and Majewski, "Les tours cannonières et les fortifications bastionées en Pologne." Dürer's thesis was well-enough known in Italy for some of the leading authors to attack what they clearly regarded as a threat to the orthodoxy of the bastion. See Maggi and Castriotto, *Della fortificazione*, book 2, chapter 30, fols. 69*v*–70, and Busca, *L'Architettura militare*, p. 109.

44. For Coron and Nauplia, see Andrews, *The Castles of the Morea*; for Verona, see Langenskiold, *Michele Sanmicheli, the Architect of Verona*, pp. 154–55; and for measured drawings, see Ronzani and Luciolli, *Le Fabbriche civili, ecclesiastiche e militare di Michele Sanmicheli*. For Assisi, see Hale, "The Bastion," p. 492.

45. Quarenghi, *Le mura di Roma*; Rocchi, *Le Piante iconografiche e prospettiche di Roma del secolo XVI*; Borgatti, "Il bastione ardeatina a Roma"; Pepper, "Planning versus Fortification."

46. Pepper, "Underground Siege," pp. 33, 38.

47. Pepper, "Planning versus Fortification," pp. 167–69. Hale describes very similar problems circumscribing the projects for the defense of seventeenth-century Vicenza: "Francesco Tensini and the Fortification of Vicenza."

48. Borgatti, *Castel S. Angelo in Roma,* pp. 234–36; de la Croix, "Radial City Plan," pp. 277–78; Marconi, "Contributo alla storia delle fortificazioni di Roma nel cinquecento e nel seicento."

49. Severini, *Architetture militari di Giuliano da Sangallo.*

50. Hale, "The End of Florentine Liberty."

51. Gurrieri, *La Rocca Paolina in Perugia.* Antonio da Sangallo the Younger was architect.

52. Hersey, *Alfonso II and the Artistic Renewal of Naples, 1485–1495.*

53. Alberti, *Ten Books on Architecture,* 5:3.

54. Machiavelli, *The Discourses,* book 2, discourse 24.

55. Quoted by Hale, "Fortezza da Basso," p. 504.

56. De' Marchi, *Architettura militare,* 1:13, fol. 3 *v.,* 1:18, fols. 5–5*v.*

57. Zevi, *Biagio Rossetti;* and Malagù, *Le mura di Ferrara;* Rosenberg, "The Erculean Addition."

58. De la Croix, *Military Considerations,* p. 45.

59. Tuttle, "Against Fortifications." See also Hale, "To Fortify or not to Fortify?"

60. De la Croix, "Radial City Plan" and *Military Considerations,* are the key general sources. For more detailed studies, see de la Croix, "Palmanova"; Hughes, "Give me time and I will give you life"; Blouet, "Town Planning in Malta, 1530–1798"; Forster, "From 'Rocca' to 'Civitas.' "

61. Braudel, *The Mediterranean and the Mediterranean World in the Age of Philip II,* vol. 2, chapter 7, provides an excellent description of frontier warfare and its related activities on the Mediterranean frontiers and far beyond. See also Pierson, *Philip II of Spain,* pp. 129–59; Merriman, *The Rise of the Spanish Empire in the Old World and the New;* Parry, *The Spanish Seaborne Empire;* Koenigsberger, *The Government of Sicily under Philip II;* and Croce, *Storia del Regno di Napoli.* Guilmartin, *Gunpowder and Galleys,* is invaluable on the military aspects of coastal warfare, as is the work of Guglielmotti, historian of the Papal navy, *La guerra dei pirati e la marina pontificia dal 1500 al 1560* and *Storia della fortificazioni della spiaggia romana.* For the Venetian building program of 1542–92 and its administration,

see Hale, "The First Fifty Years of a Venetian Magistracy." Too recent for consultation is Mallet and Hale, *The Military Organisation of a Renaissance State.*

62. Rocchi, *Le piante,* 1:239–40.

63. Braudel, *The Mediterranean,* 2:857, note 89.

64. These are, of course, indicative figures culled from Braudel, *The Mediterranean,* and Parker, *The Army of Flanders.* Wherever possible we picked data from the middle of the century to minimize the distorting effect of inflation.

65. De' Marchi, *Architettura militare,* book 1, chapter 11, fol. 3.

66. Hook, "Fortifications and the End of the Sienese State."

2

1. The early Sienese walls are shown in a drawing by Francesco Piccolomini (now conserved in the Archivio di Stato) illustrating Teofilo Gallaccini's *Informazione delle antichità di Siena.* The relevant extract from Gallaccini is published in Gigli, *Diario sanese,* pp. 490–96.

2. Alberti, *Ten Books,* book 4, chapter 3, p. 71.

3. Duccio Balestracci and Gabriella Piccinni, *Siena nel Trecento,* pp. 17–30.

4. Absence of towers made necessary the construction (and periodic reconstruction) of timber sentry boxes or guard houses at intervals along the curtains. These jobs provided frequent commissions for the architects and master craftsmen of sixteenth-century Siena and constitute a potential source of confusion for researchers attempting to discover new works of fortification.

5. Just inside the heavily restored Torrione Dipinto one can still find the short marble column that commemorates the meeting of Frederick III and his bride, Eleonor of Portugal, on 7 March 1451. Much exaggerated in size, it appears in many of the siege illustrations and is a useful reference point.

6. O. M. Orlandi, *La gloriosa vittoria di Camollia* (Siena, 1527), fol. 19*v.*

7. Vasari, *Le Opere,* 4:598.

8. The disruption of work on the major church commission, St. Peter's, represented a significant loss for Peruzzi. It is interesting that the Sienese took it upon themselves to

loan Peruzzi the money for his ransom. See the series of governmental records: ASS *Balìa* 92, fol. 247; *Balìa* 93, fol. 74*v.*; *Balìa* 571, nos. 77, 78, 86, 99; *Balìa* 1001, fol. 82*v.*; *Bicchema* 356, fols. 28, 172*v.* Despite the lack of more substantial evidence, these documents could support the assertion of Vasari in his life of Peruzzi that the Sienese had employed him on the fortifications prior to 1527. Adams, "Baldassare Peruzzi as Architect to the Republic, 1527–1535." (We have adopted the recent practice of spelling Peruzzi's first name, Baldassarre, with a double *r.* Earlier articles, including some of our own, such as that just cited, have used a single *r.*)

9. For Peruzzi's Roman activity, see Frommel, *Baldassare Peruzzi als Maler und Zeichner* and *Der römische Palastbau der Hochrenaissance*; Wurm, *Der Palazzo Massimo alle Colonne.*

10. The sequence of events is noted in ASS, *Concistoro* 2201, fols. 5, 8, 10*v.*–11*v.*

11. On the dam project, see Adams, "Architecture for Fish"; Toca, "Un progetto peruzziano per una diga di sbarramento nella 107–117." For Peruzzi as mint master, see Adams, "New Information about the Screw Press as a Device for Minting Coins." On Peruzzi's activities in the contado towns, see Adams, "Baldassare Peruzzi and a Tour of Inspection in the Valdichiana 1528–1529."

12. "Et mandaverunt significari magistro Baldassari architectori quod cum civibus electis super custodiam civitatis et cum aliis civibus et collegio vadat et procurat muros nostre civitatis Senensis et notent omnes defectus et referant. Et tres prior eligendi Iohannes Baptista Pannilinus, Nicolaus Campana, Nicolaus Franciscus." ASS, *Balìa*, 92, fol. 149*v.*

13. ASS, *Concistoro* 2205. The document is undated but looks forward to future work, and probably originates from mid-1528. Its use of the term "bastion," as will become clear, does not conform to the specialized fortification terminology of the late sixteenth century.

As is noted "Bastionare non significò sempre costruire bastioni nel senso attribuito in seguito a questo vocabulo, ma soltanto munire, fortificare un luogo, mettere le parti più esposte al coperto dalle offese." Angelucci, *Documenti inediti per la storia della armi di fuoco italiane* p. 303, n. 187.

14. Of the two no longer standing there remains convincing documentary evidence in favor of an attribution. For the Sportello,

ASS, *Balìa* 92, fols. 162*v.*–163. For San Marco, *Balìa* 93, fol. 145. For further archival references, see Adams, "Peruzzi as Architect to the Republic." See below, notes 28, 30.

15. Alberti, *Ten Books*, book 7, chapter 2, p. 135.

16. Bury, "Are Renaissance Fortifications Beautiful?"; Hale, *Renaissance Fortification: Art or Engineering?* Adams, "Military Architecture and Renaissance Art History or 'Bellezza on the Battlefield.'"

17. De la Croix, *Military Considerations*, p. 45.

18. Pepper and Hughes, "Fortification in Fifteenth Century Italy."

19. Severini, *Architetture Militari di Giuliano da Sangallo.*

20. Langenskiold, *Sanmicheli*; Gazzola and Kahne-Mann, *Michele Sanmichele*; Puppi, *Michele Sanmichele.*

21. Borgatti, "Il bastione ardeatino a Roma"; Pepper, "Planning versus Fortification"; Gurrieri, *La rocca Paolina.*

22. Dürer, *Etliche Underricht*; Malachowicz, "Fortification in Poland."

23. These weapons are described and illustrated in Guilmartin, *Gunpowder and Galleys*, pp. 159–62.

24. The subject of artillery range is an interesting one. The most complete discussion is in Guilmartin, *Gunpowder and Galleys*, pp. 162–66. Guilmartin notes that the "maximum effective range of sixteenth-century artillery was between two and five hundred yards, depending on the conditions and nature of the target. Any sound bronze cannon larger than a swivel piece could throw its projectile several thousand yards; but for a number of reasons this was of little practical consequence. First of all, a smooth-bore gun firing a spherical projectile is intrinsically inaccurate, not least because spherical projectiles which spin in an unpredictable fashion do not fly true. On top of this, undersized cannonballs were used to compensate for variations in ball size and shape" (p. 162). For breaching of fortress walls "about sixty yards was considered the optimum range" (p. 163). The kinds of renovations undertaken by Peruzzi had in mind both the long-range potential of artillery ("to annoy the enemy") and the capability to depress guns on the face batteries to engage an enemy breaching battery.

25. Bardi, *Storie senesi 1512–1556*, fols. 42*v.*–43.

26. Francesco di Giorgio Martini, *Trattati di architettura, ingegneria e arte militare;* also Pepper and Hughes, "Fortification in Fifteenth Century Italy," pp. 547–48. Although very few early ditchworks have survived, they were evidently of considerable importance in the transitional period of gunpowder fortifications and merit serious attention. Capannati, or pillboxes, on the floors of the ditch represented an effective means of flanking a medieval trace, without the massive expense of triangular bastion construction.

27. These devices are well illustrated in Heydenreich, Dibner, and Reti, *Leonardo the Inventor,* pp. 72–124. Cart-mounted, multibarreled weapons were evidently used to good effect in the Hussite Wars.

28. The significant passage that confirms Peruzzi's involvement reads: "Et audito magistro Baldassare architectore referente quod civitas nostra potest de facili offendi et est expugnabilis in loco qui dicitur lo Sportello, quia in loco in quo est situm monasterium Sancti Prosperi, si inimici civitatis ponerunt castra in dicto loco possent offendere, et esset opus ad evitandum hanc suspicionem facere et hedificare in dicto loco lo Sportello unum torrazum vocatum vulgariter/ baluardo, quod hedificium de facili fieret et cum parvo sumptu, moti iustis de causis, servatis servandis, deliberaverunt omni studio et cum maxima sollicitudine fieri dictum hedificium secundum ordinem et formam dandam per dictum magistrum Baldassarem." ASS, *Balìa* 92, fols. 162*v.*–163.

29. The first notice, for the delivery of the bricks, is from 29 October 1528, ASS, *Concistoro* 2203. The second notice is dated 10 December 1528, and records the payment of 150 fiorini to the owner of the land, a certain Giuliano di Lorenzo da Campagnatico, for the damage to his property in the construction of the bastion. See ASS, *Balìa* 1005, fol. 107.

30. ASS, *Balìa* 93, fol. 145 (14 January 1528). Expenditure on the subsequent works is recorded in *Balìa* 1002, fol. 46; *Biccherna* 357, fols. 64*v.*, 66, 66*v.*, 68, and 69.

31. ASS, Balìa 93, fol. 313*v.* (13 March, 1528) for site purchase, and *Balìa* 1005, fol. 117 (10 December 1528) for expenditure on works.

32. ASS, *Biccherna* 365, fol. 21.

33. ASS, *Balìa*, 573, no. 80 (19 May 1528).

34. ASS, *Balìa*, 583, no. 94 (9 October 1528).

35. See ASS, *Balìa* 1008, fol. 62; *Balìa* 1009, fol. 9; *Balìa* 100, fol. 81*v.* The first of these orders reads: "Per parte della Balìa eccetera: voi specialissimo Guido di Girolamo Biringucci camerlingo di zecca data et pagate ali specialissimi .vi. cittadini deputati sopra l'ornato per la Cesare Maestà ò a chi per loro vi sara ordenato tutti il retratto et denaro dello zecchino atribuiti ale muraglia delli torazzi per uno tempo di uno mese cominciato il .vi. del presente et da finire come segue. Et tanto eccetera." *Balìa* 1008, fol. 62.

Peruzzi's involvement is well documented. While in Florence (7 January 1530), at the siege, he expresses his desire to return to Siena in order to work on the triumphal arches being prepared for the entry of the emperor (ASS, *Balìa* 600, no. 16) and he is recorded later as actively working on the project (7 February 1530; *Balìa* 99, fol. 10–10*v.*). On the entry, Pecci, *Memorie storico-critiche della città di Siena dal 1480 al 1552,* 3:27.

36. Hook, *The Sack of Rome,* pp. 267–78. In 1536 the visit provided the occasion for the erection of a commemorative column. See Brinton, *The Renaissance in Italian Art,* 2:148; and "Carlo Quinto in Siena, nell'aprile del 1536." ed. P. Vigo, in *Scelta di Curiosità Letterarie inedite o raro* (Bologna, 1968).

37. ASS, *Consiglio Generale* 243, fol. 8*v.* (23 November 1528); and "Item sopra la petitione di maestro Baldassare atteso le sue virtù nota la necessità e sue virtù detto et consiglio che dectto maestro Baldassarre si radoppi el suo stipendio e quali sopra li torazzi habbino autorità di darli della pecunia del comune d'ogni torazo si ne facto havere scudi .xxv." ASS, *Concistoro* 2202 (22 November 1531).

38. "Per parte della Balìa eccetera si da licentia alli operari della fabrica di Santo Jacomo et Santo Cristofano in Salicotto poter levare dal torazzo di Santo Prospero alo Sportello tucta quella quantità di mattoni che vi fussero" ASS, *Balìa* 1011, fol. 58*v.*

3

---

1. Cantagalli, *La Guerra di Siena (1552–1559),* p. 1xxiii. See also Hook's important article "Hapsburg Imperialism and Italian Particularism."

2. Roth, *The Last Florentine Republic 1527– 30,* pp. 209–13.

3. Cochrane, *Florence and the Forgotten Centuries, 1527–1800;* Spini, ed., *Cosimo I de' Medici: Lettere;* Marini, *La Spagna in Italia nell'Età di Carlo V.*

4. Cantagalli, *La Guerra,* pp. lxxii–lxxxii. Hook, *Siena: A City and its History,* pp. 173– 85, gives an excellent and broadly based account of the internal tensions and problems facing the republic in these decades. Billeting of the troops was not popular. For example, a certain Maestro Donnino appealed for aid in 1550 from the Sienese Concistoro: "già uno ano visono divento li Spagnioli et io con la mia povara famiglia mi trovo stare apigione inel merchato vechio." ASS, *Concistoro* 2243.

5. Bardi, *Storie senesi,* fol. 238: "loro non possevano stare sicuri ne godere il loro, se non si faceva il castello." Alessandro Sansedoni, the republic's ambassador in Rome, reporting reactions to the first news of the Spanish project, 7 July 1550: "si dice che molti cittadini vogliano il castello." ASS, *Balìa* 723, no. 13. Hook, "Hapsburg Imperialism," makes the point that many Sienese, far from caring about liberty in the abstract, were merely trying to make the best political deal they could.

6. Pecci, *Memorie storico-critiche,* 3:227–29.

7. "Charles himself always drew a careful distinction between those soldiers who were billeted in the city for Siena's own good, and which he held the Sienese should pay for, and those billeted in the interests of the Empire who were, theoretically, paid from Spain. In fact, he rarely provided money to pay any of the troops at all." Hook, *Siena,* p. 184.

8. Bardi, *Storie senesi,* fol. 239, lists the seventeen towers demolished in Camollia. Postwar views of the city, however, show that many towers survived both the citadel project and the siege. Hook, "Hapsburg Imperialism," p. 286.

9. Bardi, *Storie senesi,* fols. 217v–218v.

10. Most authorities "credit" Peloro with authorship of the citadel, an attribution which in Sienese eyes was at best unwelcome and at worst an act of complicity bordering on treason. Sozzini, "Diario," p. 38, appears to be the first of the chroniclers to name Peloro. However, Bardi, *Storie senesi,* fol. 218v., attributes the model of the city done in earth to a certain "Giovambattista Romano ingegnere"

but makes no mention of Peloro. One would like to know more about this shadowy Roman. He is mentioned in a number of dispatches to Siena, notably Girolamo Tolomei, writing from Milan, 12 September 1549 (ASS, *Balìa* 719, no. 64). He may also be the Giovambattista noted in letters of July 1551 as a military captain (ASS, *Balìa* 724, nos. 60, 62, 63). There is also an important letter, confirming the attribution of work on the citadel from the Sienese ambassador, Amerigo Amerighi, in Rome, 17 June 1551, who noted his last letter on 15 June "quale portò Gio: batista Romano Archittore del Castello." (*Balìa* 724, no. 52).

11. Bardi, *Storie senesi,* fol. 218v. According to Sozzini, "Diario," p. 58, the towers of Camollia were pulled down in June and July 1551 for their material.

12. "La cacciata della guardia Spagnuola da Siena d'incerto autore, 1552," *Archivio storico italiano,* 2 (1842): 440–41.

13. Bardi, *Storie senesi,* fol. 217v., records that Tolomei was voted the prodigious salary of 150 scudi per month. Was this to cover his own expenses, to cover those of his entire party, or to offer hospitality and other "favors" at the Imperial court?

14. Sozzini, "Diario," pp. 38–39.

15. "La cacciata," p. 443.

16. "La cacciata," pp. 444–46.

17. "La cacciata," p. 446.

18. Misciatelli, *The Mystics of Siena;* Gonzi, *Brandano.* Poems were even composed on this bitter occasion. Gianmaria Nini wrote an immensely tedious protest verse (for which he was thrown in jail) from which we reproduce the following three verses ("La cacciata," pp. 446–49).

La giustizia di Cesar m'assicura
Che non darà principio all'empio freno;
Sperando ancor ch'alzendosi le mura,
Da lui meglio informato estinte sieno:
Che un'empia informazion, sinistra e dura,
Piena di tosco e colma di veleno,
S'oppon che Cesar indurato nieghi
Quel che convincon nostri giusti preghi.

Non ha sito nessun che, per alzarlo,
Gli altri edifizi tutti, in pianto e tutta
Non si ruinin, sol per elevarlo,
A potere spiantar il resto tutto:
Ogni contorno poi n'ha da sbassarla
Con tante spendio e tanto poco fretta
Che in diservizio di tua Maestade,
Per una rocca guasti una Cittade.

Chi corre la campagna, agevolmente
D'ogni fortezza tua si fa padrone:
Provoca l'empio fren tanto ogni gente,
Che in odio ti si volta ogni affezione.
Se tu lo perdi, come è contingente,
Non ti rimane amor nè devozione,
Per racquistarti i nostri ameni colli,
Con quella libertà che tu ci tolli.

19. The emperor's position is expressed very well in a report from Orlando Mariscotti, Sienese ambassador to the court at Innsbruck, who had been granted a personal audience by Charles. Mariscotti's letter describes the aging emperor ("se l'havesse visto in altro tempo certo è che non l'havei conosciuto, tanto è trasformato") but continues: "Et circa del castello che S. Mta. non solo l'havea fabricato per sua mera voluntà ma ancora per la causa che n'haveva data la città, per l'instabilità, e per levare via la causa che non si havessi e perdere la libertà e l'istessa città, et ancora dannificare li stati di S. Mta. che era stato a risolversi piu che haveva potuto, e tutto haveva fatto per mantenere la libertà a la città." ASS, *Balìa* 725, no. 85.

20. See Cantagalli, *La Guerra*, pp. 16–17, for the French planning discussions at Chioggia, near Venice, on 15–18 July 1552.

21. Quoted by Hook, "Hapsburg Imperialism," p. 287.

22. Details of the fighting in "La cacciata." See also Sozzini, "Diario," 75–88, and Bardi, *Storie senesi*, fols. 259ff.

23. Sozzini, "Diario," p. 88.

24. Bardi, *Storie senesi*, fols. 295–96.

25. Cantagalli, *La Guerra*, pp. 23–35.

26. Sozzini, "Diario," p. 88.

27. The main landscaping project was carried out between 1778 and 1781, when Leopold I, the reforming grand duke of Tuscany, evacuated the fortress and turned it and the Lizza into a public gardens. Wandruszka, *Pietro Leopoldo, un grande riformatore*, p. 347. For many years the accepted location of the Spanish citadel was that provided by the map of Francesco Piccolomini. Following the description of the eighteenth-century topographer Teofilo Gallacini, he placed the citadel between the extant Medici Fortress and the Camollia wall. To fit onto this site the citadel was shown with a somewhat smaller plan than the existing fortress. In this respect Piccolomini-Gallacini has proved most misleading. Part of the citadel certainly lay beneath the present-day Lizza gardens, but its total extent was very much greater. (For Piccolomini-Gallacini, see chapter 2, note 1.)

Fragments of walling were uncovered (but never properly excavated or published) when the new Palazzo della Giustizia was built in the late 1970s. (This building was still not open to the public in 1985!) Fragments of what look like fortifications can be seen acting as a retaining wall between the Medici fortress and Camollia in a number of early topographical studies. Francesco Vanni's view of circa 1600 was probably the earliest accurate topographic picture to employ what later was to become a somewhat standardized air view. It was copied by Rutilio Manetti in his early seventeenth-century painted view (Siena, Archivio di Stato), by Matteo Floriani's view as well as by Pierre Mortier. For reproductions, see Rombai, "Siena nelle sue rappresentazioni cartografiche fra la metà del '500 e l'inizio del '600," in *I Medici e lo stato senese 1555–1609*, pp. 91–109.

28. Biographical information on Giorgio di Giovanni (d. 1559) is provided in chapter 9. On the Biccherna covers, see Borgia et al., *Le Biccherne.*

29. This sheet will be published jointly by the authors with Daniela Lamberini, "Un disegno di spionaggio cinquecentesco," in *Mitteilungen des Kunsthistorischen Institutes in Florenz* (1987).

30. Compare the sheet with those published in the recent exhibition catalog, *I bottini: Acquedotti medievali senesi* (Siena, 1984), p. 32.

31. Compare, for example, the Pistoia sheets as illustrated by Lamberini, "Le mura e i bastioni di Pistoia."

32. Belluzzi's plan is divided into an earthen section facing out of the city and the hornwork facing the city with a brick or stone covering.

33. Florence, Uffizi, Gabinetto Disegni e Stampe, Architettura 1971. Published first in Mario Filippone's Italian translation of Monluc's *Commentaries* under the title *L'Assedio di Siena* (Siena, 1976), between pages 15 and 16. Filippone correctly dates it to the spring of 1554. See also Rombai, "Siena nelle sue rappresentazioni," pp. 94 and 105.

34. See Bardi, *Storie senesi*, fol. 263, for this debate.

35. Their activities are recorded in two collections of documents, ASS, *Balìa* 141, the "Deliberations" and *Balìa* 145 the "Order Book" of the committee. In practice the two kinds of record quickly became inseparable.

36. ASS, *Balìa* 141, fol. 3, and *Balìa* fol. 5v..

37. ASS, *Balìa* 141, fols. 2–3.

38. ASS, *Balìa* 141, fols. 3v–4 (8 August); *Balìa* 141, fol. 4 (9 August).

39. ASS, *Balìa* 141, fol. 4v., and *Balìa* 145, fol. 5v.

40. ASS, *Balìa* 141, fol. 2 (7 August 1552) resolved: "Che si facci precepto al camera dei muratori et loro manuali che sotto pena di tratti 4 di fune siano tutti li maestri et loro manuali alla fabrica con picconi et zapponi." For salary arrangements *Balìa* 141, fols. 31v–32 (12 September 1552). Payment was thereafter to be made every third evening, rather than daily, in order to save time. Evidently rations were provided at public expense, for the same order specifies payment of the bakers at the same three-day intervals.

41. ASS, *Balìa* 141, fol. 60v (4 January 1553) and fol. 66v (23 January 1553).

42. ASS, *Balìa* 141, fol. 24v.

43. See Goldthwaite, *The Building of Renaissance Florence,* pp. xiv–xv and 320–21, for terminology of Italian building trades titles and their functions. For Siena, see *Statuto dell'arte dei muratori (1626).*

44. ASS, *Balìa* 141, fol. 64 (17 January 1553) and fol. 75 (18 February); *Balìa* 145, fols. 4v, 5v, 7v (March), fols. 17 and 29 (April 1553).

45. ASS, *Balìa* 141, fols. 60v and 66v.

46. Alberti, *Ten Books,* Book 4, chapter 4, pp. 73–74, for an early account of the construction of masonry and rubble walls on lines established by the ancients. Francesco di Giorgio, *Trattati,* 1:7–8; 2:432–33, 440–41, gives details of foundations, arched counterforts and the use of timber reinforcement in masonry walls.

47. In 1509 the Venetians constructed a rampart and ditch some four miles long between Monforte and Lonigo, near Verona. An even longer work was built by Gonsalvo da Cordoba in 1503 in the semi-inundated land along the Garigliano, north of Naples. At the end of the century the Venetian defenses along the Isonzo river provided a near continuous chain of forts, ditches, and earthworks to prevent Turkish raids from modern Yugoslavia. Palmanova was the central fortress of this defensive complex, a sixteenth-century Maginot line. Although the Romans were well known to have built gigantic works of circumvallation for their sieges, this technique appears to have been reintroduced early in the sixteenth century to general astonishment. Guicciardini, *History,* 7:334–35, describes the work built by Prospero Colonna at Milan in 1522 in the following terms: "The city still remained in imminent danger of being entered by the French from the castle; to prevent which, and by the same expedient to deprive them of the power of putting victuals or other kinds of provisions into the castle, he [Colonna] set about a work highly celebrated for its invention and in the opinion of the public almost stupendous. For without the castle, between the gates that lead to Vercelli and to Como he caused to be dug two trenches, and raised of the earth taken out of each of them a bank, distant one from another about twenty paces, and extending about a mile across so much of the garden behind the castle as lies between the two said roads: and at each of the heads of the trenches he erected a very high and strong cavalier, in order to plant the artillery on them for annoying the enemy if they approached on that side. These trenches and ramparts were guarded by parties of foot lodged in the midst of them, and who at the same time prevented all sucors from entering the castle, and all egress of the besieged."

48. Belluzzi, *Nuova inventione di fabricar fortezze, de varie forme* pp. 13–25. See also della Valle *Vallo* fols. 5v–8v, for the earliest printed and illustrated account of Renaissance earthwork construction.

49. Della Valle, fols 5v–6, illustrates a casemated fortification made entirely of timber and earth and claims that this gave better shot resistance than masonry. He points out, however, that any stones in the earthwork will prove dangerous to the defenders: hence the efforts to "clean" the earth through sieves described by Belluzzi and later authors. Maggi and Castriotto also stress the need to sharpen the outward-facing tips of the timber reinforcement, to present the smallest possible obstacle to incoming shot. A "soft" rampart, of course, had to be well consolidated to stop iron shot. Francesco de' Marchi reported that Zitolo da Perugia, who commanded the Bastione della Gatta at Padua in 1509, had his arm taken off by a ball that had penetrated 30 feet of loosely laid parapet. After test firings of his own (the only such tests recorded in sixteenth century treatises), de' Marchi found that 20 feet of well-consolidated earth was sufficient to stop the heaviest iron balls at 100 paces. A heavy bombardment, however, could still yield extraordinary effects such as those observed by Sir Francis Vere at one of Ostend's works, known as the Sandhill, which "was so thick stuck with bullets that the ordinance could scarce shoot without a tautology, and hitting its former bullets, which, like an iron wall, made the latter fly in pieces into the air." *The Commentaries of Sir Francis Vere*, p. 134.

50. ASS, *Balìa* 141, fol. 77 (26 February 1553), records the construction of "grati e gabbioni della cittadella."

4

---

1. Paul de la Barthe, sieur de Thermes and Marshal of France (1482–1562) was one of the most experienced soldiers of his age. Despite a late start to his military career (due to exile following a duel), he served at Naples (1528, followed by two years of harsh Turkish captivity), Piedmont (1531), Thérouanne (1531), and Perpignan (1542) before gaining command of all the French light cavalry in Piedmont in 1543. The high point of his career was the cavalry counterattack that won the day at Cerisoles in 1544. His sieges included the successful defense of Savillan and the capture of Revel, both in northern Italy, and the capture of Addington in Scotland, where he commanded a French expeditionary force in 1549–50. In Scotland he acquired a reputation for fierce discipline by hanging an officer for leading an assault on a fort against orders, after publicly praising the man for his courage. With the title of *Lieutenant du Roi*, he assisted in the defense of Parma and Mirandola before his dispatch to Siena in the fall of 1552. Following the Corsica campaign of late 1553, he was to see further service in Piedmont and northern Europe; including the capture of Calais and Dunkerque, for which he was awarded his marshal's baton. Thermes was captured following his defeat at Gravelines in 1558, and remained prisoner until the Peace of Cateau-Cambrésis in 1559.

2. Bardi, *Storie senesi*, fol. 289; Orlando Malavolti, *Dell'Historia di Siena*, book 10, part 3, p. 157; Pecci, *Memorie storico-critiche*, 4:44. However, Sozzini, "Diario," pp. 92–93, credits the cardinal of Ferrara with the decision (*per consiglio di un suo architettore*) and says that many objected to the closed backs of the forts which, it was claimed, could be used

against the city. This reads rather like wisdom after the event and was probably not a serious criticism of works too far from the main enceinte to be covered effectively from the rear. Sozzini is generally very critical of the cardinal's leadership and may well be attempting here to exaggerate his responsibility for what was more likely to have been a military decision by Thermes. The latter, after completing his tour of the dominio, was instructed to survey the positions "around and close to the city" by the government on 12 December, 1552. ASS, *Balìa* 148, fol. 252.

3. Peloro's appointment was confirmed in the deliberations of 10 October 1552. One week later, he received a first payment of ten scudi "per cortesia del collegio." ASS, *Balìa* 148, fols. 59 and 74v.

4. See the material in chapter 8 and the biographical data and documents in Romagnoli, *Biografia cronologica de' bellartisti senesi dal secolo XII a tutto il XVIII*. This work, a longhand record of the lives of the Sienese artists is found in Biblioteca Comunale, Siena MS., L.II.1–13. This work is now available in a photo reprint edition (Florence, 1976).

5. Our plan is taken from the Codex Francesco Laparelli, in the private collection of the Contessa Costanza Laparelli-Pitti Maggi-Diligenti, Cortona. Laparelli, *Visita e progetti di miglior difesa in varie fortezze ed altri luoghi dello Stato Pontificio*, fig. 3.

6. Bardi, *Storie senesi*, fol. 300, makes it clear that the main structure was unrevetted earthwork, involving the collection of large numbers of brushwood fascines. However, he mentions that the cardinal of Ferrara personally donated money for a gate and drawbridge "now called the Porta Francia." The king of France also promised funds "to cloth all the forts in fine walling of the same architecture which had been begun in the gateway." We do not know how much, if any, of the permanent architectural *finishes* were applied to the forts themselves. But the gateway was evidently executed between April and August 1553; ASS, *Balìa* 152, fols. 12, 34v, 60, 73v, 118, 138v, 231v, and 279v (after which the record in the *Deliberazioni* ceases).

7. Cantagalli, *La Guerra*, pp. 83–110, gives a good account of these movements, drawn mainly from Florentine records. Among the most valuable and well informed of Siena's sources were Carlo Massaini (ambassador in Rome) and Ambrogio Nuti (ambassador in Florence). Massaini was particularly

useful as the Neapolitan forces made their way
northward; note his strategic intelligence in
ASS, *Balìa* 739, no. 90; *Balìa* 740, nos. 14,
25, 27, and 86; *Balìa* 742, nos. 4, 45, and 49.
Because of Florence's technical neutrality,
Nuti was able to remain at his post sending
coded dispatches on logistics and weapons
movements; cf., ASS, *Balìa* 744, nos. 9 and
25; *Balìa* 746, nos. 1, 6, and 22.

8. ASS, *Balìa* 145, fol. 65*v*, and *Balìa* 141,
fol. 66.

9. Bardi, *Storie senesi*, fol. 300. The early
activity at Camollia was given maximum pub-
licity by the Sienese regime in an attempt to
encourage other communities to exert themselves in their own defense. See for example
the letter to the Priors and Community of
Montalcino (then dragging their feet, see next
chapter) in ASS, *Balìa* 468, fol. 67 (8 February 1553).

10. Hook, *Siena*, p. 188.

11. "Libro delle deliberazioni dei quattro
provveditori sopra la guerra pel Terzo di Camullia," ASS, *Balìa* 151, fol. 2. Voting was
done by placing white or black beans (*lupini
bianchi* or *neri*) in a box.

12. *Balìa* 151, fols. 3–4.

13. *Balìa* 151, fol. 5*v*.

14. See ASS, *Balìa* 141, fol. 65*v* (21 January 1553), fols. 67*v*–68*v* (28 January), fols,
72*r–v* (11 February); and *Balìa* 145, fol. 66
(22 January), fols. 71–72 (2 February) and
fols. 74*v*–76*v* (18–25 February 1553), for details of transfer of skilled workers to the Camollia site. Generally, teams of nine or ten
skilled men were assigned to each fort. Dionigio Gori (see chapter 9) was appointed site
architect at Camollia, Letters Patent in ASS,
Balìa 468, fol. 34 (23 January 1553).

15. ASS, *Balìa* 151, fol. 7*v*.

16. *Balìa* 151, fol. 5.

17. *Balìa* 151, fols. 25*r–v*.

18. "Deliberazioni dei quattro cittadini
eletti dagli Otto del Reggimento, deputati sopra la Guerra, per le cortine del forte di Camollia," ASS, *Balìa* 153, fol. 2.

19. For these projects see Sozzini, "Diario,"
pp. 122–23, the *Deliberazioni* in ASS, *Balìa*
152, fols. 119 and 130; and descriptions in a
letter to Giulio Vieri, by then besieged in
Montalcino, ASS, *Balìa* 469, fols. 33*v*–35 (7
May 1553). Another similar letter was captured and is now in ASF *Med. Princ.* 414,
fols. 569–571*v* (16 April 1553). These fright-
ful breaches of security raise the possibility

that the letters were in some degree "plants,"
exaggerating the state of completion of these
works to encourage the recipient and deceive
an enemy.

20. Hook, "Fortifications."

21. See ASS, *Balìa* 148, fols. 71*r–v*, for appointment of commissioners to inspect food
supplies in all the fortresses of the dominio
(15 October 1552). ASS, *Balìa* 468, fols.
104*r–v* (27 February 1553) for food stockpile
instructions to the commissioner at Montalcino. Measures to fine communities for unauthorized trading in salt, a key commodity, at
Piancastagnaio are given in ASS, *Balìa* 469,
fols. 49*r–v* (19 May 1553). A special commissioner for grain collection was appointed at
harvest time, ASS, *Balìa* 469, fol. 77 (7 June
1553).

22. The billeting of "friendly" soldiers on
the Sienese civil population became a major
problem as French troops of all nationalities—
Italian, German, Swiss, Gascon—arrived in
southern Tuscany. Almost daily the Balìa received complaints of violent and destructive
behavior from their protectors and, not infre-
quently, were compelled to take strong measures against communities which refused to
accommodate troops. The people of Radicondoli were warned that unless they admitted
soldiers, both France and Siena would regard
them "as a place lost" and provide no protection at all. ASS, *Balìa* 468, fols. 177*v*–8 (9
April 1553). The inhabitants of San Giovanni d'Asso were threatened that they would
be "declared rebels and all their property forfeit," ASS, *Balìa* 469, fols. 38*v*–39 (11 May
1553). For their part, the troops complained
of miserable housing conditions and usurious
prices for food and wine. Siena responded by
fixing prices, regulating the facilities to be
provided in billets, and, whenever possible,
dispersing the troops in small groups over a
wide area. See Letters Patent for the billeting
commissioner, Pierantonio Guidini, in ASS,
Balìa 469, fol. 156*v* (21 August 1553), and
Balìa 469, fols. 173*v*–4 (7 October 1553). See
chapter 3, note 4.

23. Letters Patent for commissioners to organize road and bridge repairs on the strada
romana, the main road from Siena, through
Buonconvento, past Montalcino and thence
to Rome in ASS, *Balìa* 467, fol. 125 (28 October 1552).

24. Letters Patent for a new Bargello di
Campagna, a sheriff with summary powers of

execution and a small force of mounted men, in ASS, *Balìa* 468, fol. 76 (13 February 1553).

25. Regulations for the maintenance in a state of constant readiness of post horses and riders between Siena and Grosseto in ASS, *Balìa* 469, fols. 138*v*–9 (12 August 1553). Letters Patent of a newly appointed commissioner for *postieri* in *Balìa* 469, fol. 142 (15 August 1553). Orders that ferryboats be maintained in readiness on pain of fines by the communities of Grosseto, Istia, Campagnatico and Sasso in ASS, *Balìa* 469, fol. 164*v* (11 September 1553).

26. Hook, "Fortifications," p. 380.

27. Sozzini, "Diario," p. 171. The text of the February 1553 order is not among the "Bande" preserved in ASS, *Balìa* 825. A very similar order relating to the harvest of July 1554 raises the possibility that such proclamations served two purposes: to be obeyed at face value, or to give legal standing to the destruction of private property outside the sixteen defended towns. The Sienese were generally sensitive to private property rights and issued specific Letters Patent authorizing acts of destruction—for example, those issued to Piero di Foso and others giving powers to destroy mines in the area of Asciano, Rapolano, Serre, and Armaiuolo lest they should fall into the hands of the enemy. ASS, *Balìa* 468, fol. 157 (24 March 1553).

28. Report attached to letter to the duke of Florence from Ridolfo Baglioni, in Cortona. ASF *Med. Princ.* 423, fols. 168r–*v*.

29. For these small places the best general source remains Repetti, *Dizionario geografico fisico-storico della Toscana*.

30. Numerous maps of successive medieval and Early Modern drainage and land-recovery schemes in this area are to be found in the catalog of a 1981 exhibition organized by the Collegio Ingegneri della Toscana, *Bonifica della Val di Chiana*.

31. See Verdiani-Bandi, *I Castelli della Val d'Orcia e la Repubblica di Siena*, for the wartime history of Lucignano, Pienza, Monticchiello, Chiusi, Sarteano, and Radicofani.

32. ASS, *Balìa* 750, no. 10 (report from Grosseto dated 27 March 1553), for the best description; but see also ASS, *Balìa* 744, no. 15 (14 January 1553). A mid-sixteenth-century plan of some pre-Medici fortifications (showing a rectangular enceinte with nine bastions) is reproduced in Carmen Borrarelli,

"La Fortezza di Grosseto," in *I Medici*, ed. Rombai, p. 147. This plan is from ASF *Misc. Med.* 83, Ins. 59, c.133, and may represent an unexecuted Medici project. The fortifications, however, bear no resemblance to those described in the Sienese documents, and the topographical details of Grosseto itself are wildly inaccurate.

33. The bastion is illustrated in Maggi and Castriotto's treatise as a conventional triangular work, attached to the curtains by straight flanks. Documentary accounts of the fighting around it, however, suggest that the work was separated from the medieval walls by a deep ditch in which a large number of Imperial troops were killed. In this incident, the Imperialists had infiltrated the ditch at night and attempted to gain entry to the bastion by pretending to be reinforcements from inside the town; that is, they came from "behind" the bastion. When the Spaniards later captured this work they contemplated installing artillery within it, with which to batter the main walls at close range. Their problem was then that the work was completely overlooked by the walls of the town, from which stones were constantly thrown. It may well be, therefore, that this bastion was more of an advanced or detached work than the treatise illustration suggests, located some way down the slope of the east front.

34. Verdiani-Bandi, *I Castelli*, pp. 159–63, provides the substance of this account, drawing mainly from Sienese diarists and chroniclers. Details of defensive measures prior to the siege, as well as reports of Sienese patrols from nearby fortresses, are to be found in ASS, *Balìa* 748 and 749. Numerous dispatches from Florentine officials with the Imperial army are in ASF *Med. Princ.* 423 and 438.

35. See the following dispatches to the duke of Florence: in ASF *Med. Princ.* 423, fol. 242, from Simone d'Arezzo, gunner (7 March 1553); in *Med. Princ.* 423, fols. 243–44, from Ierolamo Albizzi, commissioner of transport (8 March); in *Med. Princ.* 423, fols. 251–252*v*, from Francesco Zati, commissioner of artillery (13 March); in *Med. Princ.* 423, fol. 322, from G. B. Belluzzi, military engineer.

36. Simone d'Arezzo to the duke of Florence, ASF *Med. Princ.* 423, fol. 481 (18 March 1553).

37. B[artolomme]o Justo to the duke of Florence, ASF *Med. Princ.* 438, fols. 5–6 (17

March 1553). Only about 30 attackers had been killed outright, he reported, but over 300 had been wounded—mostly by stones.

38. Ridolfo Baglioni from Cortona to the duke, reporting construction of the *tête de pont*, ASF Med. *Princ.* 423, no. 147 (19 January 1553).

39. Captain Concetto to the duke, reporting conference with Don Garcia ASF Med. *Princ.* 423A. fols. 577–78 (26 March 1553); and Don Garcia to the Duke, ASF Med. *Princ.* 423A. fols. 574r–v., and 578 (26 March 1553).

5

---

1. See Verdiani-Bandi, *I castelli,* for the medieval castle. The construction of the extant Medici bastion is described in Enrico Coppi, "Montalcino dopo la conquista Medicea," in *I Medici,* ed. Rombai, pp. 129–31. A short note on Maestro Giorgio's involvement in the wartime project appeared in the same volume; see Maria Paola Rossignoli, "Giorgio di Giovanni e i lavori di ristrutturazione alla fortezza di Montalcino durante la guerra di Siena," pp. 125–27. Nothing is added, however, to the material already published by Gaye, *Carteggio inedito d'artisti dei secoli XIV, XV, XVI,* and Romagnoli, *Bellartisti.*

2. The full scheme for the saddle with estimated costs is described in a letter from Annibale Tolomei, Sienese commissioner in Montalcino, ASS, *Balìa* 736, no. 86 (12 November 1552). See also the letter from Maestro Giorgio di Giovanni, *Balìa* 736, no. 36B (7 November 1552).

3. Alfonso Tolomei, successor to Annibale as commissioner, describes the setting out of cords for this work in ASS, *Balìa* 741, no. 46 (21 December 1552).

4. The first phase of the retrenchments was the section from Porta Cerbaia to San Martino. The dimensions of this section are given in a letter from Alfonso Tolomei, ASS, *Balìa* 741, no. 58 (21 December 1552). The ditch was set back 8 braccia (16 feet) from the wall and was itself 8 braccia wide by 6 braccia (12 feet) deep. Behind it was a rampart 8 braccia wide by 6 high. Assuming the heights to be measured from ground level,

the retrenchment must have measured some 32 feet from the bottom of the ditch to the top of the rampart.

5. Sozzini, "Diario," p. 109. Also Pecci, *Memorie storico-critiche,* 4:29.

6. ASF Med. *Princ.* 423A, fol. 603 r.–v. For Belluzzi's role in the war see "Giovanni Battista Belluzzi: Il Trattato delle Fortificazioni di Terra," ed. Daniela Lamberini, in *Documenti inediti di cultura toscana,* 4 (Florence, 1980), pp. 375–403.

7. ASS, *Balìa* 735, nos. 16, 24, 33, and 39 (26–28 October 1552).

8. ASS, *Balìa* 740, no. 3 (9 December 1552).

9. The colonel's views are recorded in ASS, *Balìa* 740, no. 3 (9 December 1552), and *Balìa* 741, no. 71 (22 December 1552). For Maestro Giorgio, see Gaye, *Carteggio inedito,* 3:300–304. However, a much more detailed record of their role in the construction program can be gained from the letters of the various civil commissioners in Montalcino, who reported regularly to Siena: see the communications of Annibale Tolomei (commissioner in October and November 1552) in ASS, *Balìa* 734, 736, and 738; Alfonso Tolomei (December 1552) in *Balìa* 739, 740, 741, and 742; Niccolo Santi (January 1553) in *Balìa* 744 and 755; Hieronimo Santi (first week of February 1553) in *Balìa* 746; and Giulio Vieri (February and March, and subsequently throughout the siege) in *Balìa* 746–50.

10. For the choronology of the construction program we have to rely almost entirely on the letters of the commissioners (see note 9 above). Some work on the medieval anteportal at the Porta al Cassero had been initiated, albeit wrongly, when Maestro Giorgio reorganized the project early in November 1552; ASS, *Balìa* 736, no. 36A (7 November 1552). For subsequent progress reports on the saddle fortifications (i.e., San Martino, Porta al Cassero, and the curtain joining them), see ASS, *Balìa* 738, no. 43 (21 November) and 48 (26 November); *Balìa* 740, nos. 24 and 81; *Balìa* 741, no. 17; *Balìa* 742, no. 103; *Balìa* 744, no. 82; and *Balìa* 746, no. 73 (8 February 1553). Work began at Porta Cerbaia and the west retrenchment just before Christmas: ASS, *Balìa* 741, nos. 46 and 58 (both dated 21 December 1552). The east retrenchment was started at the end of February: ASS, *Balìa* 748, no. 18 (26 February 1553). On the very eve of the siege the commissioner Giulio Vieri admitted that the "fortifications are not yet finished but are defensible, and we will continue to work on them while the enemy are all around." ASS, *Balìa* 750, no. 5 (27 March 1553).

11. "Giornale dell'assedio di Montalcino fatto dagli Spagnuoli nel 1553 di autore anonimo," p. 346 (Appendix); *Verissima descrizione e successo del Campo imperiale da che arrivosotto la città di Montalcino nel'anno MDLIII,* p. 4; Giulio Landi, "Diario dell'assedio di Montalcino," in Della Valle, *Lettere sanesi* 3:31. The separation of the different national contingents in the Imperial army was absolutely necessary. A serious outbreak of fighting occurred between Germans and Italians following the capture of Rocca d'Orcia: see ASF, *Med. Princ.* 414, fol. 472 r.–v (20 April 1553). Simone Ruffini d'Arezzo, one of Cosimo's gunners at Montalcino, reported that he feared for his life because of the subsequent bad blood between Germans and Italians: ASF, *Med. Princ.* 414A, fol. 616 (27 April 1553).

12. "Giornale," p. 347.

13. Letter to Balìa from Giulio Vieri, commissioner in Montalcino, ASS, *Balìa* 750, no. 32 (31 March 1553). Vieri enclosed a note from Giorgio Ciacchi, who was holding the Romitorio with five soldiers and a number of peasants, asking for another ten soldiers who were not afraid to face the enemy.

14. "Giornale," pp. 350–51.

15. Landi, "Diario," p. 31; "Giornale," p. 350; and "Verissima descrizione," p. 7.

16. Landi, "Diario," p. 31; "Giornale," p. 351; and "Verissima descrizione," p. 8. The details are confirmed by Giulio Vieri, Commissioner, in ASS, *Balìa* 750, no. 40 (2 April 1553). The Sienese were correct to suppose that the Imperialists had good information on the strength of the Rocca. Some weeks earlier Cosimo had sent Captain Ridolfino di Arezzo to Don Garcia to advise on the fortifications of Montalcino, where, the duke said, he had been for many days with Colonel Giovanni da Torino. ASF, *Med. Princ.* 199, fol. 41v. (12 February 1553).

17. "Giornale," p. 352; "Verissima descrizione," p. 8.

18. At Monticchiello, just before the siege of Montalcino, a Florentine half-cannon fired 70 rounds in a single day before splitting its barrel, according to the report of Simone

d'Arezzo, Cosimo's gunner, who declared that this piece had been "assassinato": ASF, *Med. Princ.* 423, fol. 481 (18 March 1553). Brandi *The Emperor Charles V,* p. 621, tells us that 1,448 rounds were fired by 36 cannon at the siege of Metz on 24 November 1552. This implies a daily average of 40 rounds per gun, or about 5 rounds per gun per hour assuming an eight-hour shooting day in November. It was reckoned to be exceptionally fast shooting and was directed by the famous artillerist, Juan Manrique. Other Imperial bombardments in Tuscany during 1554–55 failed to equal their performance at Montalcino. Casole surrendered on 24 October 1554 after receiving 300 rounds from twelve pieces, most of them full cannon. Crevole surrendered on 16 November 1554 after 350 rounds from eight pieces. In a carefully planned bombardment at Siena on 11 January 1555 (described in chapter 6), the Imperialists fired 260 rounds from nine cannon without creating a breach. High achievements in Early Modern bombardments demanded rapid fire from much larger numbers of guns than were available at all but the most important sieges. (See also chapter 1, note 20.)

19. A classic account of this type of bombardment is given in the anonymous "Diario della ribellione della città di Arezzo dell'anno 1502," pp. 216–17: "In comincio a bombardare le mura del Cassero, et a ogni colpo mandava via un merlo per modo tale no' se potiano fare alle difese . . . sempre traendo due o tre colpi a la volta."

20. "Giornale," p. 367; "sparandone dodici in un tempo"; and Landi, "Diario," p. 31, "con 8, 10 e 12 palle in un tempo, e in un istante."

21. Simone d'Arezzo to Cosimo, ASF, *Med. Princ.* 423, fol. 481 (18 March 1553).

22. G. Lotto to Cosimo, ASF, *Med. Princ.* 414, fol. 146r.–v (2 April 1553).

23. Don Garcia to Cosimo, ASF, *Med. Princ.* 423A, fol. 587 r.–v (27 March 1553). The six cannon arrived in San Quirico, between Pienza and Montalcino, on 14 April; see Tommaso Bugini to Cosimo, ASF *Med. Princ.* 414, fol. 549 (14 April 1553).

24. "Giornale," p. 355.

25. Incendiary devices were part of the repertoire of the artillery and fortification expert and, together with bombs, are treated in the *trattati* from early in the sixteenth century as in Della Valle, *Vallo,* preface, chapters 1–3.

26. "Giornale," p. 357.

27. "Giornale," p. 358; "Verissima descrizione," p. 11 for accounts of this sortie. Antonio Lupicini, son of "Il Lupo" of siege of Florence fame, served with the Imperial forces at Montalcino. In his treatise he praises Giordano Orsini for the energy of his defense and picks out this incident as an example of a well-organized and well-implemented fighting patrol. *Discorsi militari d'Antonio Lupicini, sopra l'espugnazione d'alcuni siti,* Chapter 1, p. 8.

28. Belluzzi's half of this correspondence is unfortunately missing, but see Cosimo to the engineer, ASF *Med. Princ.* 200, fol. 74 (23 May 1553); *Med. Princ.* 199, fol. 122 (4 May 1553), and fol. 136 (30 May 1553). The duke had anticipated the need for miners and had ordered some of them, together with "one with a compass or direction-finding instrument, or someone experienced in similar skills" to be sent from Pietrasanta: Cosimo to Girolamo Inghirani, ASF, *Med. Princ.* 200, fol. 32 (30 March 1553). Francesco Zati, Florentine Commissioner of Artillery with the Imperial army at Montalcino, reports discussions of the rising costs of mining operations with Belluzzi and Don Garcia: see ASF, *Med. Princ.* 414A, fol. 793–94 (9 May 1553).

29. Colonna to the emperor (26 April 1553), quoted by Cantagalli, *La Guerra,* p. 129, n. 98.

30. Maggi and Castriotto, *Della fortificatione,* book 3, chapter, 22, fol. 99*v.*

31. "Giornale," p. 358.

32. "Giornale," pp. 358–64.

33. "Giornale," pp. 360, 361, and 364.

34. Letters received from Montalcino in March, April, and June 1553 are to be found in ASS, *Balìa* 750–53. Letters now missing but known to have reached Siena are those specifically acknowledged by date in the registers of copyletters dispatched from the capital (*Balìa* 468 and 469.) (The *Copialettere,* as they are designated, preserve in fair copy letters sent out of the city.) Giulio Vieri, the chief correspondent in Montalcino during the siege, unfortunately did not regularly acknowledge receipt of letters from Siena, so it is impossible to know how many of the twenty-four Sienese communications got through the Imperial lines. On the eve of the siege Giulio Vieri had asked for a code: ASS, *Balìa* 750, no. 5 (27 March 1553). This was used for sensitive material (many of the decoded passages refer to the suspected disloyalty

of individuals) and very occasionally entire letters are encoded.

35. Maggi and Castriotto, *Della fortificatione,* book, 3, chapters 15–18, fols. 90–94*v.* Mirandola (between Mantua and Ferrara) was held by the French against the army of Pope Julius III, for whom Castriotto then served. Other discussions of the historical and contemporary use of circumvallation systems are to be found in Busca, *L'architettura militare,* p. 47, and de' Marchi, *Architettura militare,* book 3, chapter 39, p. 83 where again Mirandola is cited as an example.

36. Landi, *Diario,* p. 39.

37. This figure is made up as follows: 14,000 at the beginning of the siege; plus 3,000 Germans from the Maremma; plus 5 *insegne* (numbering some 1,300 men) from Florence on 20 April, another 5 *insegne* from Florence on 22 April and 2 more from Lucca that arrived on 29 April. The Landi, "Diario," however, gives an even higher estimate of 20,000–25,000 soldiers and 40,000–45,000 in total.

38. "Giornale," p. 368; "Verissima descrizione," p. 34.

39. De' Marchi, *Architettura militare,* book 3, chapter 44, p. 89.

40. "Giornale, " p. 368.

41. "Verissima descrizione," p. 35.

42. "Giornale," p. 368.

43. "Verissima descrizione," p. 51.

44. "Giornale," p. 372.

45. Landi, "Diario," p. 40.

46. "Verissima descrizione," p. 54.

47. "Verissima descrizione," p. 53. Possible confirmation of the poor state of the subsoil in this area comes from the report of a row between the colonel and Maestro Giorgio during the early stages of construction of San Martino. Giovanni da Torino felt that the fortifications would never be completed in time because of the slow start and their size. He was enraged to discover that the foundations had been excavated much deeper than indicated in Maestro Giorgio's plans. Possibly this was necessary because of the nature of the filled ground. Reported by Alfonso Tolomei, ASS, *Balìa* 379, no. 74 (6 December 1552).

48. As well as many accounts and illustrations of spectacularly destructive mine explosions, the histories of sixteenth-century warfare record other instances of dramatic disappointment. For example, Guicciardini's report of Pietro Navarra's mine at Bologna in

1512: "The mine at last being finished, and the army drawn up in order for immediately giving the assault . . . the same was sprung and with a horrible noise and violence lifted up the chapel and the wall in such a manner that, through the space between the ground and the wall thus heaved up, those that were without had an open view of the city within, and of the soldiers as they stood ready to defend it. But the wall immediately sinking down returned sound and entire to the very same place whence the violence of the powder had forced it, and with all its parts as firmly connnected as if it had never been moved," Guicciardini, *History*, 5:365–66.

49. "Giornale," p. 274, and "Verissima descrizione," p. 59.

50. "Giornale," p. 374, and "Verissima descrizione," p. 58.

51. "Giornale," p. 374, and "Verissima descrizione," p. 59.

52. "Giornale," p. 374: "li nimici hanno fatto scale per la faccia non guardata; quale montano su sino alla cima, traendo sassi alli nostri lavatori."

53. "Giornale," p. 374, and "Verissima descrizione," p. 65.

54. *Trombe di fuoco*, would be prepared for use in close fighting by boring out the center of a log of wood about two feet in length. The log would then be reinforced with bindings of rope or leather and fixed to a long shaft (sometimes fixed crossways so that it could be fired round a corner). The bore would be charged with powder and a load of small stones, pieces of broken glass, pots, and so on. Usually the weapon could be used only once, the wood tending to split with the explosion. See above, chapter 1 note 24.

55. "Giornale," pp. 376–77.

56. "Giornale," p. 377.

57. ASF, *Med. Princ.* 423, fol. 254 (8 March 1553), contains an abstract of the contents of captured papers.

58. ASF, *Med. Princ.* 414A, fol. 976r.–v (18 May 1553). The letter includes a copy of a circular outlining Imperial/Genoese efforts to keep the peace with the Turks.

59. Sozzini, "Diario," pp. 138–39.

60. ASF *Med. Princ.* 200, fol. 84v.–85 (9 June 1553).

61. "Giornale," p. 378, and "Verissima descrizione," pp. 66–67. Such exchanges were not entirely unknown elsewhere, for example at Padua (1509) and Vienna (1683). See the

Diarii di Marino Sanuto, 9:123; and Stoye, *The Siege of Vienna*, p. 321.

62. Sozzini, "Diario," pp. 138–45.

63. Sozzini, "Diario," p..145, and "Giornale," p. 381.

64. "Giornale," p. 381.

65. Montaigne, "Journal de voyage en Italie," in *Oeuvres complètes*, p. 487.

66. Landi, "Diario," p. 40, specifies 2,487 shots received; "Giornale," p. 382, gives 2,497. Evidently the government expected the balls to be collected for reuse or for their metal. The reply to Alfonso Tolomei's letter (now missing) of 3 July, giving the figure of rounds fired against Montalcino, expressed surprise at the small number salvaged since "we supposed there were at least two thousand." ASS, *Balìa* 469, fols. 108–108v. (8 July 1553).

67. Annibale Tolomei, serving again as commissioner in Montalcino, in ASS, *Balìa* 753, no. 95A (28 June 1553).

68. Marcel Nuti, commissioner, in ASS, *Balìa* 751, no. 95 (17 September 1553): "It will be necessary to think hard about that ruined bastion of San Martino (and to decide) either to rebuild it or to demolish it completely, because from there thousands of thefts are made each night and, although the town gates are locked, one can go in and out through (the bastion) freely."

69. "Giornale," p. 382, and Landi, "Diario," p. 40. Enemy deaths from wounds and disease were estimated at about 3,000.

70. Sozzini, "Diario," p. 51.

6

1. For general developments, see Cantagalli, *La Guerra*, pp. 133–59; Arnaldo d'Addario, *Il problema senese*, pp. 145–88; G. B. Adriani, *Istoria dei suoi tempi*, 9:365–76. The coastal operations are well described in Squarcialupi, *Diario della guerra del 1552–1556 in Maremma e nell'Elba*.

2. Giangiacomo de' Medici, marquis of Marignano (1497–1555) began his military career in the classic mold of the unscrupulous, freebooting condottiero. As a young man he served under two of Italy's leading mercenaries, Giovanni delle Bande Nere, and Francesco Sforza—for whom he murdered Ettore Visconti. Fearing with good reason that he

would himself be silenced for his part in this act, Giangiacomo seized the castle of Muzzo and held it against all of Sforza's efforts. After serving with the Imperialists in 1525, and against them in 1527, he formally entered the service of Charles V in 1528, and was created marquis of Marignano. He led the Italian contingent at the capture of Ghent in 1540 (where, as governor, he built a citadel), and held high commands in Germany, on the Danube, and at the sieges of Luxembourg (1543) and Metz (1552). Marignano served the duke of Florence from 1553 to the fall of 1555, when his health deteriorated, and he retired to Milan to die on 8 November. From his earliest exploits to the siege of Siena, Marignano's reputation suffered from charges of cruelty, and his early death removed a cause of embarrassment to his brother, who was elected Pope Pius IV in 1559. On the life of Marignano, see Missaglia, *Vita di Giovan Jacopo Medici, Marchese di Marignano*.

3. Cantagalli, *La Guerra*, pp. 151–52.

4. Piero Strozzi, Marshal of France (1510–1558), came from a Florentine banking family of great wealth and was originally destined for a career in the church. Driven from Florence by the persecution of duke Alessandro de' Medici, he joined the French for the relief of Turin in 1536. On hearing of the assassination of Alessandro, he hurried to rejoin his father and the other anti-Medici partisans; but failed to reach them before Cosimo's victory at Montemurlo (1 August 1537) where his father was captured. Exiled once more, Piero served with the French at the siege of Luxembourg (1543), Mirandola (1544), at sea in 1545, and at the siege of Metz in 1552. As a cousin of the queen, Catherine de' Medici, he became chamberlain to the king, colonel-general of the infantry, and later general of the galleys. Following his unsuccessful defense of Siena and Port'Ércole, he returned to Italy to command the army of Pope Paul IV in 1557. Piero was killed in 1558 whilst establishing a battery at the siege of Thionville.

His younger brother, Leone Strozzi, Prior of Capua (1515–1554) spent his own exile in the order of St. John, becoming a skilful galley commander in the endless naval war against the Turks. Leone commanded the French fleet sent to Scotland in 1547 to support Mary Queen of Scots and, during the War of Siena, commanded the French galley squadron based on Port'Ércole. He was mor-

tally wounded in 1554 when reconnoitering Scarlino, and was buried at Castiglione della Pescaia. The Imperialists later desinterred his body and threw it into the sea. On the lives of the Strozzi, see Trucchi, *Vita e gesta di Piero Strozzi, fiorentino, maresciallo di Francia*; Brigidi, *Le vite di Filippo Strozzi e di Piero e Leone suoi figli*; Coppini, *Piero Strozzi nell'assedio di Siena*; Picot, *Les Italiens en France au XVIe siècle*; Bullard, *Filippo Strozzi and the Medici*.

5. Cantagalli, *La Guerra*, p. 158.

6. Adriani, *Istoria*, 10:377, provides the best details of the operational planning; but see also Montalvo, *Relazione*, p. 11, and R. Galluzzi, *Storia del Granducato di Toscana* (Leghorn, 1731), 3:39. Cantagalli, *La Guerra*, p. 208, n. 2, tells us that the official cover story for the closure of the Florentine frontiers and ports was a hue and cry for an escaped murderer.

7. Sozzini, "Diario," pp. 159–60; Pecci, *Memorie storico-critiche*, 4:112–13. Marignano himself placed the initial contact at Badesse, some three miles north of Fontebecci, ASF *Med. Princ.* 1853 (28 January 1554).

8. Sozzini, "Diario," pp. 160–61; Montalvo, *Relazione*, p. 12; Adriani, *Istoria*, 10:378.

9. Marignano's dispatch describing the first twenty-four hours of the assault lays the blame for this panic on the Florentine militia, who were "more likely to throw good men into disorder than to fight." ASF *Med. Princ.* 1853 (28 January 1554).

10. Sozzini, "Diario," p. 165.

11. Monluc, *Commentaires*, 2:19. Blaise de Lasseran-Massencome, seigneur de Monluc and Marshal of France (c.1561–77), was one of eleven children born to an ancient but impoverished Gascon family. He was educated as a page at the court of Lorraine, and saw his first active service in the Milan campaign of 1521 as a light horseman in the company of the Chevalier Bayard. He was captured after the French defeat at Pavia in 1525 but—too poor to be worth a ransom—was released in time to serve in Lautrec's disastrous expedition to Naples in 1527–28, where he was severely wounded in the arm and leg (the first of seven gunshot wounds in his long fighting career). Unable to support the expense of service in the mounted *gendarmerie*, Monluc became a lieutenant of foot in 1535 and saw a great deal of action in Provence, Picardy, and Piedmont before winning official recognition

for his role in the battle of Cerisoles in 1544. At that time still a captain, he was knighted after the battle and promoted to camp-master (or brigadier general). Having caught the eyes of the new king, Henry II, and his queen, Catherine de' Medici, Monluc was given senior commands in Piedmont before being posted to Siena in 1554 as deputy to Piero Strozzi. His heroic and skillful defense of the city following Strozzi's defeat at Marciano brought him the lucrative post of colonel-general of the infantry and the rare honor of *chevalier de l'ordre du roi*. Monluc's capture of Thionville in 1558 won him further fame. But the peace of Cateau-Cambrésis (1559) and the accidental death of Henry II put the professional soldiers out of work and cost him his profitable colonel-generalcy. The Wars of Religion provided an outlet for his talents when, as lieutenant of Guienne, he became the hammer of the Huguenots in southwest France until dreadfully wounded in the face by an arquebus ball, while leading the assault on Rabestens, Navarre, in July 1570. His celebrated *Commentaires* were written in defense of his role as a loyal servant of the Catholic monarchy, while the old soldier was in disgrace following the Treaty of Saint-Germain and facing charges of brutality and peculation brought against him by political enemies. The book had its intended effect. For besides giving us one of the most colorful accounts of sixteenth-century warfare, it helped to clear his name. When the duke of Anjou (to whom it was dedicated) became king Henry III in 1574, Monluc was fully restored to favor and created Marshal of France. On the life of Monluc, see Courteault, *Un cadet de Gascogne au XVIe Siècle*, and *Blaise de Monluc, historien*.

12. Concino's report, ASF *Med. Princ.* 1854, no. 12 (19 February 1554).

13. Sozzini, "Diario," p. 173.

14. Sozzini, "Diario," pp. 173, 210, and 215; Bardi, *Storie senesi*, fol. 325*v*.; Concino in ASF *Med. Princ.* 1854, no. 53 (23 March) and 59 (4 April 1554).

15. Monluc, *Commentaires*, 2:19. The standard pike was 16–18 feet in length.

16. Sozzini, "Diario," p. 217.

17. Sozzini, "Diario," pp. 225 and 322; Concino's dispatches to Cosimo, ASF *Med. Princ.* 1854, no. 70 (26 April), no. 83 (9 May), and no. 248 (23 November 1554).

18. Giulio Ricasoli (Florentine Commander in Brolio) wrote to Concino (at the Imperial camp on the Camollia ridge) telling him of a captured woman, Florentine by birth, who had told her interrogators of a most ambitious Sienese mine. The woman was living "carnalmente" with a French engineer, who, to quiet her fears of the Imperial bombardment, had shown her the drawings of a mine which he promised would soon silence the Imperial guns. The drawing showed "a long thing like a road" ending in a large chamber in the middle of which was a cross. Asked of the significance of the cross, the engineer had replied that it marked a point beneath the Imperial magazine. Concino's report to Cosimo, with Ricasoli's dispatch, in ASF *Carte Strozziane*, I, 35, no. 101 (5 April 1554). To the best of our knowledge, no mine was sprung at Siena.

19. Sozzini, "Diario," p. 234 (20 May), reports the start of this scheme. Concino reports the testing of Sienese artillery in the completed work. ASF *Med. Princ.* 1854, no. 109 (1 June 1554). See also Bardi, *Storie senesi*, fol. 315.

20. Sozzini, "Diario," p. 238 (1 June); Concino, ASF, *Med. Princ.* 1854, nos. 106 (28 May) and 109 (1 June 1554) report the beginning of the second battery.

21. ASF *Med. Princ.* 1854, no. 36 (11 March 1554).

22. This point is emphasized in the first of Marignano's *discorsi* or position papers in ASF *Carte Strozziane*, I, 109, fols. 150–51.

23. ASF *Med. Princ.* 1853 (28 January 1554).

24. Sozzini, "Diario," p. 169, mentions half a braccia of snow on 3 February. As late as April 1554 a Sergeant and fourteen men from Belluzzi's company deserted into Siena: Marignano's dispatch, ASF *Med. Princ.* 1853 (2 April 1554).

25. The most revealing of Marignano's position papers, in chronological order, are to be found in ASF *Carte Strozziane*, I, 109, fols. 150–51, 142–43, 148, and 153–54.

26. Sozzini, "Diario," pp. 190–92; Adriani, *Istoria*, 10:391; details of the Imperial force in Concino's dispatch, ASF *Med. Princ.* 1854, no. 53 (23 March 1554).

27. Sozzini, "Diario," p. 201; Concino, ASF *Med. Princ.* 1854, no. 59 (4 April 1554).

28. ASF *Med. Princ.* 1854, no. 61 (6 April 1554).

29. Sozzini, "Diario," p. 203, and Concino, ASF *Med. Princ.* 1854, no. 64 (8 April

1554), both supply good topographical information. However, the best description of the fortifications and the events leading to their capture is in a letter from Federigo di Montaguto to Giorgio Vasari (dated 16 February 1564) in *Il carteggio di Giorgio Vasari*, p. 40. Vasari, researching for his picture of the capture of Monastero, had asked Montaguto (then serving as governor of Siena) for an account of the action and a locally commissioned sketch of the topography. Further evidence of Vasari's attitude to documentary accuracy is discussed in chapter 7.

30. ASF *Med. Princ.* 1853 (10 April): "Scoprendo l'altro hieri, che'l faceva un'altro [forte] su la man manca del Monastero sopra un poggio rilevato, che venea ad assicurare detto Monastero e che pariment si fabricava al Monastero, parvemi non differir più."

31. Presumably the rampart was fronted by a ditch of the same depth, to give a total obstacle of some eight feet.

32. Marignano's dispatch, ASF *Med. Princ.* 1853 (10 April 1554) confirmed by Montaguto; see note 29 above.

33. ASF *Med. Princ.* 1853 (12 and 17 April 1554).

34. Marignano, 2d *discorso* in ASF *Carte Strozziane*, I, 109, fols. 142–43.

35. Marignano, 3d *discorso* in *Carte Strozziane*, I, 109, fol. 148 (23 April); and Concino's earlier report in ASF *Med. Princ.* 1854, no. 65 (17 April 1554).

36. Galluzzi, *Storia* 1:2, chapter 4.

37. ASF *Med. Princ.* 1853 (16 April 1554).

38. *Med. Princ.* 1853 (22 April 1554).

39. Marignano, 4th *discorso* in ASF *Carte Strozziane*, I, 109, fols. 153–54; and his dispatch in ASF *Med. Princ.* 1853 (3 June 1554), when the general warned that the enemy had 7 *insegne* stationed in the monastery outside the Porta Romana and another 16 or 17 inside the city, besides the 8 *insegne* of the Sienese militia. See also Adriani, *Istoria*, 10:405.

40. Cantagalli, *La Guerra*, p. 244.

41. ASF *Carte Strozziane*, I, 25, no. 17 (13 June 1554). Cosimo begins his letter thus: "Chiunque a iuditio può considerare se di costa si dorme al fuoco, poi che hoggi è il terzo che le genti sono uscite di Siena, e voi state a fare buon sonni."

42. Cantagalli, *La Guerra*, pp. 245–56.

43. For the proceedings of the council at Basciano, see Concino's reports in ASF *Med.*

Princ. 1854, nos. 143 and 144 (both dated 29 June 1554).

44. ASF *Med. Princ.* 1854, no. 146 (3 July 1554); also *Med. Princ.* 1853 (3 July).

45. Marignano's dispatches ASF *Med. Princ.* 1853 (7 and 8 July 1554). Sozzini, "Diario," p. 257, mentions the construction of a battery in the garden of the monastery of Sant'Agostino to bombard the Imperial camp at San Lazzaro. Since the monastery was well inside the walls, and the camp some three-quarters of a mile outside them, a total range of a mile is suggested for the bombardment of this area target.

46. ASF *Med. Princ.* 1854, no. 152 (8 July 1554). In the event, Monastero was also held by the Imperialists.

47. It did indeed anger the duke; see ASF *Carte Strozziane*, I, 35, no. 38 (11 July), and no. 39 (12 July 1554). Adriani, *Istoria*, 10:427–28, also admits that the withdrawal got out of control and became something of a panic. It was, he observed, "poco onorevole . . . e parendo che'l Marchese fosse impaurito."

48. ASF *Med. Princ.* 1854, no. 157 (10 July 1554).

49. Sozzini, "Diario," p. 263; Bardi, *Storie senesi*, fols. 336r–v.

50. ASF *Med. Princ.* 1854, no. 168 (16 July 1554).

51. ASF *Med. Princ.* 1854, no. 168.

52. ASF *Med. Princ.* 1854, no. 170 (17 July 1554), in which Concino passes on reports of discontent inside the city because of the army's food consumption and apparent unwillingness to fight.

53. Cantagalli, *La Guerra* pp. 283–307, gives a detailed account of the maneuvers up to and including the Battle of Marciano.

54. Monluc, *Commentaires*, book 2, p. 34.

55. Bardi, *Storie senesi*, fol. 340.

56. Sozzini, "Diario," p. 272, not only describes the misery of the survivors but reports that entirely new companies were formed after the battle, with new enlistment bonuses to help rebuild morale.

57. Sozzini, "Diario," pp. 291–92; Marignano's dispatch in ASF *Med. Princ.* 1853 (3 September 1554).

58. The places captured in October 1554 are listed in ASF *Carte Strozziane*, I, 109, fol. 245.

59. The difficulties of the attack on Crevole, particularly those connected with the artillery, are described in Marignano's dispatches in ASF *Med. Princ.* 1853 (dated 5, 6, 9, 10, 11, 12, 13, 14, 17, and 20 November). The general's description of the site (16 November) seems to have been copied by Adriani.

60. Sozzini, "Diario," pp. 297–98; Monluc, *Commentaires*, book 3, pp. 57–58.

61. Sozzini, "Diario," p. 299.

62. Sozzini, "Diario," p. 301.

63. Marignano's order is reproduced in Galluzzi, *Storia*, 2:73–74. Bardi, *Storie senesi*, fol. 353, estimates that as many as 1,500 peasants were hanged in the autumn of 1554. See also Cantagalli, *La Guerra*, pp. 340–41, and the associated notes in which he describes a system of "passes" provided to civilians in occupied territory willing to take an oath of loyalty to the emperor. Not all blockade runners were summarily executed. Particularly sturdy peasants could hope to be sent to the galleys, and *prominenti* could sometimes be ransomed. It should be said in reply to Sienese complaints about *mala guerra* that the Imperialist measures represented no more than the strict application of traditionally harsh siege law. See Keen, *The Laws of War in the Late Middle Ages*.

64. ASF *Med. Princ.* 1854, no. 170 (17 July 1554).

65. *Med. Princ.* 1853 (5 October 1554).

66. Many of the Spanish and German troops should have been paid by the emperor through the Spanish viceroy in Naples. Cosimo, on Marignano's advice, agreed to stand surety for their payment. However, news of this decision did not prevent the mutiny of 19 August, when Marignano's tent was surrounded all night by a mob shouting, "Money, money!" Marignano's dispatch, ASF *Med. Princ.* 1853 (20 August 1554). Fortunately for the Imperialists, the paydays for the different units fell on different days, and the whole army never mutinied at the same time. However, there were scenes of disorder among the Germans at their 2 September pay muster when it was found that there was not enough money for all. *Med. Princ.* 1853 (3 September). On 5 September a number of Spanish soldiers were hanged at Brolio for deserting after having been paid. Florentine commissioners in the fortresses were instructed to take strong measures against men who were, evidently, quitting the army at the end of the summer. *Med. Princ.* 1853 (5 and 7 September).

ber). At the end of September, Marignano felt compelled to lend money to German soldiers "that had not the means to live." *Med. Princ.* 1853 (24 September). By the end of November, Marignano, his staff, and the gunners were all three months unpaid. *Med. Princ.* 1853 (24 November). Concino reported that on 2 December 2,000 Spaniards and 4,000 Germans were owed money. The pioneers were also unpaid, and they, he remarks, cannot even look forward to a sack! ASF *Med. Princ.* 1854, no. 254. The institution of mutiny as a means of pay-bargaining in the Imperial army is well described in Parker, *The Army of Flanders*, pp. 185–207.

67. These difficulties are discussed in the dispatches from Marignano and Concino on the following dates (all 1554): (a) shortage of gunners—30 November and 5, 20, and 29 December; (b) shortage of pioneers—3 November; (c) shortage of oxen handlers—3, 11, 17, and 25 November; (d) inexperience of oxen handlers—19 October; (e) shortage of mule handlers—6, 21, and 22 November; (f) shortage of master carpenters to repair gun carriages—19 October. ASF *Med. Princ.* 1853, 1854.

68. In April 1554, bad ammunition had actually ruined a number of guns, reported Marignano: ASF *Med. Princ.* 1853 (7 April). Later in the month the general again complained of bad powder and reported that he was sending to Milan for Maestro Giulio Bombardieri and Maestro Ambrogio to find out what was wrong; "otherwise we'll find ourselves without both artillery and ammunition." *Med. Princ.* 1853 (22 April).

69. ASF *Med. Princ.* 1854, no. 217 (4 October 1554).

70. ASF *Carte Strozziane*, I, 35, no. 57 (5 October 1554).

71. ASF *Med. Princ.* 1853 (30 November 1554).

72. ASF *Med. Princ.* 1854, no. 253 (30 November 1554).

73. ASF *Med. Princ.* 1853 (30 November 1554).

74. ASF *Med. Princ.* 1853 (30 November 1554). This is the second letter on that date.

75. ASF *Med. Princ.* 1853 (30 November 1554). To the first letter is attached a dispatch from Lione Ricasoli complaining about the difficulty of providing an extra 150 yoke of oxen (i.e., 300 beasts) and 700 pioneers at short notice (19 December). Concino re-

ported that six experienced oxen handlers had already been sent to assist Santa Fiora. ASF *Med. Princ.* 1854, no. 265 (17 December 1554).

76. Reported by Concino, ASF *Med. Princ.* 1854, no. 272 (24 December 1554).

77. Sozzini, "Diario," pp. 326–27, reported that the convent of Santa Margherita, just outside the Porta Tufi, was abandoned and demolished on 1 December. Imperial troops immediately occupied the ruins. The Fortino di San Marco was lost on 16 December (Sozzini, "Diario," p. 331). Concino, ASF *Med. Princ.* 1854, no. 262 (9 December), notes that the Imperialists put a company into the ruined church below the "casa al vento," i.e., in the valley leading to the Porta Fontebranda, on 9 December.

78. Sozzini records eleven separate proclamations between 9 November and 11 January which closed the shops in the city for one to three days so that the entire able-bodied population could work on the fortifications (9, 12, 17, 30 November; 8, 20, 23 December; and 1, 4, 9, 11 January). This was the most urgent and intensive period of fortification. On 22 October, however, Concino reported a reconnaissance by Chiappino Vitelli, who found 3,000 people working on the Porta Tufi defenses. ASF *Med. Princ.* 1854, no. 243. The text of one of the surviving Sienese proclamations is in ASS, *Balìa* 825, no. 7 (28 April 1554).

79. Monluc, *Commentaires*, 2:53 describes the organization of the civil population, who, within the hour, could put at least 1,500 people onto the construction of a retrenchment. His description tallies closely with the "Ordini fatti da Mons. di Monluc et dalli S[ignor]i Colonelli il s. Cornelio, Richerot et Combasso, et dalli S[ignor]i Otto della Guerra per la difesa di Siena per l'impresa che i nemici fanno di batterla." ASS, *Balìa* 827.

80. Orders for the bombardment in ASF *Carte Strozziane*, I, 109, fols. 158–158v.

81. Sozzini, "Diario," p. 345 (7 and 8 January 1555). Details in this and the following paragraph are from the same source.

82. Monluc, *Commentaires*, 2:50–51: "Or avois-je tousjours délibéré, que si l'ennemy nous venoict assaillir avecques l'artillerie, de me retrancher loing de la muraille où se feroict la baterie, pour les laisser entrer à leur ayse; et faisois estat tousjours de fermer les doux boutz, et y mettre à chescun cinq ou six

grosses pièces d'artillerie, chargées de grosses chaines et de gros cloux."

83. Monluc, *Commentaires*, 2:54.

84. "Il successo de la batteria," Montalvo, *Relazione*, pp. 233–36 (Document 8).

85. Monluc, *Commentaires*, 2:59.

86. Sozzini, "Diario," p. 349.

87. Ibid.

88. Monluc, *Commentaires*, 2:62–63.

89. ASF *Med. Princ.* 1854, no. 289 (11 January 1555).

90. "Il successo de la batteria" estimates as many as 32 or 34 *pezzi grossi* parked around Osservanza. Monluc, *Commentaires*, Book 2, p. 32 estimates 26 or 28 "canons, ou grandz colovrines."

91. Concino's dispatch, ASF *Med. Princ.* 1854, no. 289 (11 January 1555).

92. Adriani, *Istoria*, 13:471.

93. Sozzini, "Diario," p. 405, reports intelligence from a prisoner that the Imperialists were manning 106 *corpi di guardia* around the city with sentries posted at intervals of 5 braccia or about 10 feet (1 April 1555).

94. Bardi, *Storie senesi*, fols. 363v.–364.

95. Sozzini, "Diario," p. 407.

96. Carlotto was reported captured at the end of March: Sozzini, "Diario," p. 401 (28 March) and Marignano's dispatch in ASF *Med. Princ.* 1853 (26 March 1555). Agnolo Callocci was taken at Christmas 1554: Adriani, *Istoria*, 13:470. The precise fate of Tiranfallo is not known, although Sozzini, "Diario," p. 280, remarks on his death sometime in the future, and Cantagalli, *La Guerra*, p. 358, n. 12, found records of money voted to him after the fall of Siena.

97. Sozzini, "Diario," p. 399.

98. Monluc, *Commentaires*, 1:452.

99. Quoted in Cantagalli, *La Guerra*, p. 386. See also Adriani, *Istoria*, 12:459.

100. Pius II, *Memoirs of a Renaissance Pope*, pp. 154–55: "Gently sloping hills planted with cultivated trees and vines . . . thick forests planted by nature or man where birds sing most sweetly and on every hill the citizens of Siena have built splendid country seats."

101. D'Addario, *Il problema senese*, pp. 358–59 and 366–67, stresses the low priority in French strategy accorded to Siena in general and the capital city in particular. By February 1555 a decision had already been taken to abandon Siena and to fall back on Port'Ércole, Grosseto, and Montalcino.

102. Cantagalli, *La Guerra* pp. 377–407.

103. For the text of the capitulation, see Pecci, *Memorie storico-critiche*, 4:219–24.

104. Monluc, *Commentaires*, 2:94, describes the separate negotiations and arrangements for the royal French troops.

105. Monluc, *Commentaires*, 2:101.

106. Monluc, *Commentaires*, 2:103–4, in which Monluc describes what for him became a semitriumph as the Imperial officers honored their gallant adversary: "The Spanish camp-masters (*maestri di campo*, roughly equivalent to a brigadier general) then came to salute me, and all their captains. The camp-masters did not alight, but all the captains did and came to embrace my knee, after which they remounted and accompanied me up to the marquis [of Marignano] and Signor Chiappino [Vitelli], which might be about 300 paces from the gate, where they embraced and they placed me between them. After this manner we passed on, discoursing all the way of the siege and the particularities that had happened, attributing much honor to us."

7

---

1. Montalvo, *Relazione*, p. 157.

2. ASS, *Balìa* 136, fol. 50v. (6 October 1552).

3. Marignano to Cosimo, reporting a reconnaissance authorized on 3 October, ASF *Med. Princ.* 1853 (27 October 1554).

4. Forster, "Metaphors of Rule"; Howe, "Architecture in Vasari's 'Massacre of the Huguenots' "; and Kirwin, "Vasari's Tondo of Cosimo I."

5. ASF *Med. Princ.* 1853 (16 May 1555).

6. For the more cautious attitude of Chiappino Vitelli to this operation, see ASF *Med. Princ.*, 648, fols. 165–165v.

7. The best description of the march is that of Captain Giovanni Pazzaglia, written in Pisa on 7 August 1555, in ASF *Carte Strozziane*, I, 109, fols. 222–25.

8. Repetti, *Dizionario geografico-fisico-storico della Toscana*, 3:187.

9. Pierson, *Philip II of Spain*, p. 77.

10. Gaye, *Carteggio*, 3:242; Milanesi, *Documenti per la storia dell'arte senese*, 3:115; ASS, *Balìa*, 600, no. 33.

11. Bardi, *Storie senesi*, fols. 280–280v., says that Thermes organized the original proj-

ect. Montalvo, *Relazione*, p. 159, attributes the scheme generally to Piero Strozzi, his bête noire, and mentions specifically that the Galera fort (see below) was completed in stone by Leone Strozzi. This last may well be true, because Leone spent most of his war in the Maremma where he was killed in 1554. However, the whole scheme must have been well advanced by the time Piero Strozzi arrived in Italy in December 1553.

12. ASS, *Balìa* 136, fol. 50v. (6 October 1552): "cento guastatori in Port'Ércole per far vi i forti per li soldati."

13. ASF *Med. Princ.* 414A, fols. 848–849v. (12 May 1553); dispatch written at sea in a very shaky hand by Domenico Bottananti to Cosimo. Technically a neutral at this stage of the war, Domenico had been allowed ashore under close escort. He noted that the garrison was very alert and that a fort on top of the hill above the town had been built and was said to be held by 300 men. He doubted that there were more than 100 men in the fort, or more than 300 soldiers in the town.

14. ASF *Med. Princ.* 1853 (27 October 1554).

15. ASS, *Balìa* 469, fols. 41–41v. (11 May 1553).

16. Montalvo, *Relazione*, pp. 159–60. See also Adriani, *Istoria*, 13:495, for a similar description, which confirms many of the names.

17. ASF *Med. Princ.* 1853 (3 October 1554).

18. ASF *Med. Princ.* 1853 (25 May 1555); Montalvo, *Relazione*, p. 158, confirms that the officers leading the patrol from Orbetello disclosed what they knew of the Imperial plans when threatened with torture.

19. ASF *Med. Princ.* 1853 (25 May 1555).

20. ASF *Med. Princ.* 1853 (27 May 1555).

21. Montalvo, *Relazione*, p. 161.

22. ASF, *Med. Princ.* 1853 (27 May 1555).

23. Montalvo, *Relazione*, p. 161; Pazzaglia in ASF *Carte Strozziane*, I, 109, fol. 223.

24. ASF *Med. Princ.* 1853 (31 May and 2 June 1555).

25. ASF *Med. Princ.* 1853 (31 May 1555); for Doria's strength, see Montalvo, *Relazione*, p. 160.

26. Pazzaglia in ASF *Carte Strozziane*, I, 109, fol. 223.

27. Montalvo, *Relazione*, p. 162; Marignano in ASF *Med. Princ.* 1853 (2 June 1555); for the fate of the defenders; see ASF *Med. Princ.* 1866, fol. 292.

28. ASF *Med. Princ.* 1853 (2 June 1555).

29. ASF *Med. Princ.* 1853 (2 June 1555).

30. "Questi luochi tanto diabolici." ASF *Med. Princ.* 1853 (3 June 1555).

31. "Et se ne andato con Dio, ma non sa dove." Montalvo, *Relazione,* p. 163, and three consecutive dispatches from Marignano filed under ASF *Med. Princ.* 1853 (9 June 1555).

32. Unsigned dispatch from the Imperial camp dated 11 June, in ASF *Med. Princ.* 1866, fol. 244.

33. Marignano, ASF *Med. Princ.* 1853 (14 June 1555).

34. Unsigned dispatch dated 17 June in ASF *Med. Princ.* 1866, fol. 296v.

35. Montalvo, *Relazione,* p. 166.

36. Pazzaglia in ASF *Carte Strozziane,* I, 109, fol. 223.

37. Montalvo, *Relazione,* pp. 167–68; Marignano in ASF *Med. Princ.* 1853 (19 June 1555).

38. ASF *Med. Princ.* 1853 (20 June 1555).

39. Vasari, *Il libro delle ricordanze,* p. 201, gives the date of the commission of the wall frescoes of the *salone* as 1556. Preliminary designs were produced for whole series during the period January to July, broken by trips to Rome, Milan, and Venice in the period February to May. The Port'Ercole fresco was painted between 15 April and 8 June 1570 (pp. 100–101).

40. There are two other pictures of the Port'Ercole siege, both plainly derived from the *salone* fresco and lacking much of its detail. One of them is a low-quality fresco in the frieze of the Room of Cosimo I (also in the Palazzo Vecchio), the other is a print by Giovanni Stradano, Vasari's assistant.

41. Belluzi, *Nuova inventione de fabricar fortezze, di varie forme . . . ,* p. 108. The treatise was published posthumously long after its compilation by Belluzzi (killed 1554) and its corruption by another author, probably Antonio Melloni of Cremona; see Belluzzi, *Belluzzi:il trattato* p. 411.

42. De' Marchi, *Architettura militare,* is another posthumous publication, probably written in the 1570s.

43. Vasari, *Le opere* 8:174–75.

44. J. L. Motley, *History of the United Netherlands* (New York, 1968) 3:39, provides the following information: "He [Vitelli] was equally distinguished for his courage, his cruelty, and his corpulence. The last characteristic was so remarkable that he was almost monstrous in his personal appearance. His protuberant stomach was always supported in a bandage suspended from his neck, yet in spite of this enormous impediment, he was personally active on the battlefield, and performed more service, not only as a commander but as a subaltern, than many a younger and lighter man." Vitelli died in 1576 near Antwerp from injuries sustained when he fell off his litter.

45. Vasari's "simultaneous" documentary technique lets him down, however, when he depicts the battery of the Avvoltoio fort. As this fort had already been depressed to reveal Port'Ercole, it was evidently considered more satisfactory to show the guns firing on Fort Sant'Elmo. This is the only instance of flagrant historical inaccuracy. Vasari's view also raises the possibility of further defensive works not mentioned in written accounts of the siege. Between the Stronco and the Galera forts there seem to be three rampartlike structures which would have blocked the landward approaches to the harbor. These may be the works suggested by Montalvo, who, after describing the discovery of the plans against Port'Ercole, mentions that Strozzi "thought to fortify the roads to oppose the coming of the enemy." They might also, of course, be works of countervallation raised by the Imperialists.

46. Montalvo, *Relazione,* p. 159: "grande spesa sì, ma con poca consideratione."

47. Marc René, marquis de Montalembert (1714–1800) was the proponent of perpendicular fortification, a late eighteenth-century theory which sought to achieve numerical superiority over breaching batteries by stacking large numbers of guns in casemated tiers. Montalembert took this firepower thesis to its logical conclusion in his proposal for a wooden fort which was essentially little more than a framework for guns. While military governor of the island of Oleron he built and tested such a wooden fort (or, perhaps, battery) in the teeth of conservative opposition from the Corps of Engineers. Not surprisingly, the marquis himself established a private cannon foundry in 1750 to produce the large numbers of cheap iron guns on which his theory turned. He was also a seasoned soldier, with experience of no less than fifteen campaigns and nine sieges. Lloyd, *Vauban, Montalembert, Carnot*; part 2.

48. Count Lazare Nicolas Marguerite Carnot (1753–1823) was a career officer in the

Engineers (and supporter of Montalembert) who left the army for politics during the Revolution. He was minister of war under Napoleon, but resigned because his radical beliefs would not allow him to hold office under the empire. In 1809 he was commissioned to write a manual of the defense of fortresses and, specifically, to include a discourse on the duties of commanders. To this work, *De la défense des places fortes* (Paris, 1812) he added his own theories on "vertical defense." Carnot's theory relied on firepower from casemated mortar batteries to cover a physical obstacle that was limited to a thin curtain wall concealed at the bottom of a ditch (with a 45-degree counterscarp to facilitate sorties). Carnot argued that the curtain would be invisible and thus secure from the random fire of enemy breaching batteries. See Lloyd, *Vauban*, part 3.

49. De' Marchi, *Architettura militare*, 3:57, p. 105.

50. Girolamo Cataneo, *Dell'arte militare*, fol. 1v.

51. ASF Med. Princ. 1853 (9 June 1555).

52. Ibid.

53. ASF Med Princ. 1853 (14 June 1555).

54. Montalvo, *Relazione*, p. 160; ASF Med. Princ. 1853 (2 June 1555); unsigned dispatch from the Imperial camp dated 3 June, in ASF Med. Princ. 1866, fol. 292, gives the most details: "Vi si trovò dentro un quarto di cannone sette archibugi da poste."

55. Unsigned dispatch dated 18 June in ASF Med. Princ. 1866, fol. 296v.

56. Montalvo, *Relazione*, p. 159.

8

1. Montalvo, *Relazione*, pp. 168–71; Squarcialupi, *Diario*, p. 77. Vitelli's report of the action is in ASF Med. Princ. 438, fols, 556–57 (12 July 1555). The battle was later the subject of one of Vasari's frescoes in the Palazzo Vecchio, Salone del Cinquecento.

2. Cantagalli, *La Guerra,*, pp. 451–56.

3. A detailed account of the siege of Sarteano is in Montalvo, *Relazione*, pp. 195–97.

4. Maurizio De Vita, "L'organizzazione della difesa costiera nello Stato di Siena e nei Presidi Spagnoli," in Rombai, ed., *I Medici*, pp. 157–61.

5. The Medici refortification program is described in articles in Rombai, ed., *I Medici*, by Enrico Coppi, "L'architettura militare del regime mediceo nello stato di Siena," pp. 117–24, and "Montalcino dopo la conquista medicea," pp. 129–33; Carmen Borsarelli, "La fortezza di Radicofani," pp. 133–41, and "La fortezza di Grosseto," pp. 145–55.

6. For the Medici fortress in Siena, see Coppi, "L'architettura," pp. 118–24. Baldassarre Lanci (sometimes Lancia) of Urbino (1510–71) was another successful pupil of Girolamo Genga. After early work in Lucca his career was spent almost entirely in the service of Cosimo dei Medici, for whom he built the fortresses of Siena (1561–63), Grosseto (begun 1561), Radicofani (begun 1565), and San Martino in Mugello. He also prepared an alternative plan for the new city of Valetta following the great sige of Malta in 1565. Vasari, *Le opere*, 3:266, and Rocchi, *Le fonti storiche*, pp. 319ff.

7. Montaigne, "Journal," p. 487.

8. Severini, *Architetture militari di Giuliano da Sangallo*.

9. De la Croix, *Military Considerations*, p. 45.

10. Vauban can reasonably claim to have reintroduced the enclosed casemate in his "bastion towers" at Besançon, Belfort, and Landau (c. 1687). For plans, see Duffy, *Fire and Stone*, p. 188, and Chandler, *The Art of War in the Age of Marlborough*, p. 277. Hughes, *Military Architecture*, pp. 151–230, provides an excellent account of nineteenth-century casemated fortifications, including the so-called Haxo casemate devised by the Napoleonic engineer/general François Nicolas Haxo (1774–1838), which provided protected gun positions (open only at the rear) on top of the ramparts.

11. Illustrated in Dürer's *Etliche Underricht*. For measured drawings of the guntowers at Langres, Burgundy, see Viollet-le-Duc, *Essai sur l'architecture militaire au moyen âge*.

12. De la Croix, *Military Considerations* pp. 42–45. For Ferrara, see Zevi, *Rossetti*.

13. Celli, "Le fortificazioni di Urbino."

14. For a discussion of this much-published project, see Renzo Manetti, *Michelangiolo*.

15. The citadel, whatever its unfortunate effects, was always claimed by the Spaniards to be in city's best interests and to contribute to its defense. The Medici fortress was simply imposed, against the terms of the Sienese surrender document, on a subject state. Unlike the Florentine Fortezza da Basso, the Sienese fortress stood well clear of the walls. The stiff, simplified lines of Cosimo's Sienese fortress mark a change from the varied and well-decorated surfaces of the earlier Renaissance works. See Hale, "Florentine Liberty," pp. 501–32.

16. "E ogni volta che voi ne potete piantare piú contro il nemico, che il nemico ne può piantare contro a voi, gli è impossibile che vi offenda; perché le piú artiglierie vincono le meno." Machiavelli, "Relazione di una visita fatta per fortificare Firenze," p. 297.

17. Sozzini, "Diario," p. 170: "alli 13 detto [13 April 1554] furono messi due cannoni grossi nell'orto di Girolamo Luti, et roppero le mura per vedere il Torrione dipinto."

18. The Sienese government organized the *fascinate* (raids to collect brushwood for fascines) but continued to exercise strict control of timber, which was the chief fuel for the communal bread ovens (private ovens were banned) as well as a strategic material. The proclamation for one of the first fascinades (reported by Sozzini, "Diario," p. 220) is in ASS, *Balìa* 825, no. 7 (28 April 1554). Two days later the same body announced the purchase of various timber plantations "for public service" and heavy penalties for any unauthorized wood cutting: *Balìa* 825, no. 3 (30 April). Another order forbade the cutting of vines under any circumstances: *Balìa* 825, no. 10 (23 September 1554). By this time, however, Sozzini tells us that "closer to the city than a mile there were neither houses, nor vineyards, nor plants of any sort." "Diario," p. 220 (19 October 1554).

19 The case of Pistoia is well documented in an article by Lamberini, "Le mura e i bastioni di Pistoia:" Here, in 1544, Belluzzi reckoned to find at least 7,000 *guastatori*, or laborers, for the works. It is difficult to estimate the effective Sienese civilian labor force because the proclamations (ASS, *Balìa* 825) order all shops to be closed and all men and women to work—an unlikely state of affairs, if we recall the difficulties faced in the construction of the Camollia forts. But under siege conditions the numbers were evidently very great. Sozzini, "Diario," p. 203, reports that the fort outside Porta San Marco was completed in three days (7–10 April 1554). Concino, reporting Chiappino Vitelli, says that 3,000 people were counted by Imperial patrols working daily on the Porta Tufi defenses alone

during the autumn. ASF *Med. Princ.* 1854, no. 243 (22 October 1554).

20. Pecci, *Memorie storico-critiche,* 3:102, and Sozzini "Diario," pp. 92–93.

21. Belcaro awaits a careful restoration. Hitherto the best description is in Barsali, *Baldassarre Peruzzi e le ville senesi del Cinquecento* pp. 94–101. See also Forlani-Conti, *Rilievi,* pp. 435–66.

22. The guns brought by the count of Santa Fiora would, it was hoped, bombard the city into surrender before Christmas 1554. Marignano's orders for the operation are reported to Cosimo in ASF *Med. Princ.* 1853 (30 November and 20 December 1554). Santa Fiora's progress is reported in *Med. Princ.* 1853 (23 and 29 December 1554 and 3 and 7 January 1555). See also chapter 6 above.

23. The effect of artillery on troop movement can be illustrated by comparing Santa Fiora's painful progress with Marignano's forced march (without cannon) from Pienza to Ansedonia—right through the mountains of South Tuscany—covering at least 65 miles in five days on the way to Port'Ercole.

24. ASF *Med. Princ.* 438, fol. 129 (21 February 1554): "Perché li cannoni sono malagievoli da condurre per questi paesi, quando V[ostra] Ecc[ellenz]a havesse costì duo mezzi cannoni La prego voler loro mandare a Poggibonzi perché di essi me ne serviro molto sopra questi luoghetti."

25. Pandolfo Gaci (Poggio Imperiale) to Cosimo, ASF *Med. Princ.* 419, fol. 138 (7 March 1554).

26. ASF *Med. Princ.* 438, fol. 362 (29 March 1554): "Habbiamo qua queste due mezze colubrine se ne serviam molto, ma vi habbiamo mancamento di palle, et havendosi mandato a chiederne al Prov[v]editore ci ha risposto non esserne, e che sara necess[ari]o farne fare di pietra, i che non ci forma a proposito: voglio per questo pregar la Ecc[ellenz]a V[ostr]a che sia contenta fargli dar modo che possi far fare di detto palle di ferro acciò quanto prima ce ne mandi, mandano parimente tutte le altre munitioni che si chieggono al detto Prov[v]editore." Evidently the same problem afflicted the Sienese. Concino reported that a month after the beginning of the siege of Siena the defenders were using stone shot because they were short of iron. ASF *Med. Princ.* 1854, no. 23 (28 February 1554).

27. Concino told Cosimo that the ball came into his room: ASF *Med Princ.* 1854, no. 25 (2 March 1554). In Concino's mind the Sienese were deliberately making life difficult for Marignano's staff. Two days later, Concino reported that a prisoner had revealed that the cavalier then being raised on San Prospero was to bombard the Palazzo dei Diavoli. *Med. Princ.* 1854, no. 27 (4 March). Shortly afterwards the Sienese tried again. "Yesterday," wrote Concino, "the enemy fired two long-range shots, one of which went through the Palazzo dei Diavoli, the other fell 25 braccia short." *Med. Princ.* 1854, no. 35 (10 March). Sozzini confirms the range of the Sienese artillery. Guns at Sant'Agostino bombarded the Imperial positions at San Lazzaro, an area target about one mile away. "Diario," p. 257. Evidently this surprised Marignano, who had supposed the camp to be out of range. ASF *Med. Princ.* 1853 (7 and 8 July 1554). Sozzini also reports the testing of a repaired basilisc which fired a very heavy (stone?) round "more than a mile" before a crowd of over 1,000 spectators. The basilisc burst not long afterward: "Diario," p. 203, 204.

28. He was the father of Antonio Lupicini (c. 1530–98) the military engineer and author who served at Monticchiello and Montalcino (chapter 5, note 27, above). For the father's exploits, see Promis, *Biografie di ingegneri militari italiani dal secolo XIV alla metà del XVIII*, p. 653; Rocchi, *Le fonti storiche dell'architettura militare*, p. 405; Roth, *Last Florentine Republic*, p. 225.

29. Guilds or unions of gunners with the Spanish forces were formed, the Fraternità di Santa Barbara (with entrance tests, dues, and pension arrangements). They are set out in an appendix to Collado, *Pratica manuale*, chapter 127, fols. 92–92v.

30. See chapter 1, note 20 and chapter 5, note 18, above.

31. ASF *Med. Princ.* 1853 (12 February 1554).

32. ASF *Med. Princ.* 1853 (28 August 1554).

33.
però che come su la cerchia tonda
Monteriggion di torri si corona . . .
così 'n la proda che 'l pozzo circonda
torreggiavan di mezza la persona
li orribili giganti, cui minaccia
Giove del cielo ancora quando tuona.
Dante, *Inferno*, Canto 31, lines 40–45.

34. ASF *Med. Princ.* 1853 (28 and 30 August 1554).

35. Montalvo, *Relazione*, p. 201.

36. ASF *Med. Princ.* 1854, no. 174 (2 August 1554): "Il luogo è importantissima . . . et ben'egli lo dice, che da a v[ostra] ecc[ellenz]a la più bella fortezza d'Italia."

37. "Infratanta circondai la terra, la quale di dentro su le mura gira passi 650 di fuora su la scarpa circa mille di buona misura: la scarpa ripida a quasi tufo tutta è alta braccia 32. La muraglia presso a sedici in grossa otto palmi et più: Tra la scarpa et la muraglia v'è un poco di fossa a torno a torno da ricever' archibusieri et far altri effetti: di dentro ha per tutto la retirata spaziosa, et le mura più alte, talché la nostra batteria restava alta per di dentro circa .vi. braccia oltre che si poteva farvi fosso da renderla più profonda e più difficile." ASF *Med. Prin.* 1854, no. 178 (1 September 1554).

38. See chapter 1, notes 11 and 12, above.

39. Monluc, *Commentaires*, 4:24–26. The undated letter was addressed to Armand de Gontauld, Baron de Biron, royal envoy in South Tuscany. Somewhat surprisingly it was written in Italian.

"Io ho saputo che l'inimici hanno abandonato il forte di Montecchio, che è dietro a Munistero circa un miglio et li sta tanto, a cavaliere, che non ci può entrar ne uscir homo che non sia scoperto, et mi sono informato da persone, che ci ho mandate a posta, et tra li altri il capitano Combasso et il capitano Sciarry, che è luogo fortificato et da potersi tenere ogni volta che ci sien dentro dua compagnie di fanteria et una di cavalli. Con le qual genti, mettendo ancora in Barontoli 25 soldati et 15 al poggio a'frati luoghi li vicini, io impediro di maniera le strade che vien dal forte di Camollia, che ridurrò in pochi giorni questi di Munistero in estrema necessità . . . Però se sua Eccellenza mi mandassi fino a 500 fanti in tutto, io li ridurrei in breve a tale, o'che saria forzato il marchese o a smembrar di costa grassa bandar per rimediar qua, overo perderebbe Munistero, che l'uno et l'atro saria di grande importanza. . .

"Intendiamo ancora che Palazzo de' Diavoli i abbandonato da loro, et forse da quella banda si potria pigliare qualche luoghetto da farli grande impedimento. Et se sua Eccellenza mi manderà queste genti, io faro forza di pigliar qualche castelletto alle spalle loro per la via di Firenze, et li tagliero la strada d'haver più vettovaglie ne' forti. Et se de' forti vorranno andar con l'artiglieria a recuperarlo, ci reston si pochi, che io andro a combattere il forte, et lo torro loro. Talché se non lo vorranno perdere sara forzato il marchese a tornarsene da queste bande."

40. For example, de'Marchi, *Architettura militare,* book 3, chapter 103, p. 167.

41. On the aesthetics of fortification, its materials, decoration, and appreciation, see references chapter 2, note 16, above.

42. The late medieval Law of Arms made an important conceptual distinction between a siege and a field engagement. The latter was regarded as a "trial by battle" arbitrated by God; the former as a test of the sovereignty of the princes involved. If a "summons" to surrender was rejected by means of a "defiance," the siege would be commenced by the firing of a gun. After this a well-understood siege law came into effect, excluding the defenders (soldiers and civilians alike) from the humanitarian provisions of the Law of Arms, which in other circumstances protected the life, honor, and welfare of a Christian prisoner of war. No quarter was the rule of the siege. Almost any kind of brutality was condoned when a town or castle had been taken by storm. Property could be looted or destroyed, women raped, men gratuitously killed (indeed, it was not uncommon for the entire surviving garrison to be hanged from the battlements). Only churches and churchmen were technically immune from the sack. "The goods and indeed the lives of the inhabitants of a conquered town were not regarded as mere lawful spoil; they were forfeit to the contumacious disregard of a prince's summons to surrender . . . the sentence of justice." Keen, *The Laws of War,* p. 123. Monluc, *Commentaires,* 2:110–18, makes it very clear that these "rules" obtained in the mid-sixteenth century. For their continuity into the Napoleonic era, see Carnot, *De la défense des places fortes,* and for their influence on fortress iconography, Simon Pepper, "The Meaning of the Renaissance Fortress," *Architectural Association Quarterly* 5 (1973):21–27.

43. When Strozzi sent a herald to summons the Imperial position in the monastery of the Osservanza, Captain Luchino da Fivizano replied that he would "hold it . . . or die in its defense." Concino, who reported this brave defiance to Cosimo, noted that Marignano did not consider Osservanza to be very important and that he planned to abandon it should the enemy launch a proper attack. ASF *Med. Princ.* 1854, no. 167 (16 July

1554). Captain Luchino was right. Even the defense of an outpost at the siege of Siena seems to have been regarded legally as a "siege" and, by implication, the outwork itself as a "fortress." This indeed made the commander responsible in honor and in duty to his prince to hold the position, or die in its defense.

44. Bardi, *Storie senesi,* fol. 300.

45. Montalvo, *Relazione,* p. 160.

46. Bardi, *Storie senesi,* fol. 300.

47. Although the defense of outlying positions can hardly have been new in siege warfare, the treatise authors clearly regard the conscious tactical use of forts as a novelty. De' Marchi, *Architettura militare,* book 3, chapter 57, p. 105, presents his thoughts on the subject as original. Castriotto (who went to France in 1553) cites the Mirandola campaign of 1552 as the first use of forts. *Della fortificatione,* book 3, chapter 18, fol. 95. Girolamo Cataneo, although critical, specifies Mirandola and Siena as the pioneering campaigns. *Dell' arte militare,* fol. 54.

9

1. Ackerman, "Architectural Practice in the Italian Renaissance." See also Catherine Wilkinson, "The New Professionalism in the Renaissance," in *The Architect: Chapters in the History of the Profession,* ed. Spiro Kostof (New York, 1977), pp. 124–60, and M. Briggs, *The Architect in History* (Oxford, 1927). On the fate of Renaissance architectural education in later periods, see Millon, "Filippo Juvarra and Architectural Education in Rome in the Early Eighteenth Century."

2. For Sangallo, see G. Clausse, *Les Sangallo* (Paris, 1902); Giovannoni, *Antonio da Sangallo il Giovane;* Carli, *Firenzuola.* For Sanmicheli, see Langenskiold, *Sanmicheli;* Semenzato, "Michele Sanmicheli architetto militare." The report of the joint tour by Antonio da Sangallo the Younger and Sanmicheli through the papal states was published by Luca Beltrami, *Intorno alla relazione pontifica fata nel 1526 da Antonio da Sangallo il Giovane e Michele Sanmicheli delle rocche della Romagna* (Rome, 1855).

3. De la Croix, "Military Architecture and the Radial City Plan in Sixteenth Century Italy," 274.

4. Or, as in the case of Leonardo da Vinci, to suggest the special character of his thought. See, for example, Parsons, "Leonardo da Vinci: The Military Engineer," in his *Engineers and Engineering in the Renaissance*, pp. 43–66. Ladislao Reti also wrestles briefly with this problem in "Leonardo the Technologist: The Problem of Prime Movers," in *Leonardo da Vinci, Technologist*, pp. 65–66. Reti points out that to the Sforza, Leonardo was known as "ingenarius et pinctor"; to Louis XII as "nostre peintre e ingenieur ordinaire." Conversely, Francesco di Giorgio Martini, anything but a simple painter, is called "depentore" while involved in work on the Sienese acqueducts; see ASS, *Concistoro* 2124, no. 125. During the mid-sixteenth century the titles "ingegnere," "architetto" (or "architettore") and, where appropriate, "depentore" (or "dipinctore") are used quite freely on their own or in combination by the Sienese. Later in chapter 9 specific evidence from mid-century Siena is cited. See below, notes 64 and 65.

5. Vanoccio Biringuccio was the author of one of the best-known treatises on metallurgy, *Pirotechnia* (1540), which featured extensive comments on gun founding. Niccolò Tartaglia wrote two books including extensive passages on artillery, the *Nuova Scientia* (Venice, 1537) and *Quesiti ed inventioni diverse* (Venice, 1546).

6. Mallett, *Mercenaries and their Masters*; and Pieri, *La crisi militare*. Civilian military architects, however, seem to have been expected to conform more closely to modern concepts of "loyalty" to a state or system of government. Witness Giorgio Vasari's treatment of Michelangelo's identity crisis of 1529, Vasari, *Le Opere*, 4:603, and note also his remarks concerning Peruzzi noted by Adams, "Baldassare Peruzzi and the Siege of Florence."

7. For Martinengo, see Tadini, *Vita di Gabriele Tadino da Martinego Priore da Barletta*. The episode during the siege of Genoa is reported by Tadini, pp. 91–94. A well known case in which a military official changed sides is revealed in the contractual relations of Andrea Doria (1466–1560) with Francis I and Charles V. Doria's contract expired with Francis in 1528. He signed the same year with the Imperialists with disastrous but not unexpected effects for his former employer.

8. For Francesco de' Marchi, see Marini, *Francesco de' Marchi*, 1:1–27. For the provenance of the treatise, see de la Croix, "Radial City Plan," pp. 278 and 285–86.

9. For Castriotto, see Rocchi, *Le fonti storiche dell'architettura militare* (Rome, 1908), pp. 362–65. Information is also contained in Carlo Promis, *Dell'arte dell'ingegnere e dell'artiglieria in Italia* (Turin, 1841), pp. 101–4. For the provenance of the treatise jointly authored by Maggi and Castriotto, *Della fortificatione*, see da la Croix, "Radial City Plan," pp. 278–79.

10. De la Croix, "Radial City Plan," p. 276.

11. Lamberini, "Giovanni Battista Belluzzi ingegnere militare e la fondazione di Portoferraio."

12. All of the information is taken from the closely researched life in Lamberini, "Belluzzi," pp. 375–517. Lamberini's work significantly updates Promis, *Dell'arte dell'ingegnere*, pp. 78–81, and de la Croix, "Radial City Plan," p. 274.

13. Belluzzi, *Belluzzi: il trattato*, p. 392. On the group of military architects in the circle of Cosimo I, see Marco Dezzi Bardeschi, "Il rinnovamento del sistema difensivo e l'architetto militante." in *La nascità della Toscana*.

14. De la Croix, "Radial City Plan," pp. 273–75. The original references are to de' Marchi, *Architettura militare*, book 1, chapter 1, fols. 1–1*v*., and Antonio Lupicini, *Architettura militare, libro primo* (Florence, 1582), chapter 1, p. 30.

15. *Nuova inventione di fabricar fortezze, di varie forme* (Venice, 1598), pp. 51–53. Also quoted by de la Croix, "Radial City Plan," p. 275. Belluzzi, *Belluzzi: il trattato*, pp. 411–12, attributes this passage in the corrupted text of Belluzzi's treatise to a certain Antonio Melloni of Cremona.

16. The forces at work in this change of position are interesting. Some architects move out of the field of military architecture altogether, but the freedom of the architect may, to some degree, be resented by military men. A "free professional" was also likely to be more expensive. By contrast see the biography of the Duke of Urbino, Federigo da Montefeltro by Vespasiano da Bisticci: "A military man who knows Latin has a great advantage over one who does not. The duke wrought the greater part of his martial deeds by ancient and modern example." Vespasiano da Bisticci, *The Vespasiano Memoirs*, trans. William George and Emily Waters (London, 1926), p. 99.

17. De la Croix, "Radial City Plan," p. 274.

18. Peruzzi's work in military architecture elsewhere is not securely dated. Some may have taken place prior to his return to Siena. Zander, "Due disegni di Baldassare Peruzzi per il Castello di Rocca Sinibaldi"; Maggi, "L'opera di Sangallo il Giovane e del Peruzzi nelle fortificazioni di Piacenza." There is no mention of military architecture in the standard study of Peruzzi's early career by Frommel, *Die Farnesina.*

19. For a complete survey of Peruzzi's activity as architect to the Sienese republic see Adams, "Architect to the Republic," and the volume prepared for the celebration of the five hundredth anniversary of Peruzzi's birth, *Rilievi,* ed. Forlani-Conti.

20. On his Chiusi visit of 1528, see Adams, "A Tour of Inspection."

21. Letter from Ansano Biringucci in Ascanio to their Lordships of the Balia in ASS, *Balià* 574, no. 39. No drawings survive for these projects.

22. "Continuando c'è capitato uno maestro Baldaxarre quale fa produxione di architectura." ASS, *Balià,* 600, no. 33.

23. Adams, "The Siege of Florence."

24. Adams, "Architecture for Fish."

25. Adams, "New Information."

26. Vasari, *Le opere,* 4:607–8, and Romagnoli, *Bellartisti* 7:17ff lists his complete opus. Lari, also known as "Il Tozzo," left the service of the republic in 1543 to build a fortress for Gianfrancesco Orsini, count of Pitigliano. When Gianfrancesco was deposed by his son, Lari followed the count to Rome, where he is believed to have died about 1549.

27. Venturi, *Storia dell'arte italiana: Architettura del Cinquecento,* 11:2, p. 672 for the Palazzo Francesconi attribution. U. Thieme and F. Becker, eds., *Allgemeines Lexikon der bildenden Künstler von der Antike bis zur Gegenwart* (Leipzig, 1940), 6:178, also credit him and Il Riccio with the beginning of San Giuseppe, Siena. Promis, *Dell'arte dell'ingegnere,* pp. 106–8, and Romagnoli, *Bellartisti,* 7:171–242, provide details of Cataneo's military architectural career, which was concentrated on the coastal towns of Orbetello, Talamone, Port'Ércole, and Grosseto between May 1544 and April 1549. This work was started just after the Turkish attacks of 1543. Cataneo held patents as commissioner of Port'Ércole in the summer of 1546 and as castellan of Grosseto in 1547. For documents relating to the Orbetello and Talamone projects, see Gaye, *Carteggio* 2:247, 346.

28. *Le pratiche delle due prime matematiche con la aggionta, libro d'albaco e geometria con il pratico e vero modo di misurar la Terra* (Venice, 1559). The treatise also embraces commercial mathematics, with worked examples of currency exchanges and division of shares in business enterprises. It provides a good deal of information on exchange rates for the more obscure regional coinage, equivalencies for weights, and measures, and the like. See R. Franci and L. Toti Rigatelli, "La trattatistica matematica del Rinascimento Senese," *Gli Atti dell'Accademia delle Scienze di Siena detta de'Fisiocritici,* 14th ser., vol. 13 (1981):1–71.

29. Cataneo, *I quattro primi libri di architettura,* is discussed by de la Croix, "Radial City Plan," p. 274.

30. A rather hostile life of Peloro is given by Vasari, *Le opere,* 3:210–12, but a more sympathetic treatment is to be found in Romagnoli, *Bellartisti,* 3:385–490, and Promis, *Dell'arte dell'ingegnere,* pp. 89–91. Gaye, *Carteggio,* 2:159, 387–88 has published documents. Alfonso d'Avalos, marquis of Vasto (1502–46).

31. Reported by Biringuccio, *Pirotechnia,* p. 332.

32. ASS, *Balìa* 744, no. 21 (14 January 1553) and no. 29 (15 January).

33. Bardi, *Storie senesi,* fol. 288*v.* Documents describing Thermes's visits to Sovano, Chiusi, and Caparbio are to be found in ASS, *Balìa* 740, no. 11 (9 December) and nos. 19 and 21 (both 10 December 1552). A letter from Siena contains the unambiguous statement that Thermes had designed a bastion at Caparbio, ASS, *Balìa* 467, fol. 130*v* (1 November 1552).

34. Letter from Giulio Buonsignori, Chiusi, 14 October 1553. "Il signor Cornelio Bentivoglio arrivò qui ier sera quasi a notte, con tutto ciò prima che scavalcasse giro tutti di fuori la terra e volse ancora vedere il forte. Questa mattina poi fu in piè all'alba, e giramo tutta di dentro questa città e di poi tornarno ancor fuore al luogo più debole e dove si considerò insieme col Peloro il tutto, e stasse in due disegni . . . il sign. Corenelio dice di voler conferire col R.mo di Ferrara . . . e ha ordinato che il Peloro torni a levarne la pianta." Quoted by Romagnoli, *Bellartisti,* 4:461.

35. It was not uncommon for an architect to travel in company with a facilitator of one sort or another. Pietro dell'Abbaco, the fifteenth-century Sienese estimator, accompanied the architect Guidoccio d'Andrea on work for Santa Maria della Scala.

36. Sozzini, "Diario," p. 331 (13 December 1554) mentions the Engineer to the King. Maestro Guglielmo Francese is named in a report from Simone Franci, commissioner in Caparbia (or Caparbio), ASS, *Balìa* 746, no. 72 (8 February 1553). He was evidently a minor figure. Malagrida seems to have been very active and important. For his appearances in the dominio, see ASS, *Balìa* 468, no. 60 (5 February 1553) and fol. 152*v*. (22 March 1553): *Balìa* 740, no. 52 (13 December 1552); *Balìa* 748, no. 5 (24 February 1553) and no. 18 (26 February 1553); *Balìa* 749, no. 70 (20 March 1553); *Balìa* 751, no. 63 (20 June 1553), no. 67 (15 June 1553), no. 72 (29 June 1553), no. 73 (3 July 1553). For his work inside Siena, see Sozzini, "Diario," p. 170 (9 February 1554) and p. 216 (22 April 1554). The commissioner of Montalcino refers to him as "captain"; ASS, *Concistoro* 2248 (27 November and 13 December 1552). Borgatti, *Storia dell'arma*, 1:65 mentions a certain Francesco Malacreda, or Malagrida, or Malagreda, a Veronese military architect who entered Venetian service in 1554, later serving Don Ferrante Gonzaga and the king of France at the defense of Boulogne. If our man is the same person, his engagement by Venice would explain his disappearance from Sienese records in the summer of 1554.

37. ASS, *Balìa* 148, fol. 38 (3 October 1552) records the first deliberation. The offer was repeated in *Balìa* 148, fol. 50*v* (6 October), when the Sienese ambassador in Florence had reported that Peloro was engaged on work for Cosimo and required a "pressing invitation" to show the duke when asking for leave.

38. ASS, *Balìa* 148, fol. 59 (10 October 1552).

39. ASS, *Balìa* 148, fol. 74*v* (16 October 1552).

40. Romagnoli has transcribed the relevant documents with varying degrees of precision. His system of referencing has, of course, been superseded in the Archivio di Stato, Siena.

41. See ASS, *Balìa* 148, fol. 82 (19 October 1552), for the deliberation.

42. ASS, *Balìa* 737, no. 5 (24 November 1552). Instructions to survey the walls of Montalcino are recorded in ASS, *Balìa* 148, fols. 99*v*.–100 (25 October 1552), but the commissioners in the city never mention his appearance.

43. Romagnoli, *Bellartisti*, 1:229.

44. See Cornice, "Indagine per un catalogo dell'opera del Riccio," for a complete list of Il Riccio's building works.

45. See Romagnoli, *Bellartisti* 6:711–85, for transcriptions of the documents. The argument with Captain Leonbruno is described in a letter from Piermaria Delci, commissioner in Monterotondo, in ASS, *Balìa* 747, no. 42 (15 February 1553).

46. For the life of Gori, see Romagnoli, *Bellartisti*, 7:269–320. His treatise has been published, *Libro e trattato della praticha d'alcibra*, ed. Laura Toti Rigatelli (Siena, 1984).

47. ASS, *Balìa* 468, fol. 34 (23 January 1553). This patent seems to have been misread by Romagnoli, who interprets Gori's powers to draft labor "nela massa del nostro dominio" as a posting to Massa, the place.

48. ASS, *Balìa* 469, fol. 20 (29 April 1553).

49. Romagnoli, *Bellartisti*, 7:559–61. Some of Maestro Giorgio's letters are published in Gaye, *Carteggio*, 2:381–87.

50. ASS, *Balìa* 141, fol. 3 (7 August 1552).

51. ASS, *Balìa* 747, no. 5 (14 February 1553). He asks for compensation and permission to return to Siena to look after his wife and seven sons.

52. ASS, *Balìa* 736, no. 36B (7 November 1552); Gaye, *Carteggio*, 2:383–84.

53. For the commissioner's account, see ASS, *Balìa* 740, no. 24 (10 December 1552).

54. Commissioner's account, ASS, *Balìa* 740, no. 7 (9 December 1552). In this case the colonel supported Maestro Giorgio. *Balìa* 740, no. 3 (9 December).

55. Even before Giorgio's arrival, the commissioner in Montalcino had called repeatedly for the dispatch of an architect. ASS, *Balìa* 735, no. 4 (24 October 1552); *Balìa* 735, no. 39 (28 October); *Balìa* 736, no. 5 (4 November); and *Balìa* 736, no. 29 (6 November), when he reports: "I have cleared certain areas around the walls, collected carbon, provided timber and gabions to make bastions; but without a good architect and a large sum of money I cannot put into effect the important works to this town." Maestro Giorgio arrived later that night, and the next day the commissioner reported the results of the survey. Three places would need new works which the architect estimated would cost 600 scudi and take three months. *Balìa* 736, no. 36A (7 November). Giorgio's undated report was attached (see also Gaye, *Carteggio*, 2:383–84). The architect than departed for Chiusi, leaving the commissioner protesting that he could "do nothing without fear of error in the absence of Maestro Giorgio" and that, in particular, he was needed to advise on the ground for the foundations of the bastion. *Balìa* 736, no. 86 (12 November). See also ASS, *Balìa* 738, no. 43 (21 November), no. 86 (26 November); *Balìa* 739, no. 48 (2 December); *Balìa* 740, no. 7 (9 December); *Balìa* 741, no. 17 (18 December 1552). After Christmas the architect remained more or less constantly on site.

56. The commissioner's account is in ASS, *Balìa* 739, no. 70 (5 December) and no. 74 (6 December 1552).

57. Annibale Tolomei in ASS, *Balìa* 741, no. 99 (25 December 1552); Niccolò Santi in ASS, *Balìa* 745, no. 40 (25 January 1553), *Balìa* 748, no. 51 (1 March 1553); and Giulio Vieri in *Balìa* 749, no. 48 (17 March 1553).

58. Quoted by Maestro Giorgio, Gaye, *Carteggio*, 2:382–83.

59. Gaye, *Carteggio*, 2:385–86.

60. Gaye, *Carteggio*, 2:386–87.

61. ASS, *Balìa* 748, no. 66 (4 March 1553.

62. ASS, *Balìa* 749, no. 62 (7 April 1553).

63. ASS, *Balìa* 753, no. 25 (31 May 1553).

64. ASS, *Balìa* 162, fol. 118*v* (16 March 1555): "A M[aestr]o Giorgio dipentore ad uno homo del S[igno]re Cornelio [Bentivoglio] derno buona licentia di possere andare nella torre di piazza per disegniare la pianta della città."

65. ASS, *Balìa* 148, fol. 176 (22 November 1552), records the deliberation for payment of "den [ari] che si deve per la vettura del cavallo che ha operato M[aestr]o Riccio architettore nel andata sua a Asinalunga per conto delli fortificationi da farvi." See also ASS, *Balìa* 741, no. 21 (9 December 1552), offering Il Riccio and Maestro Giorgio 6 gold scudi for "mercede et cavallo"; and *Balìa* 148, fol. 164*v* (18 November 1552): M[aestr]o

Giorgio dipentore architettore . . . per la vettura del cavallo."

66. The importance of local tradition in these matters cannot be overestimated. As in all small towns, even today, confidence in a local man was often greater than in a supposed expert from outside.

67. This impression is also due in part from the desire of later theorists to stress the importance of drawing as the justification for the architect's involvement in military affairs. In his life of Michele Sanmicheli, Tommasso Temanza, the Venetian architect-critic, notes that his skill in military architecture was no more than the result of his skill in *disegno*. According to Temanza, he had nothing of the martial character (Temanza, *Vite dei più celebri architetti e scultori veneziani*, ed. Liliana Grassi (Milan, 1966), p. 156.)

68. Among the most beautiful are the woodcuts of Pietro Cataneo for his *Architettura*. Elaborate and richly varied in form, the drawing is treated as an "object" by being rotated through the different perspective views. The finest collection of drawings, however, is generally reckoned to be that in de' Marchi's *Architettura militare*.

69. Pepper, "Planning versus Fortification."

70. Ackerman, "Architectural Practice," pp. 3–11.

71. Cataneo, *Architettura*, book 1, chapter 1, fol. 1.

72. This was no mere artistic convention: Galluzzi describes Cosimo's use of a model for this purpose. Vasari's life of Tribolo gives a detailed account of the model of the siege of Florence made by the artist in 1529 for the Medici pope Clement VII.

73. Adams, "Tour of Inspection," p. 30.

74. Heinrich Wurm, *Baldassarre Peruzzi: Architekturzeichnungen* (Tübingen, 1984).

75. ASS, *Balìa* 773, no. 36B (12 September 1554), letter from the commissioner of Montalcino, Marcello Tuti, reporting the arrival of Cornelio Bentivoglio, Maestro Giorgio, and Peloro. (Romagnoli, *Bellartisti*, 6:450–51, incorrectly dates this visit to September 1553.)

BIBLIOGRAPHY

Chronicles, Diaries, Memoirs, and Treatises

Adriani, G. B. *Istoria dei suoi tempi, divisa in libri ventidue.* Florence, 1583.

Alberti, Leone Battista. *Ten Books on Architecture.* Ed. Joseph Rykwert. Trans. James Leoni. London, 1965.

Bardi, Agnolo. *Storie senesi, 1512–1556.* Manuscript A.VI.51. Siena, Biblioteca Comunale.

Belluzzi, Giovanni Battista. *Nuova inventione di fabricar fortezze, di varie forme. . .* Venice, 1598.

———. *Giovanni Battista Belluzzi: Il trattatto delle fortificazioni di terra.* Ed. Daniela Lamberini. In *Documenti inediti di cultura toscana,* 4:375–517. Florence, 1980.

Benvoglienti, Bartolommeo. *Trattato de l'origine e accrescimento della città di Siena.* Siena, 1571.

Biringuccio, Vannoccio. *Pirotechnia.* Ed. C. S. Smith. Trans. M. T. Gnudi. Cambridge, 1966.

Borghesi, S., and L. Banchi. *Nuovi documenti per la storia dell'arte senese.* Siena, 1898.

Busca, Gabriele. *L'architettura militare.* Milan, 1601.

Cataneo, Girolamo. *Dell'arte militare libri tre.* Brescia, 1571.

Cataneo, Pietro. *I Quattro primi libri de architettura.* Venice, 1554.

Collado, Luigi. *Pratica manuale di artigleria.* Venice, 1586. (Later Italian edition, Milan 1606; and a revised Spanish edition, Milan 1592, from which the 1606 Italian edition was translated.)

Della Valle di Venafro, G. B. *Vallo: libro contenente appertinentie ad capitani, retenere et fortificare una città con bastioni, con novi artificii de fuoco aggionti . . . et de espugnare una Città. . .* Venice, 1524.

De' Marchi, Francesco. *Della architettura militare, Libri tre.* Brescia, 1599.

"Diario della Ribellione della città di Arezzo dell'anno 1502." *Archivio storico italiano* 2 (1842): 213–26.

Dürer, Albrecht. *Etliche Underricht, zur Befestigung der Stett, Schloss und Flecken.* Nuremberg, 1527.

Francesco di Giorgio Martini. *Trattati di architettura, ingegneria e arte militare.* Ed. Corrado Maltese. 2 vols. Milan, 1967.

"Giornale dell'assedio di Montalcino fatto dagli Spagnuoli nel 1553 di autore anonimo." *Archivio storico italiano* 8 (1850): 354–85.

Giovio, Paolo. *Historie del suo tempo.* Florence, 1551.

Guicciardini, Francesco. *The History of Italy.* Trans. Chevalier Austin Parke Goddard. London, 1754.

———. *Ricordi politici e civili.* In *Opere inedite,* ed. Giuseppe Canestrini. Florence, 1857.

"La cacciata della guardia spagnuola da Siena d'incerto autore, 1552." *Archivio storico italiano* 2 (1842): 481–524.

Landi, Giulio. "Diario dell'assedio di Montalcino." In Gugliemo Della Valle, *Lettere sanesi del Padre Guglielmo Della Valle sopra le belle arti.* Vol. 3, Venice 1782.

Laparelli, Francesco. *Visita e progetti di miglior difesa in varie fortezze ed altri luoghi dello Stato Pontificio.* Ed. Paolo Marconi. Cortona, 1970.

Lupicini, Antonio. *Architettura militare, libro primo.* Florence, 1582.

———. *Discorsi militari d'Antonio Lupicini, sopra l'espugnazione d'alcuni siti.* Florence, 1576.

Machiavelli, Niccolò. *L'arte della guerra e scritti politici minori.* Ed. Sergio Bertelli. Milan, 1962.

———, *The Discourses.* Ed. Bernard Crick. Harmondsworth, U.K., 1970.

Maggi, Girolamo, and Jacopo Fusto Castriotto. *Della fortificatione delle città . . . Libri III.* Venice, 1564.

Malavolti, Orlando. *Historia de' fatti e guerre de' Senesi.* 4 vols. Venice, 1599.

Milanesi, Gaetano. *Documenti per la storia dell'arte senese.* 3 vols. Siena, 1854–56.

Monluc, Blaise, de. *Commentaires et Lettres de Blaise de Monluc, Maréchal de France.* Ed. Alphonse de Ruble. 5 vols. Paris, 1864. (See also the more recent edition edited by Jean Giono, Paris, 1964. Italian edition of the sections dealing with Siena under the title *L'Assedio di Siena,* ed. Mario Filippone, Siena, 1976).

Montaigne, Michel de. *Oeuvres Complètes.* Ed. Robert Barral. Paris, 1967.

Montalvo, Antonio di. *Relazione della guerra di Siena, scritta l'anno 1557 in lingua spagnola da don Antonio di Montalvo, e tradotta in lingua italiana da don Garcia di Montalvo, suo figlio.* Ed. C. Riccomani and F. Grottanelli; documents ed. L. Banchi. Turin, 1863.

Orlandi, O. M. *La gloriosa vittoria de Senesi per mirabil maniera conseguita nel mese di luglio del anno 1526.* Siena, 1927.

Pius II. *Memoirs of a Renaissance Pope: The Commentaries of Pius II.* Ed. F. A. Gragg. New York, 1959.

Sanuto, Marino. *Diarii di Marino Sanuto.* Ed. N. Barozzi. 18 vols. Venice, 1879–1902.

Squarcialupi, Marcello. *Diario della guerra del 1552–1556 in Maremma e nell'Elba.* Ed. E. Rhigetti. Florence, 1912.

Sozzini, Alessandro. "Diario delle cose avvenute in Siena dal 20 luglio 1550 al 28 giugno 1555." *Archivio storico italiano* 2 (1842): 1–434.

Vasari, Giorgio. *Le opere di Giorgio Vasari.* Ed. G. Milanesi. 9 vols. Florence, 1906.

———. *Il Libro delle Ricordanze.* Ed. Alessandro del Vita. Rome, 1938.

———. *Il carteggio di Giorgio Vasari dal 1563 al 1565.* Ed. Karl Frey. Arezzo, 1941.

Vere, Francis. *The Commentaries of Sir Francis Vere.* Cambridge, 1657.

Verissima descrizione e successo del campo imperiale da che arrivo sotto la città di Montalcino nel'anno MDLIII. Ed. L. Banchi and A. Lisini. Florence, 1850.

Williams, Roger. *The Works of Sir Roger Williams.* Ed. John X. Evans. Oxford, 1972.

Zanchi, G. B. *Del modo di fortificar le città.* Venice, 1564.

Secondary Sources:

Ackerman, J. S. "Architectural Practice in the Italian Renaissance." *Journal of the Society of Architectural Historians* 13 (1954): 3–11.

———. *The Architecture of Michelangelo.* 2 vols. London, 1961.

Adams, Nicholas. "Baldassare Peruzzi and the Siege of Florence: Archival Notes and Undated Drawings." *Art Bulletin* 60 (1978): 475–82.

———. "Baldassare Peruzzi and a Tour of Inspection in the Valdichiana 1528–1529." *Revue d'art canadienne/Canadian Art Review* 5 (1978): 28–36.

———. "New Information about the Screw Press as a Device for Minting Coins; Bramante, Cellini and Baldassare Peruzzi." *Museum Notes of the American Numismatic Society* 23 (1978): 201–6.

———. "Baldassare Peruzzi as Architect to the Republic of Siena, 1527–1535: Archival Notes." *Bullettino senese di storia patria* 88 (1981): 256–67.

———. "Architecture for Fish: The Sienese Dam on the Bruna River—Structures and Designs, 1468–ca. 1530." *Technology and Culture* 25 (1984): 768–97.

———. "Military Architecture and Renaissance Art History or 'Bellezza on the Battlefield.' " *Architectura* 14 (1984): 106–18.

Andrews, Kevin. *The Castles of the Morea.* Princeton, 1953.

Angelucci, Angelo. *Documenti inediti per la storia delle armi da fuoco italiane.* Turin, 1869.

Balestracci, Duccio, and Gabriella Piccini. *Siena nel Trecento: Assetto urbano e strutture edilizie.* Florence, 1977.

Balestracci, Duccio. ed. *Statuto dell'arte dei muratori (1626).* Siena, 1976.

Bardeschi, Marco Dezzi. "Le Rocche di Francesco di Giorgio nel Ducato di Urbino." *Castellum* 8 (1968): 97–138.

———. "Il rinnovamento del sistema difensivo e l'architetto militante." In *La nascità della Toscana* (Convegno di studi per il IV centenario della morte di Cosimo I de' Medici), pp. 273–94. Florence, 1980.

Barsali, Isa Belli. *Baldassare Peruzzi e le ville senesi del Cinquecento.* San Quirico d'Orcia, 1977.

Bartoli, N. "Le congiure di Siena e la cacciata degli Spagnuoli." *Bullettino senese di storia patria* 37 (1930): 361–421.

Beltrami, Luca. *Intorno alla relazione pontifica fatta nel 1526 da Antonio da Sangallo il Giovane e Michele Sanmicheli delle rocche della Romagna.* Rome, 1855.

Biagi, A., G. Neri, A. Giachetti, and M. Picchi. *Baldassare Peruzzi: 20 lugli–20 Agosto Ancaiano-Sovicille commemorazione V centenario della nascita.* Siena, 1981.

Blouet, B. W. "Town Planning in Malta, 1530–1798." *Town Planning Review* 35 (1964): 183–94.

Borgia, L., E. Carli, M. A. Ceppari, U. Morandi, P. Sinibaldi, and C. Zarrilli, eds. *Le Biccherna: Tavole dipinte delle magistrature senesi (Secoli XIII–XVIII).* Rome, 1984.

Borgatti, M. "Il bastione ardeatina a Roma." *Rivista d'artiglieria e genio* 2 (1916): 207–23.

———. *Castel S. Angelo in Roma.* Rome, 1931.

————, *Storia dell'arma del genio.* Rome, 1928.

Bracci, Mario. *Il popolo senese dall'assedio alla ritirata in Montalcino.* Siena, 1959.

Brandi, Karl. *The Emperor Charles V.: The Growth and Destiny of a Man and of a World Empire.* London, 1965.

Braudel, Fernand. *The Mediterranean and the Mediterranean World in the Age of Philip II.* Trans. S. Reynolds. 2 vols. London, 1973.

Braunfels, Wolfgang. *Mittelalterliche Stadtbaukunst in der Toskana.* Berlin, 1953.

Brenzoni, R. *Fra Giovanni Giocondo Veronese.* Florence, 1960.

Brigidi, S. *Le vite di Filippo Strozzi e di Piero e Leone suoi figli.* Montalcino, 1880.

Briggs, M. *The Architect in History.* Oxford, 1927.

Brinton, Selwyn. *The Renaissance in Italian Art.* New York, 1907–8.

Bullard, Melissa. *Filippo Strozzi and the Medici: Favor and Finances in Sixteenth Century Florence and Rome.* Cambridge, 1980.

Bury, John. "Francisco de Holanda: A Little Known Source for the History of Fortification in the Sixteenth Century." *Arquivos do Centro Cultural Português* 14 (1979): 163–202.

————. "Are Renaissance Fortifications Beautiful?" *Fort* 8 (1980): 7–20.

————. "The Early History of the Explosive Mine. *Fort* 10 (1982): 23–30.

Buselli, Franco. *Documenti sulla edificazione della Fortezza di Sarzana, 1487–1492.* Florence, 1970.

Calvi, Ignazio. *L'architettura militare di Leonardo da Vinci.* Milan, 1943.

Cantagalli, Roberto. *La Guerra di Siena (1552–1559).* Siena, 1962.

Carli, Giorgio. *Firenzuola: La fortificazione ad opera di Antonio da Sangallo il Vecchio considerazioni sulla struttura urbana della nuova fondazione fiorentina.* Florence, 1981.

Celli, L. "Le fortificazioni di Urbino." *Nuova rivista misena* 7 (1895): 5–10.

Chandler, David. *The Art of War in the Age of Marlborough.* London, 1967.

Cipolla, Carlo. *Guns and Sails in the Early Phase of European Expansion, 1400–1700.* London, 1965.

Clausse, G. *Les Sangallo.* Paris, 1902.

Cochrane, Eric. *Florence in the Forgotten Centuries, 1527–1800.* Chicago, 1973.

Collegio Ingegneri della Toscana. *Bonifica della Val di Chiana: Mostra documentaria.* (Essays by Francesco Guerrieri, Vittorio Franchetti Pardo, Giuseppina Carla Romby, and others.) Florence, 1981.

Contamine, Philippe. *War in the Middle Ages.* Oxford, 1984.

Cornice, Alberto. "Indagine per un catalogo dell'opera del Riccio." Doctoral diss., University of Genoa, 1973–74.

Courteault, Paul. *Blaise de Monluc historien: Étude critique sur le texte et le valeur historique des Commentaires.* Paris, 1907.

————. *Un cadet de Gascogne au XVIᶜ siécle: Blaise de Monluc.* Paris, 1909.

Coppini, A. *Piero Strozzi nell'Assedio di Siena.* Florence, 1902.

Croce, B. *Storia del Regno di Napoli.* Bari, 1925.

D'Addario, Arnaldo. *Il problema senese nella storia italiana della prima metà del Cinquecento.* Florence, 1958.

————. "Burocrazia, economia e finanze della Stato Fiorentino alla metà del Cinquecento." *Archivo storico italiano* 121 (1963): 392–456.

De Fiore, Gaspare, *Baccio Pontelli: Architetto fiorentino.* Rome, 1963.

De la Croix, Horst. "Military Architecture and the Radial City Plan in Sixteenth Century Italy." *Art Bulletin* 42 (1960): 263–90.

————. "The Literature of Fortification in Renaissance Italy." *Technology and Culture* 6 (1963): 30–50.

————. "Palmanova: A Study of Sixteenth Century Urbanism." *Saggi e memorie di storia dell'arte* 5 (1966): 23–41 and 175–79.

————. *Military Considerations in City Planning: Fortifications.* New York, 1972.

De la Pilorgerie, Jules. *Campagne et bulletins de la Grande Armée d'Italie commandée par Charles VIII, 1494–1495.* Nantes and Paris, 1866.

De Tolnay, Charles. "Michelangelo Studies: (1) Newly Found Autographs by Michelangelo in America; (2) Michelangelo's Projects for the Fortification in Florence in 1529." *Art Bulletin* 23 (1940): 127–37.

Duffy, Christopher. *Fire and Stone: The Science of Fortress Warfare.* London, 1975.

Filangieri, R. *Castel Nuovo Reggia Angoina ed Aragonese di Napoli.* Naples, 1934.

Ffoulkes, Charles. *The Gunfounders of England.* Cambridge, 1937.

Forster, Kurt W. "From 'Rocca' to 'Civitas': Urban Planning at Sabbioneta." *L'Arte* 5 (1969): 5–40.

————. "Metaphors of Rule: Political Ideology and History in the Portraits of Cosimo I de' Medici." *Mitteilungen des Kunsthistorischen Institutes in Florenz* 15 (1971): 65–104.

Frommel, C. L. *Die Farnesina und Peruzzis Architektonisches Frühwerk.* Berlin, 1961.

———. *Baldassare Peruzzi als Maler und Zeichner.* Vienna, 1967.

———. *Der römische Palastbau der Hochrenaissance.* 3 vols. Tübingen, 1973.

Fuller, J. F. C. *The Decisive Battles of the Western World and their Influence upon History.* London, 1970.

Galluzzi, R. *Storia del Granducato di Toscana.* 3 vols. Livorno, 1731.

Gaye, Giovanni. *Carteggio inedito d'artisti dei secoli XIV, XV, XVI.* 3 vols. Florence, 1839.

Gazzola, Piero, and Marcella Kahne-Mann. *Michele Sanmicheli.* Verona, 1960.

Gigli, Girolamo. *Diario sanese.* Siena, 1846.

Giorgetti, N. *Le armi toscane.* Città di Castello, 1916.

Giovanelli, Giovanni. "La Rocca Sinibaldi." *Bollettino dell'Istituto Storico della Cultura di Arma del Genio* 32 (1966): 407–26, 566–93; 33 (1967): 188–221, 333–64.

Giovannoni, Gustavo. *Antonio da Sangallo il Giovane.* 2 vols. Rome, 1959.

Goldthwaite, Richard A. *The Building of Renaissance Florence: An Economic and Social History.* Baltimore, 1980.

Gonzi, Vittorio. *Brandano.* Rome, 1967.

Guglielmotti, Alberto. *La guerra dei pirati e la marina pontificia dal 1500 at 1560.* Florence, 1876.

———. *Storia della fortificazione nella spiaggia romana.* Rome, 1880.

Guilmartin, John Francis. *Gunpowder and Galleys: Changing Technology and Mediterranean Warfare at Sea in the Sixteenth Century.* London, 1974.

———. "The Guns of the Santissimo Sacramento." *Technology and Culture* 24 (1983): 559–601.

Gurrieri, Ottorino. *La Rocca Paolina in Perugia.* Perugia, 1973.

Hale, J. R. "War and Public Opinion in the Fifteenth and Sixteenth Centuries." *Past and Present* 22 (1962): 18–35.

———. "The First Fifty Years of a Venetian Magistracy: The *Provveditori alle Fortezze.*" In *Renaissance Studies in Honor of Hans Baron,* ed. Anthony Molho and John A. Tedeschi, pp. 501–29. Dekalb, Ill., 1971.

———. "The Early Development of the Bastion: An Italian Chronology c 1450–c. 1534." In *Europe in the Late Middle Ages,* ed. J. R. Hale, L. Highfield, and B. Smalley, pp. 466–94. London, 1965.

———. "Francesco Tensini and the Fortification of Vicenza." *Studi Veneziani* 10 (1968): 231–89.

———. "The End of Florentine Liberty: The Fortezza da Basso." In *Florentine Studies,* ed. Nicolai Rubenstein, pp. 501–32. London, 1970.

———. "Military Academies on the Venetian Terraferma in the Early Seventeenth Century." *Studi Veneziani* 15 (1973): 273–95.

———. "Men and Weapons: The Fighting Potential of Sixteenth Century Venetian Galleys." In *War and Society: A Yearbook of Military History,* ed. Brian Bond and Ian Roy, pp. 1–23. New York, 1975.

———. "To Fortify or Not to Fortify? Machiavelli's Contribution to a Renaissance Debate." In *Essays in Honour of John Humphreys Whitfield,* ed. H. C. Davis and others, pp. 99–119. London, 1975.

———. "The Military Education of the Officer Class in Early Modern Europe." In *Cultural Aspects of the Italian Renaissance: Essays in Honor of Paul Oskar Kristeller,* ed. C. H. Clough, pp. 440–61. New York, 1976.

———. *Renaissance Fortification: Art or Engineering?* London, 1977.

Hale, J. R., and Michael Mallett. *The Military Organisation of a Renaissance State: Venice c. 1400 to 1617.* Cambridge, 1984.

Hall, A. R. *Ballistics in the Seventeenth Century.* Cambridge, 1952.

Held, Robert. *The Age of Firearms.* New York, 1957.

Hersey, George. *Alfonso II and the Artistic Renewal of Naples, 1485–1495.* New Haven, 1969.

Heydenreich, L. H., Bern Dibner, and Ladislao Reti. *Leonardo the Inventor.* London, 1981.

Heydenreich, Ludwig, and Wolfgang Lotz. *Architecture in Italy, 1400–1600.* Baltimore, 1974.

Hicks, David. "The Sienese State in the Renaissance." In *From the Renaissance to the Counter-Reformation,* ed. C. H. Carter, pp. 75–94. London, 1966.

Hook, Judith. *The Sack of Rome, 1527.* London, 1972.

———. "Fortifications and the End of the Sienese State." *History* 62 (1977): 372–87.

———. "Habsburg Imperialism and Italian Particularism: The Case of Charles V and Siena." *European Studies Review* 9 (1979): 283–312.

———. *Siena: A City and Its History.* London, 1979.

————. "Siena and the Renaissance State." *Bullettino senese di storia patria* 87 (1980): 107–22.

Howe. E. "Architecture in Vasari's "Massacre of the Huguenots.' " *Journal of the Warburg and Courtauld Institutes* 39 (1976): 258–61.

Hughes, Quentin. *Military Architecture.* London, 1974.

————. "Give Me Time and I Will Give You Life: Francesco Laparelli and the Building of Valletta, Malta, 1565–1569." *Town Planning Review* 49 (1978): 61–74.

Isaccs, A. K. C. "Popoli e monti nella Siena del primo Cinquecento." *Rivista storica italiana* 86 (1970): 32–80.

Keegan, John. *The Face of Battle: A Study of Agincourt, Waterloo, and the Somme.* New York, 1976.

Keen, M. H. *The Laws of War in the Late Middle Ages.* London, 1965.

Kenyon, J. R. "Early Artillery Fortification in England and Wales." *Fort* 1 (1976): 22–25.

————. "Early Gunports: A Gazeteer." *Fort* 4 (1977): 4–6.

Kirwin, W. Chandler. "Vasari's Tondo of Cosimo I with his Architects, Engineers, and Sculptors." *Mitteilungen des Kunsthistorischen Institutes in Florenz* 15 (1971): 105–22.

Koenigsberger, H. G. *The Government of Sicily under Philip II.* London, 1951.

Kostof, Spiro, ed. *The Architect: Chapters in the History of the Profession.* New York, 1977.

Lamberini, Daniela. "Le mura e i bastioni di Pistoia: Una fortificazione reale del '500." *Pistoia Programma* 7 (1980): 5–30.

————. "Giovanni Battista Belluzzi ingegnere militare e la fondazione di Portoferraio." In *Cosmopolis: Portoferraio Medicea secoli XVI–XVII,* ed. Giuseppe M. Battaglini. Pisa, 1981.

Lane, Frederick, *Venetian Ships and Shipbuilders of the Renaissance.* Baltimore, 1934.

Langenskiold, Eric. *Michele Sanmicheli, the Architect of Verona.* Uppsala, 1938.

Laughton, L. G. Carr. "Early Tudor Ship Guns," ed M. Lewis. *The Mariner's Mirror* 46 (1960): 242–85.

Lavin, James. *A History of Spanish Firearms.* London, 1965.

Leseur, Guillaume. *Histoire de Gaston IV, Compte de Foix.* Ed. Paul Courteault. Paris, 1896.

Lewis, Michael. *Armada Guns: A Comparative Study of English and Spanish Armaments.* London, 1961.

Liberati, A. "La Battaglia di Camullia." *Bullettino senese di storia patria* 13 (1906): 220–21.

Lloyd, E. M. *Vauban, Montalembert, Carnot: Engineering Studies.* London, 1887.

Lot, Ferdinand. *Les effectifs des armées françaises des Guerres d'Italie.* Paris, 1962.

Lusini, Vittorio. "Note storiche sulla topografia di Siena nel secolo XIII." *Bullettino senese di storia patria* 26 (1921): 241–339.

McNeill, William H. *The Pursuit of Power: Technology, Armed Force, and Society since* A.D. *1000.* Chicago, 1982.

Maggi, Serafino. "L'opera di Sangallo il Giovane e del Peruzzi nelle fortificazioni di Piacenza." *Castellum* 3 (1966): 60–62.

Majewski, Alfred. "Les tours cannonières et les fortifications bastionées en Pologne." *Bulletin de l'Institut des chateaux historiques* 40 (1982): 70–83.

Malachowicz, "Fortification in Poland." *Fort* 3 (1977): 25–30.

Malagù, U. *Le mura di Ferrara.* Ferrara, 1960.

Mallett, Michael. *Mercenaries and their Masters: Warfare in Renaissance Italy.* London, 1974.

Mallett, Michael and David Whitehouse. "Castel Porciano: An Abandoned Medieval Village of the Roman Campagna." *Papers of the British School in Rome* 35, n.s. 22 (1967): 113–46.

Manetti, Renzo. *Michelangiolo: Le fortificazione per l'assedio di Firenze.* Florence, 1980.

Marani, Pietro C. "A Reworking by Baldassare Peruzzi of Francesco di Giorgio's Plan of a Villa." *Journal of the Society of Architectural Historians* 41 (1982): 181–88.

————. *L'architettura fortificata negli studi di Leonardo da Vinci.* Florence, 1984.

————, ed. *Disegni di fortificazioni da Leonardo a Michelangelo.* Florence, 1984.

Marconi, Paolo. "Contributo alla storia delle fortificazioni di Roma nel cinquecento e nel seicento." *Quaderni dell'Istituto di Storia dell'Architettura* ser. 13, 73 (1966): 109–30.

————. *La città come forma simbolica: Studi sulla teoria dell'architettura nel Rinascimento.* Rome, 1973.

Marini, L. *La Spagna in Italia nell'età di Carlo V.* Bologna, 1961.

Marini, Luigi. *Francesco de' Marchi: Architettura militare.* Rome, 1810.

Merriman, R. B. *The Rise of the Spanish Empire in the Old World and the New.* New York, 1918–34.

Milanesi, G. *Documenti per la storia dell'arte senese.* 3 vols. Siena, 1856.

Millon, Henry A. "Filippo Juvarra and Architectural Education in Rome in the Early Eighteenth Century." *Bulletin of the American Academy of Arts and Sciences* 25 (April 1982): 25–45.

Missaglia, M. *Vita di Giovan Jacopo Medici, Marchese di Marignano.* Turin, 1863.

Misciatelli, P. *The Mystics of Siena.* Trans M. Peters Roberts. Cambridge, 1929.

Oman, Charles. *A History of the Art of War in the Sixteenth Century.* New York, 1937.

O'Neil, B. H. St. J. *Castles and Cannon.* Oxford, 1960.

Papini, Roberto. *Francesco di Giorgio Martini: Architetto.* 2 vols. Florence, 1946.

Parenti, G. *Prezzo e mercato di grano a Siena (1546–1765).* Florence, 1942.

Parker, Geoffrey. *The Army of Flanders and the Spanish Road, 1567–1659.* Cambridge, 1972.

Parry, J. H. *The Spanish Seaborne Empire.* London, 1966.

Parsons, William Barclay. *Engineers and Engineering in the Renaissance.* Baltimore, 1939.

Pecci, Giovanni Antonio. *Memorie storico-critiche della città di Siena dal 1480 al 1552.* 4 vols. Siena, 1755–60.

Pepper, Simon. "Problems in XVI Century Military Architecture: A Study of Fortifications and Siege Warfare with Special Reference to the War of Siena, 1552–1556." Doctoral diss., University of Essex, 1972.

———. "The Meaning of the Renaissance Fortress." *Architectural Association Quarterly* 5 (1973): 22–27.

———. "Planning vs. Fortification: Sangallo's Project for the Defence of Rome." *Architectural Review* 159 (1976): 162–69.

———. "Firepower and the Design of Renaissance Fortifications." *Fort* 10 (1982): 93–104.

———. "The Underground Siege." *Fort* 10 (1982): 31–38.

Pepper, Simon, and Quentin Hughes. "Fortification in Late Fifteenth Century Italy: The Treatise of Francesco di Giorgio Martini." *British Archaeological Reports,* Supplementary Series 41 (1978): 541–67.

Picot, E. *Les Italiens en France au XVIᵉ siècle.* Paris, 1802.

Pieri, Piero. *La crisi militare Italiane nel Rinascimento.* Turin, 1970.

Pierson, Peter. *Philip II of Spain.* London, 1951.

Polverini, I. Fosi. "Una programma di politica economia: Le infeudazioni nel senese durante il principato mediceo." *Critica storica* 13/4 (1976): 76–88.

Promis, Carlo. *Dell'arte dell'ingegnere e dell'artiglierie in Italia dalla sua origine sino al principio del XVI secolo: Memorie storiche.* Turin, 1841.

Promis, Carlo. *Dell'arte dell'ingegnere e dell'artiglierie in Italia dalla sua origine sino al principio del XVI secolo: Memorie storiche.* Turin, 1841.

———. *Biografie di ingegneri militari italiani dal secolo XIV alla metà del XVIII.* Turin, 1874.

Prunai, G. "L'uscita dei Tedeschi da Siena (31 gennaio 1555)." *Bullettino senese di storia patria* 8 (1937): 196–210.

———. "Provvedimenti per l'assedio di Siena." *Bullettino senese di storia patria* 11 (1940): 51–56.

Quarenghi, Cesare. *Le mura di Roma.* Rome, 1880.

Quesada, M. A. Ladero. *Castilla y la conquista del reino de Granada.* Valladolid, 1967.

Repetti, Emanuele. *Dizionario geografico-fisico-storico della Toscana.* 6 vols. Florence, 1833–1846.

Reti, Ladislao, and Bern Dibner, eds. *Leonardo da Vinci, Technologist.* Norwalk, 1969.

Rocchi, Enrico. *Le origini della fortificazione moderna.* Rome, 1894.

———. *Le piante iconografiche e prospettiche di Roma del secolo XVI.* Rome and Turin, 1902.

———. *Le fonti storiche dell'architetture militari.* Rome, 1908.

Romagnoli, Ettore. *Biografia cronologica de' Bellartisti senesi dal secolo XII a tutto il XVIII.* Manuscript, Biblioteca Comunale, Siena. 13 vols. L.II.1–13. Siena, 1835. Reprint edition, 13 vols, Florence, 1976.

Romani, A. *Le mura di Siena.* Siena, 1845.

Rombai, Leonardo, ed. *I Medici e lo Stato Senese, 1555–1609: Storia e territorio.* Rome, 1980.

Rosenberg, Charles. "The Erculean Addition to Ferrara: Contemporary Reactions and Pragmatic Considerations." *Acta: The Early Renaissance* 5 (1978): 49–67.

Ronzani, Francesco. and Giovanni Luciolli. *Le fabbriche civili, ecclesiastiche e militare di Michele Sanmicheli disegnate ed incise da FR and GL.* Verona, 1832.

Roth, Cecil. *The Last Florentine Republic, 1527–1530.* London, 1925.

Rusconi, G. *Le mura di Padova.* Bassano, 1921.

Santoro, Fiorella Sticchia, ed. *L'arte a Siena sotti i Medici 1555–1609.* Rome, 1980.

Scaglia, Gustina. "Autour de Francesco di Giorgio Martini, ingénieur et dessinateur." *Revue de l'art* 48 (1980): 7–25.

———. "Francesco di Giorgio's Chapters on Fortresses and on War Machines." *Fort* 10 (1982): 39–69.

Semenzato, Camillo. "Michele Sanmicheli architetto militare." In *Michele Sanmicheli: Studi Raccolti dall'Accademia di Agricolture Scienze e Lettere di Verona per la celebrazione del IV centenario della morte*, pp. 75–94. Verona, 1960.

Serverini, Giancarlo. *Architetture militari di Giuliano da Sangallo.* Pisa, 1970.

Spini, Giorgio. *Cosimo I de' Medici: Lettere.* Florence, 1940.

Stoye, John. *The Siege of Vienna.* London, 1964.

Tadini, Guido. *Vita di Gabriele Tadino da Martinengo Priore da Barletta.* Bergamo, 1973.

Taylor, F. L. *The Art of War in Italy, 1494–1529.* Cambridge, 1921.

Toca, Mircea. "Un progetto per una diga di sbarramento nella Maremma." *Annali della scuola normale superiore di Pisa* 39 (1970): 107–17.

Tommasi, G. *Dell'historie di Siena.* Venice, 1625–26.

Trucchi, F. *Vita e gesta di Piero Strozzi, Fiorentino, Maresciallo di Francia.* Florence, 1847.

Truttman, Philippe. *La Forteresse de Salses.* Paris, 1980.

Tuttle, Richard. "Against Fortifications: The Defense of Renaissance Bologna." *Journal of the Society of Architectural Historians* 41 (1982): 189–201.

Vale, M. G. A. "New Techniques and Old Ideals: The Impact of Artillery on War and Chivalry at the End of the Hundred Years War." In *War, Literature and Politics in the Late Middle Ages*, ed. C. T. Allmand, pp. 57–72. Liverpool, 1976.

Veen, Henk Th. van. "Cosimo I el il suo messaggio militare nel Salone de Cinquecento," *Prospettiva* 27 (1981): 86–90.

Venturi, A. *Storia dell'arte italiana: Architettura del Cinquecento.* Vol. 2, parts 1 and 2. Milan, 1924.

Verdiani-Bandi, Arnaldo. *I castelli della val d'Orcia e la Repubblica di Siena.* Siena, 1926.

Viollet-le-Duc, Eugène. *Dictionnaire raisonnée de l'architecture française du XIe au XVe siècle.* Paris, 1854–68.

Volpe, Gianni. *Rocche e fortificazioni del Ducato di Urbino.* Urbino, 1982.

Von Moos, Stanislaus. *Turm und Bollwerk: Beiträge zu einer politischen ikonographie der italienischen Renaissance-Architektur.* Zurich, 1978.

Wandruszka, Adam. *Pietro Leopoldo, un grande riformatore.* Florence, 1968.

Weller, Alan S. *Francesco di Giorgio, 1439–1501.* Chicago, 1943.

Wurm, Heinrich. *Der Palazzo Massimo alle Colonne.* Berlin, 1965.

———. *Baldassare Peruzzi: Architekturzeichnungen.* Tübingen, 1984.

Zander, Giuseppe. "Due disegni di Baldassare Peruzzi per il Castello di Rocca Sinibaldi." *Palladio* 5 (1955): 123–34.

Zevi, Bruno. *Biagio Rossetti: Architetto ferrarese.* Turin, 1960.

INDEX